Easter 2014

THE LAST CHAMPION

Jon Henderson, a sportswriter for more than forty years, has covered every Wimbledon since 1969 as tennis correspondent of Reuters and national newspapers, including the *Observer*. He is the author of one previous book, *Best of British*.

... a little

for Wimbledon 2014, ruma

love and life,

John

Also by Jon Henderson

Best of British: Hendo's Sporting Heroes

JON HENDERSON

THE LAST CHAMPION

THE LIFE OF
Fred Perry

YELLOW JERSEY PRESS
LONDON

Published by Yellow Jersey Press 2009

2 4 6 8 10 9 7 5 3 1

First published in Great Britain in 2009 by
Yellow Jersey Press
Random House, 20 Vauxhall Bridge Road,
London SW1V 2SA

www.rbooks.co.uk

Addresses for companies within The Random House Group Limited
can be found at: www.randomhouse.co.uk/offices.htm

The Random House Group Limited Reg. No. 954009

A CIP catalogue record for this book
is available from the British Library

ISBN 9780224082549

The Random House Group Limited supports The Forest Stewardship
Council (FSC), the leading international forest certification organisation.
All our titles that are printed on Greenpeace approved FSC certified
paper carry the FSC logo. Our paper procurement policy can be found at
www.rbooks.co.uk/environment

Printed and bound in Great Britain by
CPI Bookmarque, Croydon CR0 4TD

Lindy and Lucy, with love

Contents

Author's note

In more than two years researching and writing this book, I took up more of so many people's time than I had a right to expect them to give me. Only a very few became irritated. I am particularly grateful to Penny Perry for maintaining her equilibrium whenever I went to her with questions about her father. Alan Little in the All England Club library was amazing, able to summon more tennis facts in an instant than Google; his assistants Audrey Snell and Kay Crooks were endlessly helpful and courteous. John Flynn and Richard Martin at Fred Perry Sportswear interrupted their busy schedules for me on a number of occasions. The good people of Brentham, including Iver Benattar, Sue Elliott, Alan Henderson and Martin Mortimore, were invaluable in gaining me access to details of Perry's early life. Others who were helpful to a degree that is poorly reflected by a passing reference include Patty Aitkens-Mowrey, Jeanie Allen, Ronald Atkin, John Barrett, Melanie Ball, Geoff Bluett, Bob Burrows, Gianni Clerici, Bud Collins, Richard Evans, Paul Fein, George Fogelson, Heiner Gillmeister, David Godfree, Gerald Gurney, Scott Harrison, Ben Henderson, Lucy Henderson, Kaspar Hocking, Brian Hughes, Ramsay Hughes, Richard Jones, Frank Keating, Sam Keeble, Colin Kerr, Billy Knight, Jack Kramer, Chris Lewis, Sir Frank Lowe, Richard Luscombe, Kay Maule, Brian McFarlane, Frew McMillan, Paul Metzler, Elizabeth Millman, Father Martin Morgan, Rupert Neelands, Laurie Pignon, Aileen Reid, Peter Riva, Silke Ronneburg, Max Robertson, Hubert Schlosberg, Mickey Sewell, Rob Sinclair, John Sunley, Charlie Talbot-Smith, Ellsworth Vines III, Prue Wallis Myers, Inge Wegner, Bobby Wilson, Mark Winters, Sidney and Pat Wood and Pat Yeomans.

Sticklers for correctitude may be upset that I refer to the All England Lawn Tennis and Croquet Club as the All England Club but it seemed a sensible contraction. I also refer on numerous occasions to the grand slams. This was the name first given to the four major championships – Wimbledon and the Australian, French and US Opens – in 1938, when Don Budge won all four in the same year. Golf was the first sport to adopt this term from bridge after Bobby Jones won the US and British Open and Amateur titles in 1930.

It was a great joy writing this book. I suspect that like me you thought you knew most of what there was to know about Fred Perry and I hope you will be as excited as I was in discovering around each of the many corners there was so much more. So it was that the book grew from being just another tennis story to being a chronicle of the life of an extraordinary Englishman.

Jon Henderson
May 2009

List of illustrations

Section 2

Introduction

'Ruthless, full of confidence, insolent'

Standing next to his opponent Jack Crawford in the lobby of the All England Club minutes before his first Wimbledon singles final, Fred Perry felt relaxed, even a little superior. He had worked out early in his tennis playing days that there was an advantage to be gained in all things, not least the matter of appearance. His dark hair was carefully combed, parted and slicked back. His clothing was impeccable. The tailored Daks trousers fitted his lean contours, but not so tightly that they prevented easy movement. His short-sleeved linen shirt was pristine. He wore a gauze strip on his right wrist to prevent sweat trickling down to his racket hand. His plimsoll shoes were of his own design: buckskin uppers with laces going right to the toe. 'If your feet hurt, you can't play' was a strict Perry dictum. The man was more striking than any player on the international circuit: tall, strong-featured, shoulders wide and loose, hips narrow as a dancer's. 'There was never a champion in any sport who looked more like a champion than Fred Perry,' said the great American player Jack Kramer.

With moments to go an attendant gathered up their rackets, elegant implements made from laminated wood and strung with sheep's gut. Perry retained his own racket maker, who supplied him on behalf of Slazenger. His initials were inscribed on the slender, concave throat of each one. Before beating Crawford in the Australian final earlier that year, in January 1934, his racket had been painted white – he heightened the effect by unveiling it only after knocking up with an old one – and the Australian crowd yelled its excitement as he walked out with his gleaming Excalibur. He had liked that and resolved to use the tactic again at this Wimbledon.

As the players were escorted through the doors to emerge into the sunlight of the south-west corner of Centre Court, a murmur rolled down from the shadows deep under the stadium's roof, from where the first sighting of the finalists was possible. The sound gathered volume before finally breaking into rousing cheers. The Wimbledon Gentlemen's Final was the high point of the summer season, as social as it was sporting, a uniquely English institution. Interlopers were allowed in, but were easily identified, the nuances of a strict dress code eluding them. Neckties with stripes and crests signalled the right club or regiment. Hats were significant too: panamas from Bond Street, or cloches styled with the distinctive cut of the finer West End milliners. The crowd was anticipating an exceptional contest between Crawford, a popular figure who had won an outstanding final the year before against the American Ellsworth Vines, and the twenty-five-year-old Englishman whose country had not produced a Wimbledon men's winner since Arthur Gore in 1909.

Perry's entrance was a command performance that had just the effect he desired. As a young Englishman of humble origins, he knew that he was perhaps the biggest interloper of all. The other top English players were from the same public-school-educated tribe that flocked to watch Wimbledon. This was another reason he felt it necessary to have an imposing presence. 'I learned quickly the importance of getting people to watch you,' he said. No one – least of all his Australian opponent – was left in any doubt that Fred Perry belonged in an arena he was starting to regard as his own.

The sense of being somewhere special had nearly overwhelmed him when he first played on Centre Court in 1930. The architects who designed the stadium a decade earlier were rewarded for their fastidiousness with an arena that remains admired and envied to this day. They put a disc of white paper the size of a thumbnail in the middle of the court and made sure it could be seen from every seat. Down the sides of the court the seating presses up to the grass's edge, and the intimacy this creates, prevented from escaping by the overhanging roof, readily communicates itself to the remotest elevated seats. As the tournament tapers to its conclusion Centre Court becomes a walled city, no longer merely the dominant building at the heart of a bustling metropolis. By the finals, everything turns in on this place as the background noises from the packed concourses of the first week give way to silence. The tension is a shared experience felt by players, officials and spectators. Great champions feed off it. Few have grown to be more satisfyingly sustained by it than Perry.

Neither Perry nor Crawford gave any hint of the pressure they must have felt as they strode across the grass scorched by two weeks of almost continuous sunshine. The gentlest of breezes stirred the air and tempered the heat, while more than twenty photographers in trilbies jostled for pictures. Perry stood erect, his poise masking the competitive rage that churned within him. According to the French player Henri Cochet, Perry was 'ruthless, full of confidence, insolent, a rough fighter'. Crawford was the more correct and elegant stroke maker. 'No one knew better than him how to deal with savage serving,' said a newspaper reporting that 1934 final, 'what control from the baseline, what a backhand, what flint for Perry's steel!'

After the high excitement, the final was an anticlimax. From the young Englishman, said the same newspaper, there would be 'no pretty-pretty work, but a swift and painless death'. The chair umpire called 'Quiet please!' only occasionally as Perry won in straight sets to confirm his extraordinarily rapid ascent to the summit of the game. Crawford double-faulted at the finish, denying his opponent an explosive coup de grâce. He bowed towards the line judge who had disallowed his anxious first serve for a foot fault.

Before the match Perry had already carefully choreographed in his mind how he would respond if he won. He did a cartwheel and then vaulted the net, a display designed to give the impression that the match had taken little out of him. Crawford was barely halfway to the net before Perry reached him. Britain's first Wimbledon men's champion for a quarter of a century patted the Australian on the shoulder and put a consoling arm around his neck. The ramifications of the result were immense. A young man who only five years before had been unknown outside the limited sphere of table tennis – a poor-boys' sport at which he had become world champion – was now an international figure. By his example Fred Perry had, in theory, placed tennis within reach of anyone who wished to play it.

★   ★   ★

The new champion's roots were solidly working class. The early years of his childhood had been spent in semi-detached and terraced houses in the north-west of England. His father had begun his working life as a cotton spinner but rose to be a Labour MP, and in Sam Perry's drive for political advancement can be discerned the absolute single-mindedness that would make his son an irresistible force in tennis.

Fred Perry's thrust and ambition in an overwhelmingly amateur sport were not universally admired and were part of the reason why many on that day he won Wimbledon for the first time preferred to support Crawford. Reporting on the final in the *Manchester Guardian*, E.J. Sampson noted, 'The crowd in their shout for Perry had a sob in the throat for Crawford.' John R. Tunis, of *Esquire*, said that there was resentment that 'a poor boy without a varsity education should have yanked himself up to the front'.

Perry's background informed much of how he behaved as a tennis player, just as it often determined the way people reacted to him. After that 1934 final he experienced an example of the sort of prejudice that affected him deeply. Within minutes of beating Crawford, he was reminded that the son of a Labour MP had to do more than win Wimbledon to be accepted by the panjandrums of the All England Club, even if his account of what happened in the locker room, told fifty years later in his autobiography, was almost certainly closer to the truth in essence than detail. Soaking in a post-match bath in the locker room, he said he overheard the plummy tones of a committee man suggesting to Crawford that the laurels had gone to the wrong player. Crawford was handed a bottle of champagne, while the honorary All England Club member's tie that was Perry's due was left for him, draped over the back of a chair. 'All my paranoia about the old-school-tie brigade surfaced with a vengeance,' he said.

By 1934, Perry had already made a number of visits to the United States and was forming a strong affinity with that country and its citizens. His first visit in 1930 had immediately established a bond, even if the pace of New York initially overwhelmed him. He loved the access to everything that he found in America, so different from Britain, where far too many glittering events had invisible NO ENTRY signs swinging from cut-glass doorknobs. In 1931 he travelled to the West Coast and was further seduced by the American way of life. Here he encountered more evidence of the spirit of inclusiveness that distinguished the New World from the snobbery and class divisions of England, and in the late 1930s he took US citizenship.

Not only did he feel more at ease with American society, he was, we can now recognise, perhaps the closest tennis came to producing a player in harmony with the jazz years. Much of the way he played – while endlessly practised and clinically executed – was of his own devising, based on his first, and largely untutored, sporting incarnation as a table tennis player. Bill Tilden, an American still regarded by many as the greatest ever tennis player, remarked that Perry was either the worst best player or the best worst, who 'hits every shot wrong – every single one'. Had Perry played an instrument, he would have loved the improvisation of jazz musicians. His sporting and social lives were played to the rhythms of someone who relished doing things differently. They were underpinned by discipline but distinguished by originality. His famous running forehand – with the ball taken impossibly early – was the product of a conflation of these controlled, yet innovative, sides.

His private life, which became increasingly less private as he worked his way through three marriages before finding happiness in a fourth, was a paradoxical mix of the austere and carefree. The same man who advocated the spartan benefits of going early to bed and abstinence partied hard with the likes of Errol Flynn and David Niven and, at the very least, traded one-liners with Bette Davis and Marlene Dietrich.

The speed with which Perry reached the pinnacle of tennis was remarkable, even at a time when the number of players competing seriously was a fraction of today's figure. Rarely can aptitude and commitment have been combined in such measure in one person. He had soared through the table tennis rankings to take the world title in Budapest in 1929. 'I was world champion at twenty,' he said, 'so decided to retire while I was still at the top.' Within four years Perry had helped Britain regain the Davis Cup, which largely through his contributions they then monopolised until 1936, and from 1934 to 1936 he took command of the Wimbledon men's singles. George Lott, an old American adversary, reviewing Perry's career, wrote, 'Here was a man who not only possessed but also exhibited the qualities so necessary in a champion, namely, confidence, concentration, condition, coordination, courage and fortitude, determination, stamina, quickness and speed.'

Still the list is incomplete. Perry was more competitive – often archly so – than any player before him, and possibly since. It was something that not every rival appreciated. Nearly all forgave him, although some waited until their reminiscing years when resentment no longer seemed worthwhile. Later Perry owned up to 'surreptitious gamesmanship'.

One other notable aspect of Perry's story is the way, despite a parochial upbringing, he embraced travel. Throughout his life he seemed uninhibited by the notion of boundaries, either in terms of what he could achieve or where he might go. The world was opening up to sportsmen and tennis gave Perry the chance to roam, which he grasped during and after his playing career with extraordinary enthusiasm. On his travels he became the first player to win the game's four major singles titles: Wimbledon and the championships of Australia, France and the US, known as the grand slams. In later life he took assignments in such diverse locations as Egypt, Jamaica and the Soviet Union. He was, arguably, the first truly global sporting figure.

The three consecutive Wimbledon titles that Fred Perry won between 1934 and 1936 stood above all his many other successes. Some part of nearly every day of a full and colourful life that was to last another fifty-nine years referred back to the twenty-one straight wins during those summers, when the world – weary from one fight and fearful of another – looked to sportsmen such as Perry, Jesse Owens, Donald Bradman and Babe Ruth for vicarious enjoyment and distraction. Through his trilogy of monumental victories at Wimbledon he helped define an age that pointed towards a more meritocratic future. He also foreshadowed another age – more than half a century away – in which the manufacturing and marketing of celebrity were to become a huge international industry generating fortunes and idolatry on a scale that in the 1930s would have seemed incredible. His life and worldwide fashion brand resonate today with sports stars and public alike. Few British sportsmen have come close to emulating his glory and achievements. A century after his birth, Fred Perry remains the last champion.

I
A father's boy

'We come of common stock'

Spending time in the beautifully kept gardens of Vernon Park must have been one of the few small pleasures to be found in that working-class area of Stockport in which Sam and Hannah Perry lived at the start of the twentieth century. The park with its grand oaks, beeches and chestnuts, neat pathways, sloping lawns and colourful flower beds was an unlikely reward for walking half the length of Carrington Road, a determinedly unprepossessing thoroughfare in the east of the town. It is possible to imagine Hannah, whose workaholic husband Sam was rarely at home, with her daughter Edith and baby son Fred moving slowly through the park in the warm glow of a summer's afternoon. Fred may even have taken his first, tottering steps there.

The family were spared the menacing background music that now travels the short distance from the M60, a motorway whose use by an unending stream of HGVs is a reminder of this part of north-west England's robust survival as a significant centre of industry. The other end of Carrington Road from Vernon Park joins the gyratory at junction 27 of the motorway. From there, number 98 is an end-of-terrace house halfway down on the right-hand side. This is where, according to Fred Perry's 1984 autobiography, he first saw the light of day. A little further down and on the left is number 33, a semi-detached house but smaller than 98. High up to the left of the front door of 33 is a plaque, put there by the Metropolitan Borough of Stockport, which says 'FRED PERRY 1909–1995 Tennis player Frederick John Perry was born here . . .' and goes on to list his sporting accomplishments plus the fact that he was made a freeman of the borough in 1934.

The Fred Perry file in Stockport's heritage library fails to clear up the mystery of where exactly he made his entrance into the world. There is a picture of number 98 taken in the 1930s with the caption that this is where Perry was born; the next page is a copy of his birth certificate giving 33 as his birthplace. One explanation is that, by the time of Perry's birth, his father, Sam, who was then thirty-one and had already achieved an extraordinary amount for someone with a background unsullied by privilege, had bought a second house in Carrington Road. The address logged on the birth certificate may not have been the one where the family lived.

Sam Perry had spent all his early life in Stockport, which is six miles south-east of Manchester. He was born there on 29 June 1877, the son of Samuel, a cotton worker, and Annie Perry, and was steeped in the sights and sounds of its industries. Cotton manufacture, which in the age of steam and ingenuity had given rise to the great brick edifices that housed the inexhaustible, chattering inventions of men such as Sir Richard Arkwright and Samuel Crompton, was chief among them, providing jobs for nearly 10,000 people in the town. Young Sam delighted his parents by winning a scholarship to the 500-year-old grammar school for what was to prove a brief stay.

The pursuit of academic excellence through full-time schooling was an extravagance that had to be dispensed with when Samuel died. Like many other children of hard-pressed families, Sam followed his father into the cotton industry to earn money in the local mill as a half-timer. This was the system, common in the labour-intensive cotton industry in the late nineteenth and early twentieth century, that sanctioned part-time factory work by children if they were also given time to do school work.

'I was raised in a hard school,' Sam Perry said. 'I was a half-timer at the age of ten in a Cheshire cotton mill and struggle and poverty combined gave me little opportunity in my early years. It had been one of my experiences to beg pennies from door to door in order to pay the rent of a football field.' His wage of one shilling a week was a valuable contribution to the family budget. Of greater value, though, in terms of his later life, was what he earned in experience and extracted from the other opportunities available to someone of his enterprise.

In the workplace, he studied machine drawing and construction, mathematics and mechanics, showing great flair for all these subjects. Also, he quickly grasped how the human side of factory life functioned. This led to his involvement in trade unionism at an unusually young age. He was undaunted by the fact that the complexities of the cotton industry's pay and job structures were such that he had to pass a number of exams in competition with others in order to qualify as a union official. His own first job was simply as a cotton spinner. When he moved on to the self-acting mule, the spinning machine that Richard Roberts developed from Crompton's original invention, he took on the slightly grander title of self-actor minder. His fellow worker Hannah Birch, who seemed unabashed at having caught his eye, was a winder, someone who transferred cotton from bobbins to prepare it for weaving.

Sam Perry excelled in his exams, passing with first-class honours, which immediately brought him to the attention of his union elders. In 1898, at the age of twenty-one, he was elected president of the Stockport Operative Cotton Spinners' Association and went on to take up the reins of the Stockport Trades Council and later the Stockport Labour Representation Committee. In his late twenties, he was made Stockport's youngest justice of the peace, a rare honour in those days for anyone with a Labour affiliation, let alone of his young age. 'Wherever Sam Perry went he seemed to claim the confidence and arouse the enthusiasm of working-class folk,' a colleague said.

Hardly surprisingly, given his interest in trade unionism, Perry was also attracted to another cause supported by the working classes at the time, the co-operative movement, which pursued the idea of industries and commercial concerns being owned and controlled by workers for their joint economic benefit. The movement had originated in northern England and Scotland in the late eighteenth century, but the first really successful co-operative enterprise was started in Rochdale, not far from Stockport, in 1844. Perry, an intuitive co-operator, would have been familiar with this history and in 1908 he helped to save the Stockport Co-operative Society when its future was threatened by a financial crisis. At a midnight meeting called to sort out the mess, he put himself forward for the post of president and was unanimously elected. It was his first key role in the co-operative movement, which would become central to his life's work.

Like many others from his background and with his zeal, Perry had one other notable affiliation. He was a staunch supporter of the Methodist Church, with its strong traditions of concern with social welfare and promoting sobriety. He preached regularly and supported the Manchester temperance movement. This commitment to abstinence stayed with him throughout his life. He offered Fred, as a young boy, financial incentives not to smoke or drink before he was twenty-one. Fred failed to collect on the former, signing up to the popular pipe-smoking habit, but pocketed the reward for not drinking, for which he gave credit to an uncle who liked the booze and had once hung him upside down from a clothes line. Not long after, the uncle died of drink.

Beyond the dimly lit world of cotton factories, committee rooms and the pulpit, Sam Perry was a keen sportsman. He liked cross-country running, football, bowls and golf, and, in his own words, met with a fair measure of success in competitions, remaining fit throughout his life. A colleague who saw him regularly in later years at the co-operative movement's stolidly imposing building in Manchester said, 'He kept his sportsman's complexion and brisk step up Holyoake House staircases year by year with no apparent failings. When last I saw him he looked twenty years younger than his age.' He also enjoyed music and amateur dramatics. When he retired in June 1942, after nearly a quarter of a century as secretary of the Co-operative Party, one speaker at the party given in his honour said, 'He has always taken a lively interest in the brighter things in life. At Stockport he was actively connected with the repertory movement and at summer schools his musical accomplishments in the plebeian art of cornet playing always afforded listeners a great deal of pleasure.'

Sam Perry married Hannah Birch, who was also twenty-four, in a Church of England ceremony at St Matthew's, Stockport on Boxing Day 1901. Their first child, Edith, was born two years later, and Fred arrived six years after that, on 18 May 1909, the midwife being summoned either to 33 or 98 Carrington Road.

Family life was conducted according to strict Victorian principles with Sam the lord and master. He seldom if ever alluded to the women of the household and no one was in any doubt about what was and was not acceptable behaviour. 'As far as the family was concerned he laid down the rules and you had to adhere to them otherwise you were in trouble,' Fred said. 'But it was a very family-orientated atmosphere. A happy atmosphere, and it was fun.' As young children, Edith and Fred grew used at mealtimes to conversation that was invariably far harder to digest than their food. Their father's thoughts on cooperation as a political idea dominated table talk.

In his working life, Sam Perry rapidly established himself as a serious player in the co-operative movement, which meant a series of promotions and house moves. Fred remembered he was only two or three years old when they left Carrington Road, still long enough for him to be regularly referred to for the rest of his life as a Cheshire lad. Stockport showed its enduring allegiance to him when in May 1935, in front of a large crowd at the town hall, the mayor presented him with a silver tea and coffee set made by a local jeweller. (In 1997, the town bought it back for £3,600 at an auction in London, together with Perry's 1933 Davis Cup medal, for which it paid £4,200.)

The Perrys spent an equally short time in Bolton and had a brief spell back in old Cheshire, living in Wallasey, during which time Sam was asked to become a full-time organiser at the co-operative head-quarters in Manchester.

Fred Perry's first vivid memories were of the time in Wallasey, although he discovered many years later that some things were not quite as he pictured them. The family lived in Vicarage Grove in the Liscard district for two years in the First World War and Fred attended the junior school of Wallasey Grammar in Wither's Lane. He told of revisiting the house from which his father commuted to an office in Liverpool's Liver Building and later to Manchester, a much longer journey. He was surprised to find that what he remembered as a large dwelling with substantial gardens back and front turned out to be a good deal pokier than he recalled with only a few feet of land either side. The long walk to the sweet shop was no more than a few steps around the corner. The lady who answered his knock let him in, and when she closed the door he saw a plaque, FRED PERRY LIVED HERE. He never tired of expressing his bafflement at the furtive way his residence there was proclaimed.

His strongest bond with an older member of the family was with his mother's father, Grandad Birch. The two enjoyed playing board games, particularly draughts, and Fred remembered being chided, good-humouredly, as a cheat. He was banished from the house when Grandad Birch died so that he could not overhear the funeral arrangements being made.

In the last year of the war, he and his classmates from the junior school were given the day off to welcome the Mersey ferry boats *Royal Iris* and *Royal Daffodil* when they returned from the Zeebrugge Raid, the action in April 1918 at which the British tried to stop the Belgian harbour being used by German submarines. Perry and his chums were given Union flags and from the banks of the Mersey cheered the homecoming local sailors, who had performed heroically if not altogether successfully in their mission.

By 1918 Sam Perry was a key figure in the debate on parliamentary representation for the co-operative movement. The main argument was between those who supported independent representation and those who favoured an alliance with the Labour Party. Victory for those advocating direct parliamentary representation led to the formation of the Central Co-operative Parliamentary Representation Committee, which eventually changed its name to the Co-operative Party, with headquarters to be established in London. Perry became the party's first secretary. It was a time for optimism as the guns that for four years had thundered over the Western Front at last fell silent, and now the Perrys' own future was heavy with hopeful possibilities. Any trepidation they felt must have been offset by a sense of excitement as they prepared to go south to start their new life in the capital.

By the summer of 1919 they had settled in to Pitshanger Lane in Brentham, a part of Ealing in west London. The location was not particularly convenient for 19 Buckingham Street, close to Charing Cross station in central London, where Sam Perry and a small staff opened the party's new offices. Brentham's attraction was partly its pleasantness – Fred described it as 'a paradise after the bleak streets of the North' – and, what really counted as far as Sam Perry was concerned, its roots in the co-operative movement.

After a meeting in 1901 at the Haven Arms in Ealing, attended mostly by workers with the dream of building houses for themselves, Brentham moved quickly from idea to reality. One of the Brentham pioneers was a bricklayer named Harry Perry, no relation but a nice coincidence, particularly as Harry also had politics in his genes with a father who was a prominent member of the Liberal Party. Harry Perry was Brentham's first works manager, overseeing the building of 600 houses up to the outbreak of war in 1914. In fifteen years, the open fields that had been Pitshanger Farm were transformed into London's first garden suburb, providing a model for others, most notably the one at Hampstead.

The Perrys remained at 223 Pitshanger Lane, built in 1906, until soon after Sam Perry's death in 1954, when the house became known as Pooh Corner, the excuse being that it stands on the corner of Brunner Road. That name has now been dropped and there is a notice on a post in the front garden telling passers-by that they are in Brentham Garden Suburb with a quote from the current Prince of Wales describing Brentham as 'a small, yet inspiring, piece of English town planning'.

The 'paradise' of Brentham was where Fred Perry's sporting ambitions began. He blossomed almost as soon as the family moved in. A neighbour who lived opposite remembered he would leave at exactly the same time each morning for school, the first of four daily walks – he came home for lunch – of more than a mile each up and over the steepish hill behind his house. He would invariably set off whistling and often walk down the middle of the road.

It did not matter that Fred – 'Titch' to his friends – was small for his age; he played every sport that the many open spaces in the area allowed him to, football and cricket being his earliest favourites. He was forever knocking on doors pressing friends to kick a ball with him. The first known photograph of Perry participating in an outdoor activity was taken at the annual maypole ceremony in 1924, at the Brentham recreation ground. His demeanour suggests it was not quite energetic enough for him. He looks decidedly forlorn as he stands with the other children, wearing a white overall and holding a rope attached to the pole. A programme of May Day Festivities lists him as one of sixteen members of the Double Plaiting and Spiders' Web team.

His parents' determination that he and Edith should join in Brentham life as much as possible meant Fred acquired social skills that would serve him well once he joined the celebrity set. At the newly built Brentham Institute, just around the corner from Pitshanger Lane, he learned to dance. Margot Reading, who, with her brother Charles, was one of Fred's earliest tennis partners, taught him the waltz and foxtrot. Sport had just started to consume him. The *Brenthamite* magazine recorded what was possibly Fred Perry's maiden sporting triumph, victory in a three-legged race over eighty yards in August 1923. Charles Reading, who provided one and a half of the legs, was not to know that he was, in all probability, achieving a sort of immortality as the first person to partner Fred Perry to victory in an event on a grass surface. They must have been a handsome pair. Reading went on to make a name for himself as an actor of striking good looks and then at the London Palladium as the production manager who staged lavish shows starring legends of light entertainment such as Judy Garland and Danny Kaye.

The institute was where lawn tennis came into Perry's life. 'It was there that I first became interested in watching and playing sport,' he said. The decision to instal excellent sporting facilities at the institute seems almost providential given their role in Fred Perry's development.

Sam Perry's own love of sport meant he went out of his way to encourage his son's fervour for playing games. At the same time he was just as keen on instructing both his children on their general conduct and would lecture them like some latter-day Polonius, passing on 'these few precepts for thy memory'. It was important they were as good as their word and engaged with people. Perry senior could not abide stand-offishness. Edith and Fred were told to greet everyone as if he or she meant something to them, to hold out a hand and say, 'How do you do, pleased to meet you.' It was advice whose value Fred understood instinctively and carried with him into all areas of his adult life.

Sam Perry has been hailed as 'the man who made the Co-operative Party', quite an epitaph considering the lack of advantages of his early years. His dedication to the movement was based on his belief that co-operative principles were as relevant to Labour politics as trade unionism. He felt Labour invested too much faith in unionism, that by using it as the sole weapon in their battle against the right in British politics they were flexing only half their power. 'The co-operative movement supplied the other half,' he said, 'by trying to bring into industry a more Christian-like spirit.'

He was no firebrand, rather a person who preferred measured argument to high-flown oratory, by inclination a creature of the committee room rather than the debating chamber. 'He nearly always succeeded in applying the art of persuasion where forceful demands would have brought certain failure and resistance,' a colleague said. Some felt he suppressed a more flamboyant side to his character because he thought that co-operative politics needed to be 'respected and respectable'. 'He was not interested in stunts and short cuts,' an obituarist wrote, 'but he was interested in building up a specifically Co-operative group within the Labour forces.' Fred Perry's take on his father was that he did nothing to alter his image for political expediency, describing him as 'an excellent speaker, though a quietly spoken person'. It could be argued – and some people have – that Sam Perry's low-key performances did not give the party the projection it needed or make him as authoritative a figure as he might have been.

The Co-operative Party's first real foray into mainstream politics was at the 1918 general election, when the air rang with promises of a new and better country for the returning heroes of the Great War. The result was disappointing, with the railway worker Alfred Waterson, who stood in Kettering, the only one of ten Labour/Co-operative candidates to win a seat in Parliament. At the Co-operative Party congress in Carlisle in 1919, Perry, whose earlier stance in favour of independent representation went against his gut feeling for a closer alliance with the Labour Party, tabled an important motion that was passed but later ignored. It called for 'The National Co-operative Representation Committee to negotiate with the Labour Party and Trades Union Congress Parliamentary Committee with a view to a federation for electoral purposes, and with the ultimate object of forming a United Democratic or People's Party.'

In 1920, Hannah Perry and the children were introduced to the strains and deprivations brought on by having a member of the family, in those days almost certainly a husband and father, involved in front-line national politics. This was the year Sam Perry stood for Parliament for the first time when he contested a by-election in what was now (to the Perry family) the remote constituency of Stockport.

The build-up to the by-election was dominated by the participation of the jailed Irish Workers' Republican candidate William O'Brien. The publicity did O'Brien no good, his 2,336 votes leaving him last out of seven. Perry's trenchant support for Irish independence may have cancelled out the advantage of still being well known in Stockport and the co-operative movement's popularity in the area. A Labour/Co-operative candidate, Perry finished fourth in the fight for the two seats behind a Coalition Conservative and a Coalition Liberal, who were first and second, and Sir Leo Chiozza Money, the former Liberal MP, now a Labour candidate. Money was an Italian immigrant whose choice of anglicised surname seemed bizarre, particularly as it may have lost him a vote or two when he was in fact a fierce upholder of the redistribution of wealth. Perry's 14,434 votes gave him 16.2 per cent support but were more than 8,000 fewer than the winner.

In the face of criticism that by cosying up to Labour, then in a period of decline, the party had damaged its chance in the by-election, Perry gave one of his most compelling performances at the 1921 party congress in Scarborough. In unadorned language he attacked those who were against moving closer to Labour – or even venturing into politics at all: 'Only by active co-operation with our friends in the trade union and Labour movement can we achieve the objects we have set out to obtain . . . we come of common stock. We are working for the common end, and only by marching together with the trade union and Labour movements can we establish the co-operative commonwealth, which is the ideal of every true cooperator.'

More long absences from the bright new family home in Pitshanger Lane were inevitable when he stood in all three general elections that took place between 1922 and 1924. Labour's recovery to compete alongside the Conservatives and Liberals caused this eruption of political activity, which tested almost to destruction a mechanism geared to a two-party system. The first of these three elections, which, according to one commentator, represented 'a state of confusion unknown in any former election', brought the downfall of David Lloyd George and the humbling of the Liberal Party. Sam Perry, standing again in Stockport, campaigned on a platform of international cooperation, world peace, the abolition of taxes on food and a fairer system of taxation. This time he came third, although four out of eleven Co-operative Party candidates did win their seats. Perry's solidly fought campaign at least gained him 17,059 votes, a record for the party.

The major disappointment for the Co-operative Party of the 1922 election was Waterson's loss in Kettering by 128 votes. Kettering was a complicated constituency with its mix of industrial labour force and rural squirearchy. Hard-core manufacturing, mainly of footwear, and fox-hunting coexisted within two or three miles of one another. Traditionally, the town of Kettering, along with other industrial centres in Northamptonshire, voted Liberal, a practice that Labour had found hard to break. Perry knew that co-operative principles were embedded deep in the working community's psyche and felt that, with the Liberals losing ground because of their reluctance to pursue left-wing policies, he could win back the seat, if given the opportunity to stand as a Labour/Co-operative candidate.

His chance to do so came in December 1923, barely a year after he had lost for the second time in Stockport, when he faced an adoption meeting at Kettering Public Hall Baths. He was given a hard time as he tried to allay the fears of moderates concerned he might be too far to the left and overly austere. He reacted by distancing himself from communism and the Russian regime, and said he would vote against prohibition, although he was an abstainer. He even mentioned his sporting achievements, especially on the golf course.

Arguably, the Perry sporting legend started here. Not many candidates at the 1923 general election can have introduced a sporting theme into their campaigns. It did Perry no harm for he was adopted and won Kettering with 12,718 votes, beating the Conservative by 2,506 and registering twice as many as the Liberal.

Sam Perry's first stint as an MP lasted only eleven months, but this was still time enough for him to make an impression. Having established a reputation in co-operative circles as an effective organiser, he served as parliamentary private secretary at the Ministry of Health. In a speech to the House of Commons on industrial relations in July 1924, he flaunted both his working-class credentials and his preference for pragmatism, calling on both sides in the building trade to avoid unnecessary disputes: 'Having worked in the cotton trade for more than twenty years, I have been locked out or have been on strike as often as any honourable members on these benches, and I always held, and hold today more strongly than ever, that the strike is a weapon which hurts the workers ten times more than it hurts the employing class.'

With none of the three parties holding an absolute majority, the country voted again in October 1924. This time Perry was in a straight fight with Conservative Sir Mervyn Manningham-Buller, and was squeezed out despite polling more votes – 14,801 – than he had the year before. Both sides staged robust campaigns in which the antipathy of the hunting set and industrial workers was once again a feature. In one incident the police were called to the Conservative Club in Kettering when windows were smashed after Perry supporters converged on the building to confront their opponents. It may have been as a reaction against this that some members of the co-operative movement voted Conservative, an act of perfidy denounced by Perry's agent.

After the terrible losses of the Great War, people did their best to disregard signs that the peace was fragile, to forget politics and ignore matters of state. The flappers flapped in their Charleston outfits, all swinging beads and fringes, and the sounds of Louis Armstrong's trumpet and gargling voice were infinitely preferable to those of the doomsayers. Nevertheless Sam Perry remained steadfast in his determination to advance the Co-operative Party.

It meant that his family saw only marginally more of him in the years between the 1924 and 1929 general elections, when he was outside Parliament, than they had when he was engaged in three elections in less than twenty-four months. Meanwhile Hannah Perry's health started to deteriorate as her husband toured the country.

Perry encouraged local parties to affiliate to Labour. The link between the two parties at national level was more firmly ratified at the Co-operative Party congress in Cheltenham in 1927, when Perry for once bared his teeth in public. After B.H. Fletcher of Macclesfield put a well-argued case against an agreement with Labour, Perry chided: 'I want to remind him that whilst our Macclesfield friends may be against the agreement they raised little objection to the Co-operative Party and are quite prepared to take all the bene-fits that the Party . . . in the House of Commons can give them.' It also pleased him that an increasing number of trade unions now used the Co-operative Bank, a strengthening of a bond that he saw as mutually beneficial to the Labour and Co-operative Parties.

It was around this time that Sam Perry's attention to his own career, which had been pretty much undivided, started to broaden to take in the burgeoning success being enjoyed by his sporting son. By the general election of May 1929, Fred Perry, fifteen years old at the time of the previous election five years earlier, was starting to have his achievements reported in the national press. He won the world table tennis championship that year and made his first appear-ance at Wimbledon, winning through two rounds. Sam Perry's understandable and deeply felt satisfaction at having risen from the lowliest of jobs on the factory floor to a position of some eminence would soon be eclipsed by his paternal pride.

2

A world champion at nineteen

'Wholesome and boundless conceit'

Kaspar Hocking was twelve when he played Fred Perry at table tennis at Ealing County School for Boys in 1925. Eighty years later, after a full and eventful life spent mostly in Africa, he remembered the matches clearly. They were among the highlights of his school-days, although he could not recall quite why the privilege of playing a pupil four years his senior and of such palpable athletic promise was bestowed upon him. Perhaps it was no more than a neighbourly gesture towards a fellow Brenthamite who also made the daily hike of a mile and a bit over the hill, past Ealing Broadway station to the imposing school on Ealing Green.

Hocking's father was politically on the left − he chose his son's first name from a poem by the communist-sympathising writer Robert Southey − and an admirer of Sam Perry's work, which may have swung it for young Kaspar. What always remained with Hocking was the sense of having been in the presence of a games player who was out of the ordinary. 'I played table tennis with him − but never won. Lawn tennis was not played at school. After leaving school Fred became the world champion in table tennis, much to the admiration of all his school friends,' Hocking recalled.

Perry, who went first to Drayton Green Primary School when the family moved south, said he spent several very happy years at Ealing County. Two of his school friends also made names for them-selves: Dudley Pope, who played first-class cricket for Essex, and Bernard Sunley, who became one of the country's leading property developers. 'Dudley got into cricket, I got into tennis and Bernard got into making money,' Perry said.

According to Perry, Sunley would cajole his two friends into helping him sell manure from a wheelbarrow – and took all the money – in exchange for half-hearted assistance when Perry and Pope practised their respective sports. Perry's claim that Sunley was neither interested nor good at sport may not have been the case. Sunley's recollection some years later was that to start with he used to beat the future world champion at table tennis.

At Ealing County Perry had plenty of opportunities to fulfil his desire to play games, particularly the team variety. References to studying or the classroom are noticeably lacking from his school reminiscences, while he owned up to hating homework. His devotion to games was also well served by the open spaces and other facilities near his home, especially those at the Brentham Institute, where there was a football pitch, cricket field, tennis courts, bowling green and table tennis facilities.

Frank Turner was a young neighbour who grew used to being badgered by Perry to kick a ball about. Looking back, Turner was struck by the fact that Perry's earliest sporting ambition had nothing to do with tennis but was to play football for Aston Villa. The West Midlands club was remote from anywhere that Perry ever lived, but Villa had a towering reputation having reached two FA Cup Finals in the 1920s, a feat that in those days carried far greater kudos than it does now. Perry, in common with small boys of all generations, presumably found the attraction of a successful side that was far away more compelling than that of a modest one closer to home.

Perry's eventual disillusionment with team games almost certainly had something to do with his staying smaller than most of his contemporaries until quite late into his teens. 'I was good enough to be on the football and cricket teams but I wasn't a star,' he said. The physical challenges of football grew steadily less attractive, and the County School inside left in the old-style, five-man forward line finally abandoned his Aston Villa aspirations. What clinched it was being knocked about playing for the first eleven against the masters in an impromptu match that replaced a cancelled school fixture. He also turned against cricket. He disliked the hard ball, even though, as a wicketkeeper, he had more protection from it than anyone else.

*　　*　　*

If size was one factor that contributed to Perry's decision to give up team games, another was his discovery that he preferred individual sports. Gregarious in his social life, as his parents had hoped, in sport he began to enjoy being on his own as soon as he twigged that he had a singular talent for imposing himself on others in one-on-one contests that involved a ball and hand-eye coordination. Even amateur psychologists are entitled to conclude that here lay the source of the extraordinary self-confidence that enabled Perry to go on to shatter the class barriers that made tennis so elitist.

Tennis had to wait, though. While Perry dabbled in it at the Brentham Institute, he enjoyed table tennis more to start with, having been introduced to it at school. He became totally hooked after discovering he could carry on playing outside school hours just around the corner at the Ealing YMCA. It was here, he said, that his game improved no end. He was enthralled by the intricacies of table tennis – the subtleties of pace and placement, the mysteries of spin and counter-spin – and rather than shrink from being in sole charge of his destiny, he thrived on the responsibility and the freedom it gave him to express himself.

At home, his family just about tolerated his commandeering the kitchen for endless practice sessions. He cleared the kitchen table, pushed it against a wall, stretched a net across it and would lose himself in hours of repetitive hitting. Later, when tennis became his thing, Perry took over the back garden, where he learned to volley by playing the ball over a greenhouse and on to a wall of the family home. He would remark that his volley prospered even if the greenhouse suffered. Back in the kitchen, he found more to interest him than merely rallying with himself against the wall and counting how many times he could get the ball back. He was excited by developing a sense of rhythm and feeling for the game. Had he received expert tuition rather than teaching himself, he would almost certainly have held the bat differently from the hatchet or handshake grip, which would later become an important feature of the way he played lawn tennis. He had no knowledge of the penholder grip, which by now was used by most leading table tennis players.

The first time Perry played tennis is unclear. The opportunity presented itself from the moment the Perrys moved to Brentham in 1919, but he said it was not until 1923 that he started to take more than a passing interest. A year later came what Perry himself always said was the key moment when, during a family holiday in Eastbourne, he wandered away from the seafront and was transfixed by what he saw at Devonshire Park, one of the choicest tennis venues in the country.

Never before had the fifteen-year-old Fred seen tennis in all its glory. The sight of spruce young men in long white trousers and elegant, athletic women in white dresses playing on immaculately prepared, exaggeratedly green lawns awakened something deep within him. He liked the sense of wealth too – almost as much as the tennis – that exuded from all around him, from the exclusive setting to the carefully tailored clothing to the sculpted rackets to the gleaming Sunbeam 12s, MGs and Daimlers waiting to be driven off to he could hardly imagine where. 'I asked my father if all those big cars belonged to the players and he said they did. "Then that's for me," I said.' He also remembered that his father chided him for going off on his own, but Sam Perry also spent five shillings on a second-hand racket when the family returned home so that young Fred could satisfy his sudden surge in enthusiasm for tennis.

For five years table tennis and tennis vied for his attention. When he moved on from the Brentham Institute, the main attraction of the Herga club in Harrow was that it offered even better facilities for both games. In the short term, his not specialising in either sport early on was one reason for his comparatively unsuccessful efforts as a teenage tennis player, a Middlesex junior doubles title in 1926 being his most notable achievement; in the long term, it might actually have helped his tennis. Paul Metzler, the Australian tennis writer and analyst, reckoned one of the reasons for Perry's confidence as a tennis player was his having 'escaped the torments of ever being a promising junior'. In recent times, the Williams sisters, Venus and Serena, were purposely not entered for junior events by their father and mentor, Richard, because he thought they were of limited, if any, benefit.

What seems to have been the case is that just when Perry was starting to give much more time to tennis, he took off like a rocket through the ranks of table tennis, which was far less competitive at this time than tennis. Excited by this, he devoted himself almost equally to the two sports between the ages of eighteen and twenty, before deciding that tennis would give him greater fulfilment than a sport in which he could become world champion quite so quickly. The story of his brief life as an eminent table tennis player is colourfully told in an extended report hitherto consigned to a dusty basement. The author, the Honourable Ivor Montagu, was an eccentric aristocrat who would loom large in Perry's life until after he won his world title in 1929.

Montagu, the third and youngest son of the second Lord Swaythling, was the antithesis of the tradition-bound administrators Perry was starting to encounter in tennis. He was a prominent British communist who happily admitted to being a traitor to his class. He explained his affiliation by saying communism was the only political and economic system that made sense, and devoting his life to it was 'necessary simply as a mere honest act of gratitude for life'. Beyond politics Montagu's greatest passions – he was given to extreme enthusiasms – were films and table tennis. He founded the London Film Society in 1925, contributed reviews to the *Observer* and co-wrote the screenplay for *Scott of the Antarctic*. His interest in table tennis began when his father set up a table on the first-floor landing of the Swaythling country seat near Southampton. He came to see it as a sport that fitted his politics because it 'suited the lower paid, above all – since it was played indoors – in crowded towns'. At Cambridge he played for (and, it is said, saved the honour of) his university in the table tennis matches of 1924 and 1925 against Oxford.

He first met Perry, who was five years younger than him, when Fred entered a table tennis tournament in April 1927 at the Memorial Hall just around the corner from Fleet Street in the City of London. Montagu wrote that it was Perry's first table tennis tournament and that he entered the minor or second-class singles. He went on

He was 17 years old and seemed rather small for his age, but the two things that struck the eye at once were his bright red face and his boundless self-confidence.

He was a lawn tennis player then already and did not know

much about the indoor game; in fact at that first meeting he was trying to get leave from me as referee to go off in the middle of his rounds and play a club match at lawn tennis. Not expecting him to survive long, I readily and imprudently promised the sought permission, but, lo and behold, veteran after veteran fell beneath his racket, nothing would get rid of him, and eventually the whole tournament had to stand still while the promise was fulfilled. The most notable thing was that the person least astonished by his successes was young Fred himself. He took it all as a matter of course.

Montagu had been a prime mover in establishing table tennis as an international sport. He helped to frame its laws during a meeting at the London home of his parents and also to found the International Table Tennis Federation, an organisation he served as president for forty-one years. The sport had been invented in the nineteenth century by those gifted originators of indoor pastimes, British army officers whiling away their time in remote garrisons, but its initial spread beyond the regimental mess was very gradual. The first world championships did not take place until December 1926, also at the Memorial Hall off Fleet Street. There were four tables set out in a large room on the first floor, enough seats for a few hundred spectators, which were at times packed, and places set aside for the national press, who were just starting to take an interest in the sport. This was about as grand as it got. Some of the fifty men and fourteen women who took part did not bother to change out of their street shoes or clothes or take off their ties. The event was conceived as the European championships but eight Indian students turned up unexpectedly wanting to take part, which led to a retrospective upgrade at the inaugural meeting of the international federation. Montagu himself put up £300 to cover seating and hospitality for the teams. 'I could not guarantee more for it was all I had . . . and we got out just inside the guarantee,' he said.

Even given this rudimentary beginning, what Perry achieved in table tennis's hesitant nascent years as an international sport was remarkable, particularly as Britain was not in the front rank of nations as far as playing was concerned. Administrators such as Montagu were the first to establish Britain as a force in world table tennis – thus preparing the way for Mayor Boris Johnson to declare at the 2008 Olympics in Beijing that ping-pong would be coming home at the 2012 games in London. Hungary and Sweden were the countries where the standard was highest in those early days after table tennis acquired a world body. Two Hungarians, Dr Roland Jacobi, a thirty-five-year-old lawyer, and Maria von Mednyanszski, the dominant female player throughout the 1920s, won the singles titles at those first world championships.

Montagu and Perry met again in January 1928, when Perry entered the trials to represent England at the second world championships, to be held later that month in Stockholm. 'He was still not much of a player,' Montagu said. 'He had no strokes or style at all, but simply by agility and determination in defence put up a fair show in the trials and set out for abroad reckoned about fourth best of the team of five making the journey. When he was chosen he jumped for joy and confessed he had been working hard, determined he, too, would play for England ever since seeing an exhibition.'

The trip to Stockholm was Perry's first overseas and, undaunted, he once more startled Montagu, who as England captain picked him for the opening team match against Czechoslovakia. Montagu decided to rest his best players for this encounter and try out the next three. The two most successful of these would be rewarded with places against Hungary's powerful team in the evening. Montagu reckoned Hungary to be to table tennis what France's dominant Davis Cup side were to tennis at that time and Finland's renowned endurance athletes were to long-distance running. 'I know whom I expected to have to drop: Perry.'

That Perry kept his place was down to a huge slice of luck against the weakest Czechoslovak, who would have won by two games to love had it not been for a scoring error. Montagu described what happened:

> The score was being called in Swedish, which none of us properly understood, and not until too late, and referring to my notes, did I realise the score had been called 20 all instead of

21–19 to his opponent. By that time Perry had scraped the game 26–24 and his opponent was leading in the third. I did not intervene then, for I make it a rule, for or against my side, never to intervene if the two players are satisfied. A gain in accuracy is not worthwhile at the expense of unsettling and making nervous both players. Intervention would have meant a heated argument in two or three languages, very likely no concession in the score by the umpire and his opponent being left in a worse state than if the mistake had been realised at the time. In the end, Perry recovered to take the decider. He beat the other two Czechoslovaks on the crest of his triumph, walked into the team in the evening and wiped the floor with two Hungarian world champions. From that moment he was a made player.

By the final day of those 1928 world championships, 29 January, Perry was through to the quarter-finals of the singles, the last four of the mixed doubles and the final of the doubles, in which his partner was Charlie Bull, a first-class cricketer who played for Kent and later Worcestershire. On top of this, Perry had team duties to fulfil in the morning.

In the deciding match against the best Austrian player, he was leading 15–5 in the first game when he tripped over a raised floorboard, turned an ankle and lay yelling in agony. A Hungarian doctor raced to his assistance. 'He had him squirming on the table as he dragged the ankle back into place with a click,' Montagu said. 'That night the foot was bound in plaster and England's attempts on the titles had ended for the year.'

Despite this, the records show that Perry played his singles quarter-final, losing to the eventual runner-up, the Hungarian Laszlo Bellak, and also lost the doubles final, failing to win a game in either match. Perry's world ranking reached seven that year and a spectator at the world championships, referred to by Montagu as 'a foreign expert', told the England captain, 'The greatest attacking stroke we have seen is Perry's forehand drive.' Montagu replied that in England Perry was known only as a defensive player, before going away to record, 'It is true, Perry learns with every match he plays. He had built up his game in the course of that one tournament.'

As hosts and acknowledged masters of table tennis, Hungary's team were expected to dominate the 1929 world championships held in January in their capital city; no foreign player had ever won a tournament in Budapest. They started by securing the team title and were represented in each of the singles and doubles finals on the closing day. Montagu's account of the men's final is splendidly graphic but statistically inaccurate if the official scorecard, which gives the result as 14–21 21–12 23–21 21–19 to Perry, is to be believed. He wrote:

Perry is 19; following sensation after sensation he faces in the final Hungary's newcomer of the year, Miklos Szabados, a 17-year-old genius, who had defeated the title holder by a wide margin in the previous round. A great hall. Packed tiers on tiers, three thousand people, cabinet ministers like Christmas trees in evening dress, shouting students, a pushing crowd crammed against the police on every staircase, adding and oozing into every exit. Fred and I walked a little in the fresh air, then in the corridor to get used to the closeness, talking of other things than the night's fate. A last word, 'Keep it off his forehand,' and the match begins.

Perry is now a little taller, very lean, his face keyed tight as it will go. Szabados short, stocky, expressionless. Neither is easy [in] the first game, each is feeling for control and it will not come. The ball seems dead. I whisper to the Hungarian captain that neither players trusts the ball, but each is reluctant to make the first complaint. It is apparent to us both that the ball is bad but we decide not to interfere for fear of causing unsettlement. Szabados wins the first game to 18. A new ball is now commissioned. Perry increases speed; he is playing very fast now, smashing the ball to the backhand or short across court every time it rises. He wins the second to 19. Playing flawlessly, he wins the third to 16. Szabados, imperturbable, blinks slightly and takes a quick lead with two great forehand strokes. Perry fights back, goes ahead, leads 19–14. But Szabados is never finished. He closes desperately, 15–19, 16–19, service change, 17–19, 18–19. The next must be the crucial point. It seems the rally will never finish. Perry hits, hits again, again; Szabados is driven back, again. Szabados is fishing the ball back almost from the floor beneath the gallery, 35 feet behind the table, almost the longest get I've ever seen in table tennis. It comes curling in the air. Will it go over? Just, no, yes – it is right. Perry tries to drop it short as the crowd goes into a frenzy. Szabados has run all the way up and just reached it once more. The crowd is hysterical and Perry, with a last effort, not oblivious to but still tauter for the noise, drives it back, fast, past his opponent stumbling to recover. The game is over, from 20–18 it goes still to 20–19 before it is won, but one feels it is over.

Another account of the 1929 world final was included in a profile of Perry that appeared in a 1937 American table tennis magazine. The author, Sandor Glancz, also diverged from the official score.

The match started and the enthusiastic and cheering crowd suddenly quieted. The Englishman was taking the lead. Oh, well, they said, it would only be for a short time. But they were wrong, the Englishman continued to produce brilliant play and he scored repeatedly against the Hungarian. The first game went to Perry. Then something unusual happened. The crowd realised they were witnessing a match in which an outsider was actually trimming one of their native sons, but the outsider's dashing play, brilliant tactics and his ever present smile caught their fancy. The silence that had existed as the Hungarians realised their favourite was on the road to defeat turned to cheers for the Englishman as he continued to play in masterful manner. Fred Perry won the second game of the match but dropped the third. In the fourth game, leading 20–16, Perry was unable apparently to gain the point that would give him the coveted title. The score became close and finally 20–19 . . . but on the next service Fred flicked a beautiful backhand for the point, game and championship. The crowd went mad, rising to its feet and giving Perry an ovation that lasted more than 10 minutes.

Montagu assessed the new world champion as a man and player:

This is the excellence of Perry, character and quickness. Sir Wallis Myers [tennis correspondent of the *Daily Telegraph*] has written somewhere that his strokes at the outdoor game are peculiar, not truly lawn tennis strokes, but developed from taking the rising ball at the much faster indoor game. This is not correct. Perry has always been a lawn tennis player, even in reaching number one in table tennis's world ranking. He does not use the rising ball at table tennis; he does not play the typically table tennis top-spun strokes; he cannot half-volley. His game indoors is an amazingly fast and active chop defence, enabled by feet that have become speedy at lawn tennis, and a lightning, plain-hit forehand off a high-risen ball, a purely lawn tennis stroke.

His success in the one sport is not due to success in the other; both come from his inner qualities – quickness of thought and act, quickness to learn and a tremendous self-assurance. No player can reach the heights at any game without wholesome and boundless conceit, a conviction that nobody and nothing is too difficult for them to overcome, the ability to imagine themselves succeeding at any obstacle even if to others it looms like a mountain. Some cling to this inner star nervously on edge each moment lest a little thing should part their hold on it, such were Suzanne Lenglen and Bill Tilden; others mask it tightly by unchanging face, like Henri Cochet, Helen Wills and René Lacoste, but their hold is in reality no less precarious; the third group, the most attractive – or, to put it otherwise, those most difficult to quarrel with for long – are cheerfully open, gaily inviting everyone to share their own belief in their abilities, of such are Inman, Charles Fry, Jean Borotra and Perry.

Nothing is too difficult for Perry. The harder the task, the greater the company, the more likely he is to shine. When he won the world championship at table tennis it was the first table tennis tournament he had ever won. This is a feat perhaps unparalleled in any sport. He had lost event after event in England to his team-mates, but the occasion found him ready, gay and impertinent. That is why table tennis players all over Europe are backing him to win at Wimbledon. They have never seen him play lawn tennis, they do not care about the form books, they only know that, at any game, Perry will yet shock his betters.

Perry's win in Budapest brought barely a ripple of recognition back in Britain beyond the small table tennis community, which, thanks to the patronage of Montagu and his friends from Cambridge University, was probably as much upper crust as working class. Perhaps the most lasting legacy of Perry's win was the trophy presented by Montagu's London table tennis club just off Ludgate Circus, St Bride's, to honour the new world champion. Perry received a trophy from the Hungarian national association for his victory in Budapest, which he kept – and latterly, his daughter remembered, would be used to throw quarters in when the family lived in the US – but the St Bride Vase is still presented by the sport's world governing body to the men's winner.

The sport's toffish patronage and the lack of credit Perry received for winning the world title may explain why he played down the achievement. He became almost dismissive of it. 'I have now finished with serious table tennis,' he told his father soon after his triumph in Budapest. 'This after only two years at the game!' Sam Perry wrote, before recording the rest of their conversation: '"What are you going to do now?" I asked him, and the answer came in very definite terms, "I am going to win my Davis Cup colours in four years' time." Ambitious, indeed, but as a matter of fact he actually won his place in the Cup team two years later, in 1931.'

Before 1929 was out, Perry, having won an indoor tennis event at Queen's, told reporters that he preferred lawn tennis to table tennis and said it was impossible to play both for a variety of reasons. Explaining one of them, he said, 'Compare the weight of a table tennis bat, which is only a few ounces, with that of a lawn tennis racket.' In his 1934 autobiography he dealt with table tennis in a few lines. It was, he wrote, 'a game at which, before my lawn tennis developed seriously, I won the high-sounding title of world champion'. An American magazine reported, 'Perry now prefers not to hear about his youthful exploits with a paddle.' In his later autobiography, Perry said, 'I was world champion at nineteen, so I decided to retire.'

There is, though, plenty of evidence that deep down Perry never completely lost his affinity with table tennis and gave up playing seriously only with some reluctance. He went on competing in table tennis events for some time, even after ending any doubt that tennis was his first preference when he qualified for Wimbledon in June 1929. The sort of attention Wimbledon received compared to table tennis really excited him. But it would take more than this and a scary portrayal by his father of table tennis as a health hazard to put him off completely. Once Sam Perry had overcome his incredulity at hearing Fred announce that he had done with serious table tennis just days after winning the world title, he counselled his son: 'You play table tennis at night under lights in a smoke-filled atmosphere and on Sunday mornings you look like death warmed up. You've won the world championship, what else is there to win? Why not concentrate on tennis? If you're going to be a Jack of all trades you can be master of none.'

Perry's enduring enthusiasm for table tennis was evident in March 1931, when he won three titles, including the singles, at the West Middlesex Championships in Ealing having that morning gone by train to Bristol to play tennis for Middlesex in the inter-county hard court championships. He won two singles in the West Country and arrived back at Paddington in the evening in time for a car to whisk him to Ealing.

He went on competing at the English Open table tennis championships until 1933, when the event was played at the Pavilion Gardens in Buxton and he won the consolation singles. In Paris, where he was playing tennis, he took part in an exhibition rematch of the 1929 world table tennis final and once again outplayed the formidable Szabados. He was even talked into turning out, at short notice, for England in a table tennis international against Hungary in London soon after returning from a tennis tournament in South Africa in 1932. In preparing for this match, he injured his right wrist as he tried to regain his old form in the space of three days. It was the last time he prepared seriously for a table tennis match.

Still, more than half a century later, Perry demonstrated that his passion and talent for table tennis lived on. In 1987 he attended a promotional event at a London hotel and played a few points against Johnny Leach, the Englishman who won the world title in 1949 and 1951. 'We were just knocking up for fun, or so I thought,' Leach recalled in a written tribute when Perry died, 'but it soon became apparent that Fred didn't intend that I should score a single point against him. He really hated to lose at anything, even at the age of 77, as he was then.' Leach said that Perry still had a quick eye, lightning reflexes and immaculate ball control. 'I was told that his only possible weakness was a sometimes suspect backhand. Weakness? You could have fooled me.'

Another thing Leach remarked on was that Perry played table tennis in the same style that he had seen him play tennis, using a topspin forehand off an early ball to make an opening for an attack. It reminded him of Andre Agassi, the American who won Wimbledon in 1992. In fact Leach slightly missed the point, because what Perry did, regardless of what Ivor Montagu had to say, was play certain tennis strokes, notably the early forehand drive, in the same style that he played table tennis as a young man. What Leach was seeing in that 1987 exhibition was the older man reprising some of the strokes that he forged with a table tennis bat and found were as effective when played with a gutted racket.

Bunny Austin, who would become Perry's main accomplice in Britain's domination of the Davis Cup, had no doubt about the origin of his tennis strokes. They first met in the spring of 1929 at the indoor tennis courts in Dulwich, and apart from Perry's greeting – 'Hello, I'm the table tennis champion of London, Middlesex and the world' – Austin was struck by his distinctive shot making. 'The table tennis influence was immediately noticeable,' he said. 'He had transferred unchanged onto the court the strokes he played on the table, the flicked forehand, the stabbed backhand. And though he was wild at that time, there was no mistaking his great promise.'

In Perry's own words, he played this forehand shot with 'the wrist brought well over the ball at the moment of impact and it speeds, in theory at any rate, down the sideline'. It is unlikely many players could have replicated the Perry forehand, particularly holding the racket with the so-called continental grip that he brought with him from table tennis – palm of the hand on top of the handle (rather than behind or underneath it) – without his immensely strong wrist.

Perry also retained from his table tennis days the unusual habit for a tennis player of holding the racket in only one hand as he prepared to receive serve, and a backhand drive or volley played on the forehand side of his body. This was a typical piece of Perry improvisation that came in useful when he had no elbow room to play a ball coming slowly at him.

The speed with which Perry's tennis developed evidently caused some friction at the Brentham Institute. It was bad enough for him to be caught practising on the bowling greens when the tennis courts were all occupied, but when some members lobbied for the impudent lad to be given a trial to represent the club there was an even stronger reaction from on high. 'This was too much for the powers that were,' Sam Perry said, 'who imagined the worst if a mere boy were included in the team.' Perry did eventually get picked before he decided to switch to playing at the Herga club, which entailed swapping the short walk round the corner for a journey of a few miles north of the A40.

It was a Brentham member called Jenkins who actually advised the move to Herga (the Anglo Saxon word for Harrow), where, Perry said, they took an interest in juniors. Also the new surroundings met Jenkins' suggestion that Perry find 'a better-class club where the members looked as if they were going places'. Even so, Perry never underestimated the role the Brentham Institute played in his early development as a tennis player and a painting of the club presented to him after he won Wimbledon for the first time hung prominently on a wall at his home.

It was not long before the promise Perry showed playing at Brentham and then Herga was revealed to a wider audience. In 1926, two years after being ticked off by his father for sneaking off on his own to watch tennis at Devonshire Park in Eastbourne, he entered the Middlesex Junior Lawn Tennis Championships. Playing with the five-shilling racket, whose strings were now even more frayed, the seventeen-year-old Perry and his Brentham colleague Harold Melhuish were the surprises of the tournament when they won the doubles against a pair which included one of the country's top young players, Bob Tinkler. Still, though, size was against him when he played on his own, and he was swept off court in an early round of the singles by Ted Avory, another star of the junior circuit, whose forehand overwhelmed Perry.

The rickety old racket finally let him down completely when, soon afterwards, he played in the British Junior Championships, held each autumn on the hard courts at Wimbledon. The antiquated implement came apart in his hand as he fought what was anyway a lost cause in a second-round match against Tinkler, who had Perry's measure in a one-on-one contest. This was one defeat Perry survived without going into a sulk – he said immediately he started playing tennis competitively it was the end of the world when he lost – because of his excitement at being allowed to hang his clothes in the locker used by René Lacoste, one of the great French players. 'Fred thought this was a great honour,' Sam Perry said. He was far more delighted by this, apparently, than by the far more practical benefit of being presented with a replacement racket by the British Davis Cup player Cyril Eames, who had been impressed by Perry's play. Perry would go on to repay Eames by beating him in a doubles match with Frank Wilde, the player he teamed up with at Herga in what turned into a successful partnership over a number of years.

Perry's own, brutal assessment of himself as a junior, delivered more than fifty years later, was, 'I was generally a competent quarter-finalist.' The turning point, said Perry, came when he met A.R. 'Pops' Summers at the Herga club. 'For some reason,' Perry remarked disin-genuously, 'Summers took a liking to me.'

Summers' interest in juniors, his understanding of every aspect of the game, the psychological side in particular, and his job working for the equipment company Slazenger, which meant he was able to supply Perry with free equipment, would all come in useful. One of Summers' first contributions was to suggest Perry enter the annual tournament for schoolboys at Queen's, the club in west London that still stages the pre-Wimbledon grass-court event. Perry and his father both wrote about what happened in this tournament, not because of how Perry played, which was not well enough to win, but because it opened their eyes to the alien world at the top of the contemporary tennis scene, where admission seemed to be by public-school accent only.

As an active socialist from a working-class background, Sam Perry took particular delight in his son's infiltration of this world, seeing it as proof of an improving society in which ordinary people could make something of themselves. 'Fred's progress in lawn tennis was rapid, and may be unusual,' he said. 'It has been by way of the organised games at elementary and secondary schools, and later through the channels of the lawn tennis clubs, rather than a university. I think this illustrates how a boy may achieve some success through the facilities that are open to the average youth.'

On a later occasion, though, Sam Perry backtracked a little, stressing instead that while it was possible to achieve success it was not easy for poorer families. At a lunch given by the Co-operative Wholesale Society in Manchester in 1935 to honour Fred, who was a former employee, Sam Perry said if tennis were made more democratic hundreds of boys and girls could do equally well, if not better, than his son. There had to be a new orientation if the children of working-class and middle-class families were to have the opportunity to reach the top. The cost of tournament entrance fees, typically nearly two pounds, railways fares and hotel expenses limited the progress of children whose families were not comfortably off.

Sam Perry referred to his son's experience at the Queen's tournament as 'an entertaining incident' but may not have been so benevolent had things worked out differently. Fred was so eager to play at Queen's that he arrived before nine on the morning of the first day of the tournament and persuaded the club secretary, Commander E.B. Noel, to let him take part even though entries had closed. 'Fred rushed home and packed his few things, including his one racket,' his father wrote in an account that bore out his son's intrepidness.

On arriving back at Queen's he was challenged by a commissionaire, who inquired: 'What school do you represent, sir: Eton,

Marlborough, Harrow, Repton?' Fred looked astonished and replied: 'Ealing County School.' The commissionaire replied: 'Never heard of it. Where is it?' 'At Ealing,' was the reply. 'I'm afraid there is no room for you here,' was the reply – accommodation having been reserved for the various public-school representatives. 'Never mind,' said Fred, 'I can change on the floor.' Just then Jimmy Nuthall [a friend of the Perrys] came along. 'Where does Jimmy come from?' asked Fred. 'Repton,' was the reply. 'All right, then I will go with Repton,' said Fred, and that is how he 'went to Repton'. He was the first non-public schoolboy to compete in the tournament.

Perry, giving his account of the tournament much later, added that at Queen's he bumped into Jenkins, the Brentham club member who was acting as a dressing-room supervisor. He greeted him as Mr Jenkins and was told by a supercilious Queen's official that this was not the way to address an attendant. He replied that he had known Mr Jenkins much longer than he had known Queen's and would address him as he wanted. 'I was a determined young cuss even then,' he said, 'and was very conscious that I was regarded as being from the wrong side of the tracks.'

He never really grew tired of flaunting this cussedness. Dan Maskell, who was a year older than Perry and rose from the same social background to become a confidant, coach and lifelong friend, said that Perry possessed a social chip that he wore quite prominently on his shoulder and made him doubly determined to show the establishment he could beat them. 'In a sense he was not typically British,' Maskell said, 'for there was an aggressiveness and dedication about him that was out of step with the contemporary attitude towards sport.'

A story told by someone else who knew Perry well over many years, Teddy Tinling, bears this out. Tinling, a moderately good player who became renowned as a designer of tennis fashions, recalled that after Perry went with a club team to play at Cambridge University it was politely suggested that it might be best not to include him in future matches. Tinling, who had himself taken teams to Fenner's, where the university played, described it as a place where the noise level rarely rose above a restrained ripple of applause and a muted call of 'Jolly good shot.' 'It wasn't just Perry's accent,' Tinling said, 'but his consuming drive to win at all costs that ruffled the feathers of the more tradition-bound centres of the game.'

Tinling also made an observation on the way Perry spoke. He said that it was regarded as curious in the strictly public school tennis world of those days and aroused antagonism towards him, 'which neither his handsome hero's looks, often enhanced by a flashing smile, nor his glib, wise-cracking tongue were able to break down'. According to Tinling, Perry was only the second successful English tennis player, after his frequent doubles partner Pat Hughes, to speak with a non-U accent, a term popularised in the 1950s by the author and aristocrat Nancy Mitford. In the end, though, Tinling said, he forced people to accept him, and this was entirely because of his belief in himself.

Apart from brief spells at the Co-operative Wholesale Society and the sports goods company Spalding after he left school, Perry's only workplace until he reached middle age was the tennis court. Sam Perry was instrumental in fixing him up with a job with the CWS in 1925 and then providing him with the means to concentrate fully on his tennis from 1929 onwards. The job at the CWS was as a clerk in the central London office. Perry joined the tea department with a view to going abroad to work in a supervisory role on a plantation on the Indian subcontinent. He did not like office routine, which evidently reminded him of being in class at school as it involved sitting behind a desk on a high stool and writing in ledgers.

Staying on in this job would have been as big a mismatch of his talents as going back to where the family came from to follow his forebears into the cotton industry. He was set on devoting himself to tennis. 'When I first went to work, I used to continue practising my tennis strokes with the aid of my umbrella on the twenty-minute walk to Ealing Broadway station,' he said. 'I'd clip the tops of hedges and flowers when nobody was looking.' His only other employment, at Spalding, at least placed him in a setting that was more sympathetic to this ambition even if he still had to seek special leave to play in tournaments.

His need for sporting success was reflected in another switch of club. Although he retained friendly links with Herga and, crucially, Pops Summers, he reckoned his game would benefit from being based at Chiswick Park, where Laurie and Reggie Doherty, who between them ruled Wimbledon for the best part of ten years at the turn of the century, had played. He was attracted by the club's record of dominating competition in Middlesex for many years and remained faithful to it as a player for the rest of the time he lived in England. He described it simply as 'a great club'. He even chose to represent Chiswick Park in the Middlesex Championships in the build-up to Wimbledon rather than play in the London tournament at Queen's, which attracted most of the other top international players preparing for tennis's main event.

At the 1995 service of thanksgiving to celebrate Perry's life, Emlyn Jones, a friend and broadcaster, recalled chiding Perry that his name did not appear on the winners' board at Queen's. Perry had put him straight: 'I never played in it because on the Saturday before Wimbledon I always played for my club.' Jones reflected, 'Sentiment and loyalty. Just imagine a Wimbledon champion playing for his club today immediately before the start of the championships.'

In the 1940s, the grass courts of Chiswick Park went the way of so many well-appointed community tennis clubs that tried to peg prices at an affordable level when a compulsory-purchase order secured them for building. Later, the Herga club suffered a similar fate after it was bought by a developer. A country that has so indifferently built over such amenities, burying the heritage of its greatest player beneath bricks and mortar, should not perhaps be surprised that replicating what Perry accomplished has proved so elusive.

As Perry approached his twentieth birthday in 1929, the recently crowned world table tennis champion already had his sights fixed on what he now regarded as his life's great purpose, the conquest of Wimbledon. To achieve this, though, a lot of work still needed to be done.

Perry's inborn ability, his obsessiveness and the assistance of everyone from his father to sundry passing coaches had all been factors in lifting him to the level where a future dedicated to tennis had started to look viable. His father's support was by far the most important. The financial help he gave his son that enabled him to play tennis full time was only part of it. Even though tennis was not his sport, Sam Perry also provided valuable advice based on what he had learned during his rise from factory floor to the floor of the mother of parliaments. He impressed on Fred that 'it was not this, or that, particular match or tournament that mattered, but what might happen three years ahead'. He told him he must take the long view, and never sacrifice his strokes or game just for the sake of winning a match. So sure of this was Sam Perry that he offered it to a wider audience in a contribution to Fred's 1934 autobiography. He wrote, 'May I be allowed to urge most strongly upon all young players the necessity of taking the long view? Try to improve your game, strengthen your weak strokes, do not be too keen on just winning a tournament in your early years.'

Certainly Fred marked these words, quoting the long-view theory back at his father if ever he chided him for losing a match. More significantly, he implemented his father's advice when considering how to improve his game, which was in danger of stalling at a mediocre level. His own view was that it was generally safe, but vulnerable against a hard-hitting player. This was why he put on hold the wider development of his game and, with the help of Summers, set about the lengthy process of developing a stroke of penetration that would transform him into a Wimbledon contender.

Helpfully, Perry now at last added the necessary inches to reach the ideal height for a good tennis player, which then as now is somewhere between six feet and six feet four inches. In two years he shot up nine inches, a fact noted by Anthony Sabelli, the secretary of the Lawn Tennis Association, who asked for Perry's passport ahead of an overseas trip in 1930. Sabelli expressed surprise that when the document was issued only two years earlier, for the table tennis championships in Sweden, Perry's height was only five feet three inches and he was now six feet. Sam Perry's theory was that this sudden upward surge was the result of his son having taken up swimming.

The extra height was just what Perry needed as he worked on upping the destructive capability of his strokes. The early, snapped forehand, played with the shortest of backswings, would be the main weapon. Summers recognised that he could really make something of this stroke. Not only was Perry familiar with it from when he attacked the rising ball in table tennis, he also had great wrist strength, even more than is common in most good racket-sport players, a prerequisite of playing tennis effectively.

Summers' aim was for Perry's forehand to emulate that of Henri Cochet. The Frenchman's game was well known in Britain as he had completed a sensational Wimbledon success in 1927 by winning quarter-final, semi-final and final all from two sets down. Cochet's early forehand allied to his blend of touch and toughness was what Summers aimed to reproduce in Perry.

After his growth spurt, Perry was taller than Cochet, and his forehand, once perfected, was even more potent. That he did perfect it was testimony to his commitment. He spent a whole winter at it and persisted despite his overall play going into decline, which his father had preached was a price worth paying. 'Though I held the singles and the doubles championship at the Herga club, my play suffered to such an extent that I was dropped from the match team,' he wrote. 'The ball either went sailing out of court or into the bottom of the net; but I saw the advantage of persevering and gradually mastered the new method, though sometimes, when things go wrong, I wonder whether I really have mastered it even yet!'

Summers enlisted the help of players from the Herga and Chiswick Park clubs to feed the Perry forehand. 'Literally hundreds of people would come in relays and hit quiet shots at me while I learned to take the ball on the rise,' Perry said. And what he meant by 'on the rise' was so soon after the bounce that it was tantamount to playing a half-volley. Many years later, Maskell recalled that Perry's attempts to develop an early-ball technique along the lines of Cochet and Jean Borotra were derided by his critics as being too risky, 'But he knew that if he could ever perfect a running forehand with the ball taken on the rise his athletic physique and superior fitness would enable him to overcome most opponents.'

For a while Perry was close to despair as the misses and uncontrolled hits far outnumbered anything remotely resembling what he was trying to achieve. Years later, Perry maintained that, on what he described as a magical Sunday morning at the Herga club, the shot suddenly clicked. He leaned into an early ball and it fizzed to exactly the point he had intended, the action of coming over the ball helping to produce a late dip that brought it down just inside the baseline. Presumably this had happened before but the difference was that until now Perry had never felt in complete control of the stroke. Summers told him to stop there and savour the triumphant execution of the shot rather than risk spoiling the moment by trying in vain to repeat it, and come back in a week's time. The advice worked. The following Sunday, Perry found not only could he still play the stroke but keep on doing so at will. One of the best accounts of the shot that Perry was now close to perfecting came years later from Peter Ustinov, the writer, actor and lifelong tennis enthusiast: 'He took the ball so early that it seemed almost as unfair as body-line bowling to those who regarded tennis as a kind of prescribed choreography in which the strictest orthodoxy was de rigueur.'

Perry himself, reflecting on his career, put the shot in perspective: 'I had a sort of all-court game, not serve-and-volley like Ellie Vines. Everything I did was built on the fact that sooner or later my opponents had to hit the ball short on my forehand side. That was the end of the point as far as I was concerned.'

3

First glimpses of tennis glory: 1929–30

'Fred is the most promising player I've ever seen'

Quite possibly Sam Perry wanted to test whether his son had inherited any of his genes as a robust political animal when he suggested Fred join his campaign team for the general election of May 1929, which took place twelve days after Fred's twentieth birthday.

Sam Perry's target was to regain Kettering, where once again hunting folk and horny-handed sons of toil lined up against each other. Fred recalled that Young Conservatives showed up at meetings wearing dinner jackets. They goaded his father with questions such as, 'Which flag do you stand for, Perry, the red flag or the Union flag?' Hannah and Edith Perry attended some of the meetings, which, particularly in view of Hannah's failing health, prompted the Perry camp to hire minders. One of them, a Welshman called Jennings, a good amateur boxer, would be positioned at the front of the hall to discourage anyone from approaching too close to the stage. This time Sam Perry faced only a single barrel from the Conservatives. Sir Mervyn Manningham-Buller had switched to Northampton and Colonel J. Brown, an architect who specialised in war memorials and was certainly less formidable in name if not in manner, stood as Perry's most dangerous rival in a three-way contest.

Perry, as ever standing as a Labour/Co-operative candidate, won reasonably comfortably, his vote of 18,253 beating Colonel Brown's by 2,784 in a general election that brought Ramsay MacDonald back into office. Perry again served as a parliamentary private secretary during the second Labour government of 1929–31, a time of mounting economic turmoil, on this occasion to the president of the Board of Trade.

If Sam Perry had hopes of broadening his son's ambitions beyond sport at the start of the election campaign, he must have realised by the time it was over that despite his success in holding on to his seat he had not bred someone with an interest in public affairs. The competitive element of the fight to take Kettering might have excited Fred, but he showed no sign of connecting in any way with the political side of the contest, and it was not long before his fixation with tennis deepened when he won through to his first Wimbledon. What vestige of interest in a Westminster life might still have existed in Fred's mind would soon be extinguished completely by a family tragedy but for the moment the prospect of sporting success was all the disincentive he needed.

In reaching the main draw of the 1929 Wimbledon championships in late June, Perry also gave a hint of a steep improvement in his game under Pops Summers and offered the first glimpse of the glories that were to come. He negotiated three qualifying rounds without losing a set, the twelve games he dropped in a 6–4 6–4 6–4 win over H.F. Cronin being his closest match. 'Oh, the wonder of it,' was how Perry summed up his feelings at qualifying. What really pleased him, he also said, was that a competitor's badge secured him free admission for the whole of the tournament.

Up to this point he had precious little form as a tennis player. He had not won one of the big domestic club competitions, the type open not just to members of the host club, and he himself seemed surprised that 'my limited junior successes and one or two performances in senior tournaments' had secured him a place in qualifying. That he then qualified quite so easily to play at the All England Club must have taken aback even those few people closely associated with his tennis who appreciated how much potential he possessed. No wonder the national press took little notice as he launched his Wimbledon career.

Perry's first ever Wimbledon singles was on Monday 24 June 1929 on Court 16 against an Italian, Roberto Bocciardo, who experienced Perry's competitive will in a contest decided 9–7 in the fifth set. The next day, on Court 13, Perry beat Norman Dicks of Britain in four sets to reach the last thirty-two. Still his victories were no more than a footnote, if that, as the press box concentrated on the star players from abroad. These included two of France's Four Musketeers, Henri Cochet, who would claim his second title, and Jean Borotra, and the thirty-six-year-old American Bill Tilden, winner in 1920 and 1921 but still a formidable player, who would be crowned champion a third time a year later.

In fact it was not just the dailies who gave barely a mention to Perry. His own record of what happened was also brief in the extreme. 'I got through two rounds before being beaten by John Olliff, one of my contemporaries from the other side of the fence – public school.' Olliff showed the right sort of modesty when he recalled the match in one of several books he wrote on tennis some years later, describing his victory as a fluke. The reality was that he was a more experienced and probably a much better player than Perry at this stage, and the result was a most unfluky 6–2 6–3 6–3.

Perry's performances at his first Wimbledon did however catch the eye of those who ran the British game. This had the happy consequence that he joined up with Dan Maskell, who with Summers was the great coaching influence on the early part of his career. Maskell was newly installed as the All England Club's first teaching professional when Perry was sent there soon after his promising run at the 1929 championships. The two had much in common. Not only were they close in age, Maskell being the older by a year; they had working-class roots that united them in their distaste of the snobbish clique who stood sentry over the British game. 'We had an immediate rapport,' said Maskell, who grew up in the poorer part of Fulham in west London, and this friendship would last until his death over sixty years later.

The great difference between them was the career paths they chose within tennis, which at this time, in common with most other sports, was doing nothing concerted to bring together what were then the conflicting hemispheres of the amateur and professional. Amateurism would remain a precious creed of the English tennis elite until the post-war years, helping as it did to exclude those not wealthy enough to play for nothing. They would never admit this, of course; instead they defended their stance against professionalism on the grounds that it encouraged cheating and a lack of sports-manship. The difficulties that this sort of thinking created would complicate Perry's life for most of the 1930s.

Firmly guided by his father, whose left-wing views coexisted with strong, small-c conservatism, Perry at this stage rejected the idea of earning a living from tennis; Maskell, on the other hand, opted to draw a wage from the sport as a coach. In other words, he tainted himself with trade as far as the amateur establishment was concerned, and it was the tradesmen's entrance at Wimbledon that was opened to him when he became the All England Club professional. Before this, from the age of fifteen, Maskell had been on the staff of Queen's Club, rising to become the pro there. Alan Mills, who was the Wimbledon referee for more than twenty years and knew Maskell well, said that at Queen's Maskell was distinctly below stairs. 'In addition to his duties coaching the club's members,' Mills said, 'he had to string their rackets and fulfil other manual and menial tasks. He was emphatically not allowed to enter the members' bar. Good heavens no! A professional in the bar – it was quite unthinkable!'

Given that the press gave little space to the professional game, Perry was the one who would dominate the headlines as a player, although Maskell's record of sixteen British professional titles between 1928 and 1950 was worthy of greater recognition than it received. In August 1934 a newspaper report on the first professional tournament managed by the Lawn Tennis Association said, 'Experts think that Maskell would on occasion beat Perry [the newly crowned Wimbledon champion], whom he has often coached.' In later years, when both were broadcasters, Maskell made the greater impact as the voice of the BBC's television coverage from 1951 to 1991. 'Oooh, I say' was a Maskellism that had as much resonance as any stage entertainer's premeditated catchphrase, and his ability to make technical points in such a way that they were easily assimilated by the lay viewer helped to popularise Wimbledon.

Maskell did not take long to assess Perry. 'From the first I could see that he was very single-minded . . . He was a stubborn and sometimes truculent character who believed totally in his own ability.' Perry's friend also ascribed to him guts, character and vision, which made him widely respected by all while earning him, unfairly in Maskell's opinion, the reputation of being arrogant.

If Summers was the coach who did most to develop the Perry forehand, Maskell can be credited with helping to bring his backhand up to a standard that was not nearly as bad as some have made it out to be if not quite as good as he would have wanted it to be. 'Fred never saw his sliced backhand as a weakness,' Maskell said, categorising it, like Perry's forehand, as a table tennis shot played with very little backswing and with an open-faced racket soon after the bounce. 'Without risk, therefore,' Maskell said, 'he could manoeuvre an opponent about the court until the moment came when he could run round his backhand to sweep the running forehand deep into a corner to set up his winning shot.'

Maskell and Perry had an interesting way of working on the backhand. They would thread the handle of a racket through the top of the net about six inches from the sideline. As Maskell came in behind a deep approach shot in the middle of a long rally, Perry would take the ball early with a blocking action and aim for the racket head that stuck up above the net. When he could hit the racket almost at will, he moved on to perfecting a short, cross-court, angled pass using the same sliced blocking action. 'This was an essential part of his armoury to keep his opponents guessing,' Maskell said. Perry did not feel the need to develop a lifted or topped backhand, and if he had, Maskell reckoned, he could and would have perfected one. 'The whole emphasis of Fred's preparation with me at this stage was to make a world-class shot of his blocked backhand.'

Nor did Perry see any reason to develop a mighty serve. Old film shows him serving in a way that looks antiquated by today's standards. There are good reasons for this, among them the equipment. The balls in the 1930s had a pure wool cover that made them softer than the nylon-finished modern balls. This made them easier to control, which encouraged the sort of artistry with the racket that is rarely seen any more. The wooden rackets also provided an explanation of why players of Perry's era preferred a more crafted approach. Although these rackets were capable of generating scorching pace – Americans such as Ellsworth Vines and Les Stoefen possessed immense service power – keeping up the speed as consistently as top players can now with modern materials was not an option.

Another reason the serve was so different then was that players had to stand behind the baseline and keep one foot on the ground until after contact. In later years, Perry advocated a return to making it a foot fault if the forward foot did not stay on the ground. He said this would make the serve less dominant while not affecting the essence of the game. He was horrified by the modern serve and in his radio and TV commentaries would describe with an air of astonishment how Arthur Ashe, the 1975 Wimbledon champion, would stand well behind the baseline, throw up the ball ahead of him and then leap after it; or how Boris Becker, who won Wimbledon three times in the 1980s, would hurl himself forward, having hit his serve while several centimetres above the ground. At times he was scathing about the way grass-court tennis had been reduced by the big servers: 'The server bangs the ball into play and grunts; the other man hits it back and grunts. End of point.'

Perry used an orthodox slice when serving and saw the shot as a method of starting a rally on his terms rather than as a point winner. Paul Metzler, in a book on the styles of the game's great players, said of Perry, 'His favourite method of play was to gather in a rising-ball forehand en route to the net and arrive there a split second after his own shot had crossed it . . . He always preferred playing like a millionaire to playing like a miser. Attack was his nature, but he could also play grand defensive tennis when the situation demanded it.'

The progress that Perry made in partnership with Maskell prompted Sam Perry to accompany his son to one of their practice sessions at the All England Club. He watched them work out for two hours and, having waited until Fred was in the shower, took the young pro aside. 'What about this young man of mine?' he asked. 'He seems determined to take this game seriously. Do you think I should give him a year?' Maskell, towelling himself down, said, 'All I can tell you, Mr Perry, is that Fred is the most promising player I've ever seen. He seems to have exactly the right attitude to the game and is prepared to do whatever it takes to succeed.'

This commitment was rewarded when Perry secured his first open title in October 1929, winning against a field of high-class domestic players. The tournament was at the New Malden club in Surrey, which now nestles in the lee of the Kingston Bypass. Perry's hardest match was his semi-final against W.A.H. Duff, in which he passed up five match points in the second set before winning 6-4 6-8 7-5. He then outclassed W.R. Freeman in the final.

Fred Perry suffered a terrible blow on 8 January 1930, when his mother died, 'shattering my exuberance at the progress I was making in tennis'.

Hannah Perry's death certificate gave the cause as cancer of the uterus. This differed from Perry's recollection that a nervous illness had killed his mother. Possibly he was shielded from the real reason. In those days 'cancer' was almost a swear word, and people used it sparingly, particularly in front of the young. Perry even expanded on the nervous disease: 'The doctors seemed to think it had been brought on by the strain of being associated with my father's political life. It wasn't a long illness, but her death upset me very badly. I would never play on the anniversary of her death.' Some years later, in a newspaper interview, he repeated this diagnosis of why his mother had died at the age of fifty-two: 'Electioneering for the Labour Party in those days brought terrible family pressures. I'm convinced the strain of it killed my beloved mother. I vowed that when I grew up I would never, ever cast a vote.' He never did.

Quite how badly his mother's death affected Perry is hard to say. When the American news magazine *Time* put him on their front cover in September 1934, as he prepared to defend the US title, it made this dramatic claim: 'In 1930, when he was 20, his mother, to whom he was devoted, died after a long illness. Her son's nervous and physical condition was then so poor that doctors despaired of keeping him alive . . .' This seems a little fanciful, but it is just possible that Perry did suffer some kind of nervous reaction and, when writing about his mother's death many years later, muddled his own condition at the time with hers. The *Time* report is also interesting in that it corroborated stories that Hannah Perry had in fact been poorly for some time whereas her son said it was a short illness.

With Fred to be nursed through the ordeal of losing his mother, Sam Perry remained quiet about his own feelings during the brief period that he stayed a single man. His only expression of emotion at around this time, possibly provoked by Hannah's death, was when he showed spikier form than usual in parliamentary debates, to which he was a regular contributor. During a heated set-to on the economy, he turned on the Independent Labour Party MP James Maxton, a single-minded Scot who had spent a year in jail for campaigning against the First World War. Perry said dismissively that he did not know what Maxton's political philosophy was and that none of his interventions, along with the general position of the ILP, had included a single constructive proposal. Disturbed by the gathering economic crisis that led to the formation of the National Government in August 1931, Perry also attacked MacDonald's view that the general election that followed in October that year was not concerned with party politics. He said if he had supported the National Government he would have been a candidate backed by the Tories and his portrait would have been hanging in the Conservative Club.

Fred said in his memoirs that by the spring of 1930 he had recovered enough from his sadness 'to want to test my early-ball skills in the British Hard Court Championships in Bournemouth'. This tournament started at the end of April, by which time he had in fact taken part in the British Covered Court Championships at Queen's Club, losing early on in the singles but reaching the doubles final with Frank Wilde.

A real fillip came when the Davis Cup selectors included him for the first time in the trials at Wimbledon in mid-April. He lost a tight match to the experienced Charles Kingsley and the LTA magazine recorded in its report that Perry 'did enough to convince us that his time for Davis Cup honours will not be long hence . . . He has the full equipment of strokes and when experience and greater physical development have given him the ability to put his undoubted skill to complete use in the highest company he may become a very formidable proposition indeed.' The report's complimentary tone faltered when it referred to Sam Perry as 'an indulgent parent' for having stepped in before the hard court championships with financial help so his son could give up his job and concentrate on tennis. Perry senior described giving Fred this assistance as a bold decision, but not everyone agreed and a fairly petty dispute, built on the shifting sands of what constituted amateurism, took place with newspapers debating the propriety of such a step by a Labour MP.

It may have been that Sam Perry intended the money to bring

Fred some comfort after his mother's death, but it was a practical consideration that initiated the move. To play in Bournemouth Fred needed to get time off from the Spalding shop in Cheapside in the heart of the City of London, where he was earning four pounds a week and spending about three pounds of it on tennis equipment. Unfortunately for him, the boss of his department also wanted to go to Bournemouth, to watch, and two people could not be away at the same time. Fred discussed the situation with his father and Pops Summers, after which 'my father told me to resign my job and he would support me financially for a year, unless, of course, I made the grade sooner than that'.

The controversy illustrates the then-current view of the privileged classes that young men and women unlucky enough not to have independent means should take a proper job to support their pursuit of such frivolous pastimes as tennis. Parental handouts, relieving the necessity of going to work, could be seen not just as indulgent but as flouting the amateur code. Sam Perry was indignant at the criticism he received. He wrote later that his support merely amounted to giving Fred a twelve-month paid holiday – 'I could not have carried him much longer' – and added, 'Who had the right to criticise my action and the sacrifice involved? (And it was a sacrifice.) Let those who would blame me attempt to visualise my early years. Should it not be the aim of all of us to give our children a better chance than we have had?' He also cited the backing of his parliamentary colleagues: 'It might be supposed that if any objection to my decision were expressed it would come from my immediate friends in the Labour Group in the House of Commons. But they backed me to a man and wished us the best of luck.'

Fred Perry described the hard court championships in Bournemouth as 'my first tournament as a free man', and his performance also suggested that as a result of the shock of his mother's death he had acquired a sharper focus on what he wanted to achieve in tennis. It was as if he had been handed a release from the familiar prescriptions of how someone from his background should live his life. He started by winning a tough five-setter against Herman David, who at that year's Wimbledon would beat the emerging Australian Jack Crawford on his way to a place in the last sixteen, and the next day played the match of his young life when he came within a point of beating Bunny Austin, a Wimbledon semi-finalist the previous summer, in the second round.

One report reckoned that Austin, three years Perry's senior and arguably the best player Britain had produced in twenty years, was thoroughly rattled and a little lucky to survive over five earnestly contested sets. 'If Perry had not been overanxious when dealing with sitters and loath to believe he was in a position to force his presumed master in the fourth set he would have won. He had match point in the fifth set and on play taking it all through was the stouter-hearted and superior performer.'

In typical British style, the defeat was seen as a good thing for Perry, akin to a character-building early-morning cold shower and preferable to a cascade of warm praise, which might turn the lad into a swollen-headed softy. The press thought this, and so did Pops Summers, Perry's early mentor, who said, 'I felt like throwing my hat in the air for joy when Fred missed that match point. It was too soon. Had Fred won the public would have expected him to live up to it. Give him time.' Even Perry himself acknowledged there might have been a grain of truth in this, but only grudgingly – and after a pause of two years. 'Everybody was surprised that I had done as well as I had,' he said, 'but to lose like that seemed black tragedy at the time. Now it doesn't seem to matter half so much. Perhaps, even, that defeat did me no harm.'

What was evident was that a social class that hitherto had provided the nation with many excellent professional footballers, jockeys, golfers and boxers had now, for the first time, delivered an amateur tennis player with the potential to outperform all those emerging from the game's traditional milieu. Whisper it, but Britain might even have a player who could go on to challenge the might of France and the US, whose players were hogging most of the big prizes. The report of Perry's narrow defeat by Austin finished, 'he has a fore-hand that may become famous. It is not a new sort, but it is newly exploited. It does the irregular thing in a thoroughly regular way. At present Perry's weakness is his "middle register", the shots upon which stability is built and retained. He hands out too many gifts.'

Precious little largesse was evident two months later, when Perry started his second Wimbledon campaign with straight-set wins over British players Brame Hillyard and Orson Wright. Out on Court 10, Hillyard distinguished himself only by becoming the first man to play at the championships wearing shorts. In time of course Hillyard's daring outfit would be adopted by everyone, but it took a while. It was three more years before Austin, intrepidly, went bare-kneed on Centre Court. Apart from his legs, all Hillyard exposed in his singles against Perry was a game that was no match for his opponent's, which was maturing by the week and was underpinned by his speed and inexhaustible confidence. Perry's third-round win was of a different calibre altogether. Sam Perry said that in Fred's 1934 autobiography he did not think that his son wrote 'quite enough about the match at the 1930 Wimbledon championships that was the turning point in his tennis career'.

The contest he referred to was against the colourful Baron Umberto de Morpurgo. The baron held an Italian passport although his home city of Trieste had been part of the Austro-Hungarian empire when he was born and was annexed by Italy only after the First World War, during which the baron had gained a reputation as an air ace. He was both eccentric and typical of the sort of European aristo-crat who had helped to give tennis its elitist image – in other words the type who would cast a leery eye over a low-born such as Perry. His entourage included his beautiful Viennese wife, with whom he rowed constantly, his pet dog Tschao, his doubles partner Signor Gaslini and his protégé Giorgio De Stefani. Gianni Clerici, an Italian player who became one of the foremost writers on the game, recounted the story of the time De Stefani had the impertinence to beat his mentor for the first time. He ran to the net to shake hands, but 'the baron left him in the middle of the court, flabbergasted, with an outstretched arm and a red cheek after being slapped'. Playing in small tournaments was beneath de Morpurgo. He won a medal at the 1924 Olympics and, although he cared only for the major championships, was ranked in the world's top ten between 1928 and 1930.

He was thirty-four and seeded seven when he played Perry. The match was held on Court 3, the nearest Perry had been to Centre Court, for what was expected to be a taxing but negotiable contest for the baron. The small crowd, mainly Perry's fellow Chiswick Park club members at the start, grew rapidly so that by the end the space around the court was packed and people perched wherever they could to get a glimpse of the drama. Perry's own account of how he beat 'the Italian Davis Cup player with a mighty "kick" service' 10–8 4–6 6–1 6–2 was more graphic than detailed, which may account for his father's censure that it was too sparse. 'Do not ask me to describe the hurricane match,' Fred wrote. 'I suppose victory was due to the speed I was able to generate by "hitting an early ball", in accordance with the advice of Mr Summers. It was a touch-and-go match, for had he won the first set when leading 5–1 and set point the story would probably have been different. Victory and defeat at lawn tennis are indeed delicately balanced!'

The significance of Perry's win would prove to be far greater than merely confirming his talent. During the match a committee of the LTA was holding a selection meeting in a room overlooking the court. The last place on a four-man team to represent Britain in the United States in the autumn, and then join up with female members for a mixed visit to South America, was under discussion. The excited noises from outside prompted the committee to suspend its deliberations and go to the window. Soon after, Fred Perry's name was inked in as the fourth male player. 'I date the beginning of my tennis career from that day at Wimbledon in 1930,' he said.

Not all the reaction to Perry's win over de Morpurgo was entirely positive. Sam Perry recorded this incident: 'I was much surprised to hear one of our leading authorities, after congratulating Fred, say, "You are bound to have a reaction in your next match. Don't be surprised if you play terribly badly." It seemed to me undesirable to dampen confidence thus. Why not let a youngster carry on with faith in himself? If the reaction comes then there is time to offer him consolation.'

As it happened, Perry did lose in the fourth round, although it was not as a result of playing terribly badly. Now within one victory of reaching the quarter-finals at only his second Wimbledon, he was rewarded with his first appearance on Centre Court on the middle Saturday, 28 June. He would be up against Colin Gregory, a member of the Beverley and East Riding club in Yorkshire and the only other of the six British players who had reached the third round to progress to the last sixteen.

Frank Burrow, the tournament referee, a no-nonsense little man who chain-smoked cigars, summoned Perry to his office on the Friday. Knowing Burrow's reputation, Perry remembered suffering the same sort of attack of nerves brought on by an unexpected call to the headmaster's study. In fact Burrow invited Perry to accompany him on a familiarising visit to Centre Court before play started the next day. The pair strolled around the deserted court and, at Burrow's suggestion, Perry threw up a ball to get used to the background and begin to sense the atmosphere.

'Nothing in the world can prepare you for the Centre Court,' Perry said. He explained the greatest difficulty when playing on the court was caused by the longer than usual runback, beyond which there was a further space before the front row of the stands. When the ball was thrown up by the server above the level of the backstop, he said, it could be seen by the player receiving serve clearly enough, but it appeared to be several miles away. In reality, of course, the distance was only seventy-eight feet, but players who were not used to it imagined they had more time than was in fact the case. This was why what he called Centre Courtitis afflicted so many inexperienced players who could not 'hit their hats' until they fully understood the unique setting. He also pointed out that inexperienced players tended to appear on the court only because their opponent was a seed or some other star turn, which was another factor in fazing them.

In this instance, Gregory, six years older than Perry, was the established player, a Davis Cup veteran who had already been a Wimbledon quarter-finalist in 1926 and in 1929 had been the first British male to be seeded at the championships, the system having been introduced two years earlier. Also, Gregory had won the Australian title the previous year, hailed by the LTA as 'the best thing an English player has done for many a long day . . . a feat of which both the hero and his countrymen are entitled to feel proud'.

Perry would say that he started the match against Gregory poised and confident and suffered the nerves of a Centre Court debutant only when King George V turned up, from which point 'my play

was up and down like a fiddler's elbow'. The score of the exciting
five-set match certainly suggests an uneven performance by Perry.
The king did not arrive until after the younger man had made a
good start, winning the first set 6–3. Later, the royal party went for
tea, which might have been around the time Perry won the fourth
set. In the end, Gregory dominated the fifth set, winning it 6–1.

The story of Perry's first match on Centre Court was a particular favourite of his father's. A mere stripling, in Sam Perry's words,
Fred had little knowledge of the protocol the players should observe
and awaited a dig in the ribs from Gregory to signal the moment
to turn and bow towards the royal box. 'In the House of Commons,
this incident was the subject of much favourable and amusing
comment,' Sam Perry said. 'Many of my Conservative friends who
had been at the match were evidently impressed that the son of a
Co-operative Member of Parliament should bear himself so smoothly
in the royal presence. One prominent ex-cabinet minister, himself a
keen lawn tennis player, and his wife, were present at the match. He
complained to me that his wife had gone into raptures about Fred's
neat appearance on the court and remarked that not once had he
to hitch up his trousers! "Why could not her husband be the same?"
I'm afraid however it was a question of girth!'

The fact that everyone at Westminster 'from the Prime Minister
to the police constables on duty at the House of Commons' took
an interest in his son's exploits made the old warhorse of the left
positively misty-eyed. He commented that this 'kindly evidence of
good sportsmanship is characteristic of British parliamentary life; it
transcends all talk of class distinction and bitter party feelings. Members
of Parliament looked upon Fred as one of themselves and there were
many instances of their practical help and guidance, which were
gratefully accepted.'

During those 1930 championships, Fred and friends dined more
than once with Perry senior at the Commons and attracted a
cavalcade of national leaders to their table. 'We were delighted and
encouraged when the Prime Minister, Mr Ramsay MacDonald,
Mr Stanley Baldwin, Mr Lloyd George and the great sportsman,
Lord Derby, came along and wished Fred every success,' Sam Perry
said. 'On one occasion Miss Mary Heeley, Fred's partner in the mixed

doubles, accompanied us and departed the proud possessor of the autographs on her visiting-card of the Prime Minister, Mr Stanley Baldwin and Mr Lloyd George.'

Sam Perry's appreciation of the camaraderie of Westminster extended also to the pairing system, which enabled him to slip off to watch Fred play when he might have been expected to shore up the Labour vote in one of the many close divisions at that time. Invariably he could count on one sympathetic collaborator in this exercise, Victor Cazalet, a Conservative MP. Cazalet was a tennis enthusiast and the practice partner of choice of Helen Wills Moody, whenever the American, who won eight Wimbledon singles, came to England.

Even though Perry lost to Colin Gregory he was now established as a player of substance. 'His play is never forced,' one report said of his Centre Court debut, 'for he does not appear to be striving greatly, but it is none the less effective.' An indication of how quickly Perry overtook Gregory came less than two years later when, playing for Middlesex, he beat the Yorkshire doctor 9–7 6–4 in the hard court final for county teams at Bournemouth and a national newspaper marvelled at Gregory's effort in detaining the younger man for twenty-six games. Gregory kept on playing for many years after this, even making a Davis Cup appearance at the age of forty-eight as a last-minute replacement for an injured Geoff Paish.

As a result of Perry's vigorous and sudden blooming as a player, good enough to be picked to represent Britain, his father's financial support, which had caused such a stir earlier in the year, was already surplus to requirements. His international selection meant he became eligible for benefits from the LTA. There were other perks, too, for touring amateurs. Five years later, twelve months before he turned professional, Perry referred to champion players who travelled the world living on £4,000 a year, which, using the index of average earnings, is the equivalent of more than £300,000 in the early twenty-first century. An American sportswriter referred to such incomes wryly: 'Small wonder that many of the top-notch amateurs linger long in the simon-pure ranks vainly endeavouring to make up their minds to make the jump to professionalism.'

The selectors' judgment in sending Perry abroad despite his lack of experience was fully vindicated. Not only did he take to travel-ling with extraordinary enthusiasm for someone whose upbringing had not obviously equipped him to view the world as his oyster, he learned quickly from the new school of tennis in which he found himself. He exceeded all expectations by reaching the last sixteen of the 1930 US Championships, his first appearance overseas in a grand slam event, and did the same on his debut in the French Championships on his return to Europe.

Nor could the timing of his selection to tour the Americas have been much better, as the trip took him away from Brentham at the most opportune of moments, as far as Perry was concerned. On 22 January 1931, just a few days after the first anniversary of Hannah Perry's death, Sam Perry married for the second time. Olive Gardner, from Highgate, became his wife at a ceremony at Brentford Register Office. She was a secretary at the Co-operative Party headquarters and twenty-seven years younger than Sam. A profile of Perry senior that appeared in the *Co-operative Review* some years later stated, 'every-body was delighted by a co-operative romance that has lasted and grown with the years and added a daughter to the cheery clan'.

In fact, not quite everybody was delighted. Older residents of Brentham remembered that the speed with which Sam Perry remar-ried caused a good deal of surprise among those who knew the family well. Fred was least delighted of all, happy only that he was on the other side of the Atlantic when the nuptials took place. His relationship with his stepmother, just four years his senior, was never much better than cool. About the only evidence he ever had anything to do with her is that he asked her to type out the transcript of his 1934 autobiography, *My Story*, which she duly did. He seems to have little other contact with her.

When, having been in the United States more than a decade, he returned to visit Britain after the Second World War, he spent some time at Pitshanger Lane. 'I stayed at the old house in Ealing for part of the time, though my father had remarried a couple of years [*sic*] after my mother's death and things weren't therefore quite the same,' he wrote succinctly. He could not even bring himself to mention his stepmother's name. It was as if he wanted to keep his second family, the one he was presented with when his father married again, a secret, although there is some evidence that he had a soft spot for Sylvia, his half-sister. Sylvia Perry was due on the day Fred won his first Wimbledon title, but arrived a few days later. When Fred started making regular return visits to England, he would take Sylvia with him to exhibition events and make sure 'my kid sister' was looked after.

The close relationship Perry enjoyed with his full sister, Edith, is demonstrated by an anecdote their father told about the day of her marriage in 1926 to Walter Kerr, a Scotsman living in Ealing who worked for the British India Steamship Navigation Company. Fred was playing in the Middlesex Junior Lawn Tennis Championships in Harrow that day but was determined not to miss the wedding. A car picked him up after two semi-finals in the morning and took him to the church before returning him to the courts for a final in the afternoon. 'He was rushed to a car without changing his tennis kit, all excited and fearful of being late for the wedding, and immediately began changing his clothes without pulling down the blinds,' Sam Perry said. One of Edith's sons, also called Walter, would briefly make a name for himself as an outstanding rugby union player for London Scottish. In 1953 he gained his one international cap at flanker for Scotland against England at Twickenham, a match England won comfortably. Fred and Edith spent most of their adult lives on different continents but lost none of their affection for one another. Visits to Purley in Surrey to see his big sister, who died in 1982, were one of the rituals whenever Perry returned to England.

Perry admitted to being taken aback at first by the febrile pace of life in New York when he arrived in the United States for the first time in 1930. He was only twenty-one and picking him had been a big gamble. Until recently he had been viewed primarily as a table tennis player. It was still less than a year since he had won his first open title in domestic competition at New Malden.

Crucially, Perry still had an open mind about his future. Unlike the public-school-educated members of the tennis fraternity he had not been imbued with a romantic view of amateurism. He did not regard tennis as a sort of elevated hobby, offering him a topping diversion before he settled down to an office job. He already had the idea that, for him, tennis was a career opportunity, and when he stepped ashore in New York he found himself in a land where very few taboos on making money existed. 'The LTA had descended on me like a fairy godparent,' was how Perry described the decision to send him to the US. He said he could not believe his luck until he was aboard the ageing but still luxurious RMS *Mauretania* at Southampton with his team-mates Leslie Godfree, John Olliff and Harry Lee.

Godfree, the husband of Kitty Godfree, who as Kitty McKane had won Wimbledon in 1924 and regained the title two years later under her married name, was Perry's captain. A man from the old school, he moved quickly to acquaint Perry with the rules, summoning the young buck to his cabin for tea and a good talking-to. He was to practise regularly, to watch and learn from the senior members of the party and to observe codes of dress and behaviour on and off the court. The penalty for not conforming would be an immediate return ticket to England and disqualification from national team selection.

Perry, not unhappy to be given such instruction in an entirely alien environment, observed the tenets laid down by Godfree to extract as much as he possibly could from the tennis-playing and social opportunities that came his way during those late-summer weeks on the East Coast. He constantly pleaded with Americans to practise with him, an eagerness that meant he would return to England a hardened competitor with an improved backhand that no longer represented a guaranteed source of points for opponents.

He had mixed results in matches. In a contest between England and the US, he played Ellsworth Vines in the first meeting of what would become one of tennis's great rivalries. The tall, elegant American won, and Perry reflected some years later that Vines stood in the way of his ambitions more often than any other player. Encouraging results that offset this early defeat included reaching a doubles final in Westchester, after which Harry Lee, his partner, graciously allowed Perry to send the silver trophy back to his father. Most notably, though, he surpassed expectations by making it to the last sixteen of the US Championships, his first time in an overseas grand slam after his two Wimbledon appearances. The American Johnny Van

Ryn ended his run by beating him in four sets in the fourth round.

On the social front on that first trip to America, Perry revelled in the affluence of the set – redolent of the characters in F. Scott Fitzgerald's 1920s novel *The Great Gatsby* – who hung around tennis. He estimated that at least half a dozen millionaires entertained them during one week at Newport, Rhode Island. These included Arthur James, reckoned to be the world's second-richest man from his copper and railroad interests, aboard whose luxurious yacht *Aloha* the British party were taken to watch trial races for the America's Cup. The fourteenth series of this took place in mid-September with Britain's challenger *Shamrock V* being outclassed by *Enterprise*.

In time, Perry also came to know Stuart Duncan, another of the great plutocrats of Newport, whose family fortune had been made from Lea & Perrins sauce. Duncan ran a team of servants at his imposing home, Bonnie Crest, which had a prominent position over-looking the harbour and was built from stone imported from Scotland. While staying there Perry could not help imagining what his socialist forebears might have made of him as he tested water brought to him in a bowl so that the butler knew what temperature to make his bath. Duncan added a ballroom to his property for his daughter's coming-out party rather than use the only one in Newport big enough to accommodate the bash, which was owned by a rival.

In late September, their trip to the United States at an end, Perry and Lee sailed on the *Northern Prince* to South America, where they were to team up with another contingent of British players. This group, led by Eric Peters, also included Phoebe Holcroft-Watson and Ermintrude Harvey, the sort of highfalutin names Perry was becoming used to having around him. They had travelled directly from England to Brazil aboard the RMS *Asturias*.

The main destination for both groups was Argentina, the tennis authorities in Buenos Aires having asked for a visit by a team from Britain because, the LTA explained, 'Although the Argentine has been honoured with visits from other players of fame such as Borotra, Brugnon, Boussus, Alonso, etc., the local "fans" have always expressed the desire to see in action representatives of the country where true sportsmanship is the rule and not the exception.' This po-faced remark encapsulated the assumed moral superiority that was still prevalent in Britain's ruling class and irked not only young tennis players seen to have ideas above their station.

Perry and Lee played some matches in the Brazilian cities of Rio de Janeiro and São Paulo en route to joining their new team-mates in the port of Santos. Because of revolutionary unrest in the area, not all the matches they were scheduled to play took place, and when they practised it was often in the presence of armed guards. The trouble also meant their meeting with the party aboard the *Asturias* was delayed after the ship was initially refused permission to dock and sent away. 'In South America a revolution is not generally a very serious affair,' Peters wrote on his return, 'and is usually merely a rather violent way of changing Government, and there is little bloodshed. The Brazilian Revolution, however, was rather more serious and looked like turning into almost a bad Civil War but the Government were eventually overthrown with less resistance than expected, and all was quiet on our return [to Santos].' So quiet in fact Peters reported, 'On our return we landed and had some fine surf bathing in a wonderfully warm sea.'

In Argentina, Peters' team were too strong for the locals, losing only one match out of twelve in two contests between the countries, and at least one British player appeared in each of the finals in the Argentine national championships. Perry won his first national title in the singles. It was not a first-class honour in the eyes of the tennis world, but it was not completely overlooked in Britain. 'It is a far cry from London to Buenos Aires,' one national newspaper reported, 'and not often are the Argentine championships a matter of compelling interest to players in this country. But that an English player should win a foreign championship is a notable event nowadays; and the English player who has shown most improvement during the year, F.J. Perry, has just done so.' Perry played well, too. Peters, the losing finalist, said Perry produced 'the finest tennis I have seen an Englishman play for some time'.

The party's South American adventure then took them across the Andes by train – Perry was smitten by the scenery, reporting, 'I have never yet found anything quite so inspiring in all my travels' – to play matches in Chile, before finishing up back in Uruguay. Here, at a reception in Montevideo, Perry learned to his cost that he was allergic to shellfish. After tasting lobster for the first time he was carried out of the dinner and confined to his cabin for the whole of the voyage home.

4

A player of substance: 1931–3

'A Goliath rejoicing in his strength'

Perry had served his apprenticeship as a tennis player by the start of 1931. Almost as important as anything had been his discovery in America that the game could exist without social class being of the slightest concern. This invigorated him and underpinned his self-belief with a real sense of purpose. Over the next two and a half years he drove on with steely determination, dismayed but not discouraged by the inevitable disappointments, towards achieving all the objectives he had set for himself. And the impact of his success as an individual would be broadened through his contribution to the nation's Davis Cup effort. All too briefly, tennis would become a rallying point for the British public rather than a niche interest for the garden-party set.

It is easily forgotten that Britain's failure as a tennis power since Perry's time is not the first long spell of underachievement. The following might have been written at the start of the twenty-first century: 'For years our men have been going on court with an inferiority complex, doomed for the least lapse to adverse criticism and carrying the back lash of it as a handicap.' In fact it appeared in the summer of 1931 and the paragraph finished: 'Now Fred Perry and Bunny Austin are respected at their worth.'

Soon after he returned from the 1930–1 tour of the Americas, Perry reinforced the impression he had made on his travels with a solid performance in London's 14–7 win in the annual match against Paris. The improvements in his game were noticed straightaway and passed on to readers of the national press. In the words of one report, Perry showed that 'he understands the importance of hitting the ball

as soon as ever it can conveniently be done; another thing he understands is that a really good volleyer can make himself extremely
obnoxious to the other fellow'. He then secured his Davis Cup place
at the trials held at Queen's in early April. Although he lost to Austin
in the trials, he reached a peak of irresistible form before fading in
their five-set match. A report of this encounter remarked on progress
of a different kind made by Perry, who had grown into a strikingly
athletic figure: 'Austin, pale and small in comparison with his tall
and ruddy-faced opponent, looked a David with a stoneless sling
against a Goliath rejoicing in his strength.'

The Goliath was brought low in the Davis Cup tie that followed
– not by a defeat but by a fall, the effects of which were still troubling him less than a week later when he lost to John Olliff in the
third round of the British Hard Court Championships. After this, as
the weather grew warmer, he healed quickly – to the relief of the
Davis Cup selectors and to the benefit of Perry's own desire to make
a good impression at his first French Championships. In Paris, where
no British player had been successful in the tournament's six years
as an international event, Perry overcame his lack of experience on
the slow surface of Roland-Garros to reach the last sixteen – his
run being ended by Giorgio De Stefani, Baron Umberto de
Morpurgo's put-upon pupil, whose quirky style confused many other
players besides Perry. 'I do not think that there is anyone in the world,
good or bad, who plays the same way,' Perry said. 'When the ball
comes on the right side of his body he hits a right-handed drive.
Then you whip down a hard shot to his backhand corner – at least
that is what you think, for by a peculiar sliding movement he has
transferred his racket to his left hand, and back comes a powerful
drive of full length. So smoothly is the transferring of the racket
accomplished that unless you are watching closely it is hardly noticeable.' Perry's plan, to try to catch De Stefani as he switched the
racket over, proved useless. 'I was two sets down before I realised De
Stefani's left hand knew exactly what the right hand was doing.'

Despite the defeat by De Stefani, Perry's progress had been such
that a mere twenty-four months after he had slipped anonymously
through qualifying at his first Wimbledon he was fifth seed for
the 1931 championships behind Henri Cochet, Jean Borotra, the

American Frank Shields and a third Frenchman, Christian Boussus. He had overtaken Austin, who was seeded six. Perry would surpass his seeding by gaining a place in the last four, a performance that for the first time eased him into the ranks of the world's best players. In other respects, though, it proved a thoroughly unpleasant two weeks with an unknown person spoiling his tournament while almost certainly contributing to a lacklustre performance when he was within one match of the final.

Little seemed to be amiss as he won his first five matches without dropping a set. He beat Baron Gottfried von Cramm, the German who would become one of his great Wimbledon adversaries, in the fourth round, and the good American Johnny Van Ryn in his quarter-final. 'An Englishman in the semi-final at Wimbledon! When did that last happen? The memory of man would have to run a long way to ascertain this fact,' one national newspaper said, overlooking the fact that Bunny Austin had reached the last four two years before. The author's mistake was understandable, though, because Britain's record in the men's singles at Wimbledon had been dismal for some years. Austin and Gordon Lowe, in 1923, had been the country's only semi-finalists since the abolition of the challenge round after the 1921 tournament, and neither had made it to the final.

According to Van Ryn's veteran countrywoman Elizabeth Ryan, who was now a commentator on the game, Perry was the master in every aspect of play with the possible exception of the serve in winning his quarter-final. He showed, said Ryan, that Britain had a great player for the future. Herbert Roper Barrett, Britain's Davis Cup captain, who since Perry made the team in April had started to influence the way he played, watched from the stands. He was there as a reminder to Perry that he should crowd Van Ryn at the net. In due course, Roper Barrett joined Pops Summers as a regular court-side assessor of how he was playing, with a series of prearranged signals to be used if he identified any lapses in Perry's play.

Nothing was obviously wrong with Perry's frame of mind as he won the third set against Van Ryn from 3–0 down to maintain his unblemished record. Behind the scenes, though, a series of practical jokes was undermining his morale. Someone, he never found out who, was ordering articles of clothing, including shoes, trousers and suits, and having them delivered to him at the All England Club. On another occasion, trousers he was due to play in were removed from the dressing room and sent to the cleaners. Whoever it was even involved the press at one point, summoning photographers to Wimbledon for a phantom photo shoot involving the young Englishman.

Most bizarrely of all, the malicious prankster started a transaction to buy a house in Perry's name. 'If he had completed the transaction by paying for it I should have minded less,' Perry said. He was not so wry in his general comment on the incidents. 'I allowed these mysterious activities to worry me and get on my nerves, instead of being philosophical about them, and carried into court the knowledge that these pranks were being played on me. This did not benefit my play.' One thought that might have brought him the merest hint of consolation was that he was now someone worth bothering with, even if the attention was of such an unwanted nature.

The mood of Perry's semi-final opponent, Sidney Wood, could hardly have been more different. While the Englishman brooded over the identity of the person who had it in for him, the young American was transported to victory on the wings of his love for one of the day's great entertainers – at least this was how he told the story more than seventy years later.

Younger than Perry by eighteen months, Wood was the most engaging of characters, whose charm survived into grand old age despite the loss of his hearing in his mid-nineties. The object of his affection in that summer of 1931 was none other than Gertie Lawrence, who at the time was a huge star of stage and screen on both sides of the Atlantic. Noël Coward's hit play *Private Lives* was thought to have been about Lawrence, and Wood became part of an unlikely triangle. Wood's fond memories were palpable as he recollected what happened. 'Every single day Gertie and Noël Coward would pick me up in the Bentley from the Grosvenor House Hotel and we would drive down together to the tennis. They would sit in my seats in the players' box and when she was in the stands I didn't even know I was on the court. I was just transported. I walked through those championships as if I wasn't even in a tournament.'

He remembered particularly his four-set semi-final victory over

Perry, who was seeded two places ahead of him. 'Gertie would wave this little lace handkerchief and I would look up and I didn't even know Fred was on the other side of the court. It sounds ridiculous now, doesn't it?' Lawrence was thirteen years older than Wood and the romance proved fleeting. 'It was a short summer. Gertie wanted me to go to Majorca to stay with her there for a while, but the call of tennis . . . I had to go back to America and play there. We remained good friends forever, but that was the end of that excitement.'

It was quite a line-up – Wood, Perry and Wood's US team-mate Frank Shields, who won the other semi-final at those 1931 Wimbledon championships – as dashing a trio of troubadours as any sport can have ever produced at the same time. All of them had romantic scrapes, some of which found their way into print but many did not, with the press not nearly as concerned with these things as they would be in fifty years' time. Wood had his fling with Gertie and Perry himself created a huge stir at Wimbledon some years later when he took the American actress Loretta Young there, causing, he reckoned, players to hit more bad shots and line judges to make more mistakes than ever before.

Shields, whose family name would again become widely known many years later through his actress granddaughter Brooke Shields, had any number of amorous adventures, including one that Perry rated as 'the all-time caper of my time in tennis'. It involved Shields' pursuit of an American girl across Europe when he should have been competing in a tournament in Berlin. His last desperate act to win the girl was to borrow money from a friend and, with no passport and only the clothes he stood up in – a dinner jacket – to board the same US-bound ship as her. He had been at sea for three days by the time he was tracked down to the girl's cabin, which he had been able to leave only in the evenings when his clothes were not out of place.

Had Perry realised what was going on between Wood and Lawrence during that Wimbledon semi-final, he would probably have been thoroughly envious. As it was, both men had difficulty concentrating. This was reflected in press reports of a surprisingly unsatisfactory contest. 'The match was disappointing in many ways and it followed

Round the maypole in Brentham. Perry (third boy from left) joins in an annual ritual during his schooldays.

Off to the World Table Tennis Championships. Perry won the title in 1929, aged nineteen.

Perry with his father, Sam, who served two brief terms as a Labour MP.

Joan Hartigan, Perry, and Eileen Fearnley-Whittingstall as cigarette card collectables.

A model player demonstrates a selection of his strokes.

Perry carried in triumph at Victoria Station after returning from Paris
where Britain regained the Davis Cup in 1933.

Charles Tuckey,
Bunny Austin, Perry
and Pat Hughes
before the 1935
Davis Cup Challenge
Round against the
USA at Wimbledon.

Perry celebrates winning…

Headline news after winning the first of his Wimbledon singles titles in 1934.

Perry shakes hands with Princess Helen Victoria after Britain retain the Davis Cup at Wimbledon in 1934.

At full stretch during the French Championships in Paris in 1936.

Waiting to watch
Perry – a queue
forms on the pavement
outside Wimbledon.

Perry, squatting in long
trousers, prepares for
training at Arsenal FC.

Perry plays his last match at Wimbledon in the 1936 Davis Cup Challenge Round against Australia.

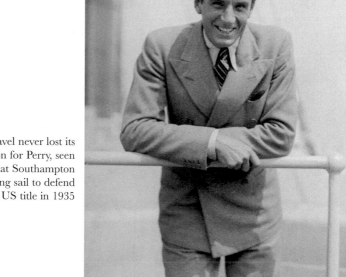

Sea travel never lost its fascination for Perry, seen here at Southampton before setting sail to defend his US title in 1935

FRED PERRY

AT HARRODS

May 24th to 29th

Wimbledon Champion three times
—five times Champion at Bournemouth—unbeaten in Davis Cup
Matches in the four years Britain has
held the cup—victory in the United
States—and now back home to tell you,
exclusively at Harrods, how it's done!

TALKS

DAILY at 11.30 and 3
(Saturday 11.30 only)

Fred Perry himself will be in our
Sports Department daily, at your
service, to advise you and show you
how to set about rivalling his own
mastery of the game!

*Seating accommodation in our Private
Theatre (first floor) is limited. You will
be well advised to be early for these
valuable and exclusive Perry 'Talks.'*

Special Displays of Sports Needs
and newest Sportswear Fashions

Harrods

Harrods Ltd   Knightsbridge S W 1
            Tel. SLOane 1234

*He will gladly advise
as to the right Rackets
for your individual needs.*

Perry's first appearance on his return to Britain as a professional in 1937
was in the Harrods private theatre.

a strange course,' one report said. 'Neither player gave of his best and both struck patches in which they were unable almost to do anything right.' Without the post-match press conferences of later years at which players were subjected to extensive grillings, the reasons for the distracted performances did not emerge straightaway. Perry's only comment at the time merely hinted at his problem: 'When the ball is right on my racket and I volley out or into the net, there is something wrong with my game.'

Understandably, Perry felt particularly frustrated at losing to Wood because the American went on to win the title when Shields withdrew from the final with a knee injury. 'If only I had managed to beat Wood I would have been champion at Wimbledon that year without needing to hit another ball,' Perry said. However, Shields might well have played in the final if Perry had beaten Wood. The US Davis Cup officials who insisted Shields withdraw from the final almost certainly did so only because the title was certain to go to an American. As Wood pointed out, he and Shields played doubles together the day after the semi-finals. 'But then our Davis Cup committee, in their infinite wisdom, decreed that Frank should default from the singles final to save him for the Davis Cup, which was going to be played two weeks later in Paris.' Thus saved, the sprightly Shields would inflict a first Davis Cup defeat on Perry in the inter-zone final just a fortnight after he had been considered unfit to compete in the Wimbledon final. 'It was the most stupid affront to Wimbledon you could imagine,' Wood said, 'but our Davis Cup committee were a bunch of old guys with badges and you know what badge-wearers are.'

Wood responded to his walkover victory by handing over the Wimbledon trophy to a lady called Maud Barger-Wallach who travelled everywhere with the US team. She was to keep it until Wood and Shields had played each other on grass to decide who was better on the surface. It would be 1934 before Wood finally accepted the trophy after beating Shields in the London Championships at Queen's.

After losing to Shields in the inter-zone final in Paris, Perry beat Wood two days later to reverse his Wimbledon defeat and guide Britain to a victory over the US that put them in the Davis Cup final – or challenge round as it was then known – for the first time since 1919. Britain would lose the final to France but neither that team defeat nor the one in the singles semi-final at Wimbledon could detract from a summer of achievement in Europe that had transformed Perry's life.

One indication that Perry's popularity was growing was that he and Austin were signed up to write newspaper columns. They were able to do this without infringing their amateur status through one of those absurd rules that kept amateurism going while slowly undermining its credibility: it was all right as long as players did not comment on matches in which they took part. It was with money from his journalism that Perry saved £140 to buy an Austin Seven with a sliding roof. A little waspishly, Perry contended that he was hired first by one London evening paper and Austin was then signed up by its rival. They occasionally wrote about each other, although checked before doing this after the occasion when a poster proclaiming a column by Austin on Perry stood adjacent to one advertising Perry's views on Austin. Once Perry turned professional he was free to write as he pleased and he remained a fairly prolific scribe well beyond his playing days. If he had ever known this, the English teacher at Ealing County School who had had so much trouble persuading Perry to do his homework would no doubt have been astonished.

Perry evidently enjoyed his journalism. To start with, he put his name to some fairly superficial, meandering pieces about the game, mostly in the *Evening Standard*. Never mind the quality, the newspaper still gave him maximum promotion. The F.J. Perry byline was accompanied by a strapline that proclaimed him 'the brilliant young London player'. In due course, though, he became much more diligent in his writing and broadcasting and was not afraid to use his contacts. Mick Jefferson was a young reporter on the *Scarborough Evening Telegraph* when recruited by Perry in the early 1950s to phone in his copy to a national newspaper during an event at the Yorkshire Lawn Tennis Club. 'I learned a lot from Perry,' Jefferson said, 'such as that the really good exclusive stories are liable to come not from watching play but from talking to people in the know.' He learned also that Perry was not so grand that he took assistance for granted. A few weeks after the tournament, Jefferson received a letter with a continental postmark. It was a handwritten thank you from Perry, now reporting on an event in West Germany.

Much had changed by the time Perry returned to New York in 1931, again aboard the *Mauretania*, on this occasion with Pat Hughes as his captain. New York had acquired some significant landmarks with the mighty Hudson River Bridge (later the George Washington Bridge) nearing completion and the Empire State Building having shot up in just 410 days to overtake its art deco rival, the Chrysler Building, as the world's tallest construction. Perry, too, had changed from being 'England's most promising colt', as Jack Crawford had recently described him, to the mature performer who had upset the pride of American tennis a few weeks earlier in the Davis Cup in Paris.

What followed was both a continuation of the rising arc of his success and a chastening reminder that whenever he had Ellsworth Vines in the opposite corner winning could still be an awkward business. His several matches against Vines on this trip were the start of an intertwining of their lives that would involve a business partnership as well as many more meetings on the tennis court. Not surprisingly, given that they were singular but very different characters – Vines, whose father owned a chain of Pacific coast meat stores, was far more subdued with 'a quiet and subtle sense of humour', as Perry put it – their relationship was a complex one. Perry wrote nice things about the Californian with 'the Irish cast of countenance'. These included that Vines was more than ordinarily well liked by players of all nationalities and that 'You never hear anyone say a word against him – and you cannot say that about every tennis player.' And yet during the years when they spent weeks together they constantly maddened one another.

Within a week of landing, Perry secured his first title in America with victory in the Eastern Grass Court Championships in Westchester, finishing off with a straight-sets win over the quite good American J. Gilbert Hall. But he then kept being gunned down by Vines, who had not been thought good enough to make the Davis Cup team which had just suffered defeat against Britain in Paris. Perry lost to him in the final of the Newport Casino Invitation event and in the semi-finals of the US Championships. He still had not identified the missing ingredient that would make him a grand slam winner and, lacking the necessary fitness, he allowed Vines to come back from two sets to love down to go through to the US final.

Vines himself was no fitness fanatic, either at this stage or later in his career; Jack Kramer even reckoned he was a lazy guy, which partly accounted for his winning only three grand slams before he turned pro at the end of 1933. But he was blessed with so much natural ability and could whip up such a storm with his serve and forehand that no one was secure against him if he was in the mood. When he followed up his win over Perry by beating George Lott in the 1931 US final, he became champion at the age of nineteen.

Regardless of his problems with Vines, Perry's new status as a leading player meant everyone now wanted to see him play. His appeal reached across the continent, and easily the most significant event of his second visit to the US was his first summons to the West Coast. Here, where tennis and the wider world of entertainment intermingled, Perry's empathy with the relaxed formulas of American life would deepen into what would become a lasting attachment to the country.

The Pacific Southwest Championships followed straight after the US Championships and were a highlight of the Los Angeles social and sporting calendar. Perry's invitation to take part arrived via an intermediary acting on behalf of the Southern California Tennis Association. As Perry would relate the story, the intermediary first asked Hughes for his personal terms and definitely batted an eyelid when told by the debonair Englishman that a date with a rich and attractive blonde would secure his participation. The same question was then put to Perry – redundantly, as he would have had to go if Hughes went – and the junior player, emboldened by Hughes's terms, actually nominated who his date should be, a certain pulchritudinous film star.

The trip to Los Angeles necessitated Perry's first coast-to-coast train journey. He and Hughes set off late at night from Grand Central station in New York aboard the *20th Century Limited*, then a mere twenty-nine years into its sixty-five-year working life and to become known as the 'Most Famous Train in the World'. In Chicago, they crossed town from LaSalle Street station to Dearborn to catch the Santa Fe Railroad's *The Chief* bound for LA, which was nearly three days down the line. These were still the high days of rail travel, when the train companies catered for all tastes, from those of the rich and famous to those with more mundane requirements. *The Chief* and its successor *The Super Chief* were sometimes referred to as the 'Trains of the Stars' and at some of the halts children with autograph books would climb aboard to seek out the celebrities. In time, Perry himself became a target.

As with his South American train journey the previous autumn, Perry loved the experience, from sitting in the observation car on the first leg from New York as they passed along the Hudson River valley to simply enjoying the pampered living on the long haul from Chicago. One morning he eagerly accepted the offer of fresh mountain trout for breakfast, the fish to be delivered at a stop as the train entered the foothills of the Rocky Mountains. Not for the first or last time, Perry would reflect, what was a lad from Stockport doing in a place like this? However his sense of wonder never overwhelmed him. Nor did he recoil from the glitz and glamour of the la-la land into which he now stepped. He happily engaged in its sybaritic rituals, while being astute enough not to go beyond that point where it might compromise his status as a headline sportsman.

In no time at all, he said, he was very much a man-about-Hollywood. He made a distinction, though, between this and 'going Hollywood', which he said he never did, a claim borne out when he migrated to Florida in 1947. By then he understood that Hollywood's infatuation with tennis was a seasonal thing. He was struck by this in 1935, when for the first time he visited Los Angeles in the spring. He found his stock noticeably diminished from when he had been playing in the Pacific Southwest tournament in late summer and shared top billing with the movie stars. For the rest of the year tennis was simply a chic form of exercise for those in the film world, in the days before yoga, Pilates, t'ai chi, body jam and all the other New Age keep-fit fads arrived. 'Tennis is one form of relaxation which its devotees in filmdom take seriously,' the *Los Angeles Times* said. 'In the privacy of their own gardens, or those of friends, actors, actresses, producers, writers, directors and others connected with the industry gather frequently to enjoy the exhilaration of the game.'

Each September the stars would converge on the Los Angeles Tennis Club for the Pacific Southwest, which first took place in 1927 and was the reason Perry went to California in 1931. The magazine *Western Tennis* ran a social column in which it quoted Mrs Alfred John Murrieta, the 'efficient entertainment chairman', as saying, 'These [Pacific Southwest] tournaments are becoming more important socially each year. Why, everyone is seen at the matches every day!' Among those who had boxes at the event were Harold Lloyd, Bebe Daniels, Marlene Dietrich, Clark Gable, Charlie Chaplin and the Marx brothers. *Western Tennis* told its readers, 'Movie queens swooped in with their retinue of friends, to receive the acclaim of their admirers. Gallant movie heroes likewise were the cynosure of all eyes. And socially, the event was decidedly outstanding.'

With his good looks, athletic build and attention to sartorial detail, Perry was never in danger of passing unnoticed. Before long he was right at the centre of the celebrity whirl. Even on that first visit to the West Coast in 1931, he and Hughes plunged straight into the social maelstrom. The choice of where they would stay gave an early signal that they were going to be spoilt, the Hollywood Roosevelt Hotel having two years earlier staged the first Academy Awards ceremony, and before the night was over both had been out acquainting themselves with the stars. At least there were some perks to counteract the pain of two more disappointments against Vines. Perry's fitness failed him once more when, having lost the longest set he ever played, he folded to a 6–3 21–19 6–0 defeat in San Francisco. The crowning disappointment came when he ran out of puff yet again in the final of the Pacific Southwest tournament, which Vines won in five sets.

From Los Angeles, Perry had to hasten back to Europe for one last appearance before the year was out, an engagement that in terms of his advancement as a player was an enjoyable irrelevance.

As he and Pat Hughes prepared to return home from California they received a cable from the LTA telling them that they had been invited by Gustav V, king of Sweden and a tennis fanatic, to play in a match in Stockholm between his country and Britain. They duly headed straight off again after arriving in England, booking into the Grand Hotel when they made it to the Swedish capital. Having been on the go almost non-stop for more than a month, they were ready for a rest, but this was denied them a little longer. No sooner had they arrived in their rooms than they were summoned downstairs, where the king was holding a party for the visiting tennis stars. Finally, well after midnight, they were told to pack their things to move to the royal palace.

They stayed at the palace for the week of the match, guests of the Swedish monarch, who had been smitten by tennis when introduced to it in Britain in 1876. On returning home, he founded his country's first tennis club. Later on, when Perry went to the south of France for some winter tennis, he would run into Gustav and be his occasional doubles partner in handicap doubles matches, with the king playing under the name of Mr G. They won two tournaments, and the king, in return for pocketing the prizes, about 6,000 francs worth of vouchers, promised to compensate Perry with a commemorative gift. Perry's expectations of something a little special were disappointed when a Swedish official tracked him down at Wimbledon to hand over a signed photograph of His Majesty. It was not even framed.

It was not just the king of Sweden who was eager that Perry should return to Europe in the autumn of 1931. Once again Sam Perry's political team prevailed on Fred to raise the profile of his father's efforts in Kettering in the October general election. 'Politics as a rule are no great concern of mine,' Fred said, 'but I just had to give my father any assistance I could in his campaign.'

In fact, Fred refused to speak at meetings. This was almost certainly a reflection of his deepening dislike of the Westminster scene following his mother's death, a dislike that in time crystallised into solid contempt and a decision 'to steer clear of anything remotely political in future'. But he undertook other tasks during that 1931 campaign with noticeable gusto. He would say, with the brightest of twinkles in his eye, that his job had been to secure the support of newly enfranchised women voters by going around kissing the factory girls. Another stunt was less successful. In trying to emulate the Olympic hurdler Lord Burghley, who would impress audiences at election rallies by jumping onto the stage 'as only an athlete could', Fred misjudged the height of the platform and fell flat on his face.

Sam Perry's attempt to keep his seat in Parliament suffered much the same fate. Standing once again as a Labour/Co-operative candidate, he lost to the Conservative John Eastwood by more than 8,000 votes. He ended his connection with Kettering in 1932 and would never again be an MP. The pull of party politics did not disappear altogether, though. There were persistent rumours that he might contest Ealing and then, when he stood down as secretary of the Co-operative Party eleven years later, a speaker told the gathering at his leaving do, 'Mr Perry is now prospective Co-operative candidate for the Bilston division of Wolverhampton and many of his friends in the movement look forward to the day when he will once again be sporting MP after his name.' It never happened, leaving him, in terms of time served in Parliament, with a disappointingly slim return for someone who fought six elections: an aggregate of not quite three and a half years in two stints representing Kettering.

The measure of political achievement that pleased him was the distance he had advanced the cause of the Co-operative Party. Here he could claim his endeavours had been genuinely successful. 'His work in the Co-operative Party has resulted in the idea of co-operative politics being acceptable to 70 per cent of the movement's membership,' a speaker at his retirement party said. 'This was a task not easily performed considering the conditions that prevailed in 1918 and in certain societies during the intervening twenty-five years. The hard core of political resistance has now been largely liquidated and the way prepared for a new period of political penetration.' The *Co-operative Review* said, 'His reward was forthcoming in his own lifetime when he was able to appreciate and participate in the glory of 1945, with two statesmen in the Cabinet and a solid Co-operative Party Group in the House of Commons numbering 23 MPs, and even two in the House of Lords!'

Sam Perry himself was offered a place in the Lords, which he turned down. Fred recalled that Lord George-Brown, Labour Prime Minister Harold Wilson's second in command in the 1960s, told him many years later that the party had begged his father to go into the upper house. 'Your father was a great man,' George-Brown said. 'Those people who stomped around the country in the 1930s did more for the Labour movement than anybody.' It said something for Sam Perry's preference for spreading the word of socialism on lecture tours rather than from a leather-upholstered bench and dressed in ermine in Westminster that George-Brown should remember it so long afterwards.

Sam Perry also declined a position on the Transport Commission. There was no question, however, of his withdrawing completely from a life of service. After losing his seat in Parliament in 1931, he not only stayed on as secretary of the party but kept up his work in the public sphere as a JP for Middlesex and chairman of the London Regional Advisory Committee of the Ministry of Information. He also busied himself with church work, playing and watching sport and travelling.

An amateur Fred Perry may still have been, but by now he played tennis full time and set sail again from Avonmouth on 19 January 1932 as part of a Britain team bound for Jamaica, where he developed a lasting taste for this particular corner of the Caribbean, and Bermuda. He won the championships of both islands before coming home to win the singles at the British Hard Court Championships, the start of a five-year reign at the West Hants club in Bournemouth that lasted until he turned professional. After Perry came back from two sets down to beat the Ireland Davis Cup player George Rogers in the Bournemouth final, one correspondent reckoned he divined in Perry's performance a departure from the game's old Corinthian ways: 'In Perry we have a master more rugged and more ruthless in his methods, more scornful of orthodoxy if less polished in ways and means, but so in a measure is the game nowadays; if less polite, it is perhaps more practical.' It was a discerning observation, identifying Perry, the unmannerly intruder, as a key figure in the process that would yank tennis away from its genteel moorings. The irony would be that in later life, when he had transferred to the commentary box, Perry thoroughly disliked some of the changes that he had helped to effect.

So obviously was he destined for great things as a singles player that Perry's first grand slam title, the mixed doubles with Betty Nuthall at the 1932 French Championships, passed with little comment. In all there would be six doubles titles at the major tournaments, including the French and Australian men's doubles with Pat Hughes. In the singles at the French that year, Perry did rather better than he gave himself credit for in his sweeping dismissal of the British effort, 'We all failed as usual.' In fact he made it to the quarter-finals, where he lost to Roderick Menzel of Czechoslovakia. Menzel, a figure of the extreme right, was another member of Europe's cast of oddball tennis players in the days before having to commit at a very early age to the game ironed out personalities before any wrinkles could form. Menzel was as eccentric as Baron Umberto de Morpurgo, although a very different personality. One pithy profile is worth recording: 'An enormous, shaggy-looking Czech, who frequently plays in shorts, he is celebrated off the court for writing mediocre poetry and novels, speaking five languages and teasing his 4ft 11in wife by putting her on a closet shelf from which she is too small to clamber down.' His win in five sets was the only time over five matches in major events that he beat Perry.

Wimbledon seeded Perry four in 1932, but after a commendable win over the 1930 runner-up, the Texan Wilmer Allison, in the fourth round, he lost in the quarter-finals to Jack Crawford of Australia. This meant he was upstaged by Austin, who reached the final where he met Ellsworth Vines. 'In the final Austin struck Vines in tip-top form – and that means about the best tennis of which human beings are capable,' Perry said. 'So English hopes were dashed.' Fittingly, given the renowned venom of the Vines serve, the match finished with an ace. Austin swung at the ball and it seemed to vanish; he did not even know which side of him it had passed. As one report put it, 'It was a cannonball delivery to end all cannonball deliveries.'

Austin had surpassed what was expected of him, while Perry had one of those lapses against Crawford that in about two years' time would be about as rare as a batting failure by Don Bradman. Perry complained that his hectic schedule meant he had only two days' practice on grass before Wimbledon, a Davis Cup tie in Warsaw having been squeezed in after the French Championships. Austin could have claimed the same and Perry was clearly dejected by his defeat. 'All my ambitions and hopes were deferred for another year.'

The early-August transatlantic crossing was now a part of Perry's life, and the 1932 trip presented him with a chance opportunity to get to know Vines better as a person. In fact, with the pair kept apart on court by some unexpected losses by Perry, they spent more time together socially that year than they did playing one another. The top British players and the US Davis Cup team, who had just lost to France in Paris in a highly charged challenge round, found themselves on the same ship when the Americans embarked at Cherbourg. In a letter home, from 'On Board RMS *Olympic*', Vines gave a brief insight into how sea travel gave international sportsmen the chance to unwind: 'Had breakfast about 10 and spent the rest of the morning playing games with Fred and John [Olliff]. We played shuffle-board and several other games that I don't know the names of. After this we went to our rooms and listened to records. Perry had some and we heard his and then we listened to Allison's and mine.' At least in this respect the players of Perry's generation were much the same as their twenty-first-century descendants with the obvious difference that PlayStations and iPods have become the new shuffle-board and vinyl. The voyage was a perfect antidote for the Americans, some of whom were still boiling about the 3–2 loss against France. Their anger stemmed from what they regarded as another 'home' decision by a French line judge, a double fault by Jean Borotra being overlooked with Wilmer Allison a point away from winning.

The defeats that kept Perry apart from Vines in 1932 included his upset in the fourth round of the US Championships, when he threw away another two-sets-to-love lead, this time against Sidney Wood. It was after this that he finally resolved to do something about his fitness – a decision that would play a major part in his reaching the final of ten of the last twelve grand slams in which he took part. But at least he signed off 1932 with an auspicious victory in the Pacific Southwest tournament in Los Angeles. After he beat Austin in the final, Perry said that the members of the tournament committee told him there would be no need to stage the US Championships the following year because he was bound to win. The pattern of the winner of the event at the LA Tennis Club going on to triumph at Forest Hills had been established over the first five years that the Southwest had been played.

Perry's defeat by Wood at the US Championships, coming on top of his losses against Crawford at Wimbledon and Menzel at the French Championships, particularly worried Sam, who remarked on the depressed tone of his son's letters home. Perry senior blamed those who he said should have known better than to instruct Fred to play safety-first tennis. A pep talk from Sam Hardy, a former manager of the US Davis Cup team who had befriended Fred, proved the turning point. Hardy took Perry aside, having noticed how flat his game had become, and told him, 'You are Fred Perry with your own game and temperament. Be your old happy self and we will watch the results.'

This was a message that resonated with Perry. There was something else, though, that kept nagging at him. 'Tennis had always been a bit of an intellectual exercise,' he said. 'But I wanted to make it a physical test, too.' The fact that getting fit for tennis beyond a certain norm had never been considered by British players, who even regarded sweating and training away from the tennis court as a little infra dig, did not bother Perry in the slightest. If anything it spurred him on. As soon as he got back to London, he made the typically bold move of contacting Tom Whittaker, who had transformed the training methods of the Arsenal football team. There was no question of settling for any old club; it had to be the team who had won the 1930 FA Cup and were about to reel off three Football League titles.

Arsenal said they would help if he made a deal with them: to report to the ground at nine each morning whenever he was in London. This he did, regardless of conditions, to subject himself to the training routines that were established practice at professional football clubs at the time. 'I must have run around that pitch hundreds of thousands of times,' he said, 'and up and down those stands five million times. Eddie Hapgood, David Jack, Cliff Bastin, Alex James – they used to kill me.' Perry also played in weekly football practice matches. He told of once being chided by Whittaker for upending Herbie Roberts, Arsenal's fine centre half, because Roberts was valuable. 'So am I,' Perry replied. Another of his stories was that the

Arsenal players bet him shillings he could not score penalties against their goalkeeper, Frank Moss, which he became so proficient at, with either foot, that it helped to supplement his income.

When winter turned to spring, Perry considered himself the fittest man in tennis. As a result he adopted the strategy of playing as hard as he could in the first set, which he did not mind losing as long as it went to numerous games and wore out his opponent. By his reckoning, he lost only two five-set matches in his remaining years as an amateur, which ended after the 1936 US Championships. 'Arsenal put a lot of power into me,' he said, 'and when I got to play in those big finals I could just go on running. Perhaps I did change the game a bit, made it tougher, a bit more competitive, and if I did I'm proud.'

It would become a debating point as Perry started to dominate the amateur game whether he was a great tennis player who was also a very good athlete – or the other way round. John Olliff, the first player to beat Perry at Wimbledon, was one of those who placed his athleticism ahead of his tennis playing. Bunny Austin, on the other hand, said that Perry was a greater player than many of his contemporaries gave him credit for, while conceding his greatness owed a great deal to his exceptional speed. Austin asked, 'Has anyone ever seen Perry unable to reach a drop shot or get back to a lob that has fallen over his head?' Perry, Austin said, never appeared to be running particularly fast, 'but without apparent movement he is everywhere in the court at once'. Roger Federer and Pete Sampras were much the same many years later.

The benefits of Perry's new physical training regime were not obvious straightaway. He went on to tour South Africa with a Britain team who lost all three Test matches in Durban, Johannesburg and Cape Town. His own form was patchy with two wins in his three singles against the left-hander Vernon 'Bob' Kirby and three wins in six doubles, in which he played with Pat Hughes in men's matches and with Mary Heeley and Betty Nuthall in mixed doubles. More significantly, Perry made an offhand remark that the South Africans regarded as disparaging their success in the Test series that rebounded on him later in the year.

In nearly every respect other than his modest showings in South Africa and at Wimbledon, 1933 was a huge success for Perry. He played a prominent role in Britain's triumph in the Davis Cup, the trophy for men's national teams being regained for the first time since 1912; again reached the quarter-finals of the French Championships, where he showed further improvement on the slow surface before losing to Japan's Jiri Satoh – a semi-finalist soon afterwards at Wimbledon; and won his first grand slam singles title at the US Championships, upholding the theory that winning the previous year's Pacific Southwest tournament was a happy omen for Forest Hills.

Having guided Britain through the early rounds of the Davis Cup, Perry arrived at Wimbledon also having retained his title at the hard court championships in Bournemouth with a four-set win over Austin in a rain-interrupted final. At Wimbledon he comfortably beat André Lacroix, a Belgian who had also lost his opening match on his three previous appearances in the tournament. Perry's defeat in the next round was a mighty upset, the earliest he lost in any of his twenty-three grand slams, and, as it turned out, the last time he would lose a singles at the All England Club. Norman Farquharson, a South African, was the man who capsized Perry's ambition.

Farquharson, two years older than Perry, was a fine all-round sportsman who had gone to Cambridge University, where he shone at tennis and played football for the university. He was also a useful cricketer. He played at nine Wimbledons but never achieved anything quite like his singles victory over Perry. He was more highly regarded as a doubles player and with various partners had beaten Perry on three occasions in the Test series the previous winter. Some years later, Farquharson wrote his own account of his Wimbledon meeting with Perry for a South African newspaper and why he had been so fired up for the match. 'Fourteen thousand spectators made the best of the lovely sunny weather and packed Centre Court at Wimbledon to watch Britain's leading player, Fred Perry, in his second round singles match. The year was 1933, and I was his opponent,' Farquharson wrote.

Although I had played at Wimbledon five times before, I was particularly keyed up for this match. Nobody gave me much of a chance of winning. I was unseeded while Perry was seeded fourth. Even so, I was confident enough and there was something which made me determined to do well.

Perry had toured South Africa with a strong British team the previous winter and yet South Africa won all three Test matches. Perry's comment was, 'This is on hard courts, which don't really count. Wait until we play you on grass.' I felt a little annoyed that he had not given us credit for our performance at home and perhaps this helped me to produce my best form that day.

Another account of what had gone on in South Africa stated that Perry made his disparaging remark about the condition of the courts after overhearing something that Farquharson said. Having withdrawn from a match against Perry because his wife was ill, Farquharson was claimed to have told an official with Perry in earshot that he thought he would have beaten the Englishman based on Perry's performance against his replacement. In this account, it was because Perry heard this that he snapped back, 'Just wait until we get you in England. It is impossible to play properly on these courts. But we'll show you how to play tennis as it should be played when your team lands in England.' Whatever the truth, the goodwill of a few weeks earlier, when Perry had spent Christmas with Farquharson and his parents in Johannesburg, had evidently evaporated.

When Wimbledon arrived, Farquharson remained eager to put Perry in his place, although he shared the general expectation that he would lose. A journalist who spoke to Farquharson just before he went on court said that the player told him he thought he had a better chance in the doubles with Kirby than in the singles.

Farquharson won the first two sets, during which he reckoned Perry was a little too casual. Perry himself said the reason for his defeat was that his opponent 'went for me with an intensive volleying campaign. On that day he played what I consider to have been super-tennis and rushed me to defeat.' The report in the LTA magazine agreed that Farquharson's superb volleying was the reason he won: 'Everything comes alike to him at the net, whether at his feet or down his lines. He has few equals at the fade-away cross-court volley.' F.T. 'Skipper' Stowe, who had captained Perry when he first played for Middlesex, was even more glowing in his praise for Farquharson: 'It takes a pretty daring player to go in right from the baseline on a backhand shot which he had sent to Perry's powerful forehand but the South African not only did it, but made it look the simplest and most natural thing in the world . . . In the latter part of the first set, and practically throughout the second, Farquharson made Perry, though he was playing his best, look like a second-rater.'

Perry did stir himself to win the third and fourth sets before Farquharson played a magnificent fifth, producing tennis, it was said, worthy of toppling one of the title favourites. Farquharson wavered only when he arrived at match point for the first time. In his own words, 'Imagine my feelings when I served – and was foot-faulted for the first time in the match. Of course, in my excitement I might have overstepped the line but it was a pretty nerve-racking experience, and I lost the point. I reached match point again and this time I was able to put away a winning volley.'

The result prompted the sort of outpourings from the British press that would become familiar many years later, long after Perry had won Wimbledon and the wait to find his successor had stretched into the twenty-first century. 'Again criticism was renewed,' Perry said of the reaction to his defeat by Farquharson. 'Lamentations were frequent about the slump in our men's tennis. Why did the foreigner always win? – and suchlike questions.' Defending champion Vines, who had been due to play Perry in the quarter-finals, reacted slightly differently in a letter to his wife: 'The big talk of the town tonight is Perry's defeat by Farquharson. Of course I'm not bothered by this at all as it removes Fred from my path. Perry was lousy while Farquharson was making volleys off his shoestrings.'

With time to kill, Perry took a break in Brighton, where the band leader Jack Hylton, with whom he had struck up a friendship in Paris two years before, was performing. Dance music was a passion of Perry's and he thanked Hylton for moderating the pain of his early loss at Wimbledon.

Farquharson recorded that the full realisation of what he had achieved did not strike him until he drove back into London with his parents after the match. 'On every street corner we saw the newspaper poster, "Wimbledon sensation – Perry beaten".' Subeditors would never again have the opportunity to write such a headline.

5

Davis Cup hero – scaling
the peak: 1931–3

'Horror of horrors! – the ambush, the massacre!'

Carhullen, a club with four red-shale courts tucked away in an exclusive residential area of Plymouth, had one moment in the tennis spotlight – at least it would have if the full significance of the event it was staging had been realised at the time. Instead, the dull glow of a miserable West Country afternoon was all that illuminated the start of a story that did as much to make Fred Perry an international figure as his performances in the grand slam tournaments. In those three years starting in 1931, during which Perry marked himself out in the great singles events, he also laid the foundations of one of the Davis Cup's most distinguished careers. It all began at Carhullen, where Britain played Monaco in late April. From this remote corner, Perry and his team-mates set off on an improbable journey. They would achieve unimagined success while encountering diverse dramas and a wonderful cast of misfits and originals, very different from the monochromes who proliferated when tennis became a much more serious business.

Perry's role in what would become Britain's domination of the men's team event, which had grown from only two entries, the US and Britain, in 1900 to thirty-one and would eventually be truly global, was so overwhelming that a huge amount of the glory reflected solely on him. Even before he won his first Wimbledon title in 1934, Perry's Davis Cup exploits had made his name as recognisable as that of any politician or showbusiness star in Britain. If anything, the run in the competition that Britain enjoyed in 1931, soaring from the lowest of bases, was the most remarkable in the six years of Davis Cup that Perry played, even though it fell just short of securing the trophy.

The Lawn Tennis Association chose Carhullen as the venue after sending out a circular in February that asked clubs 'desirous of holding the match' to contact the association's secretary. Carhullen's approach found favour presumably because, with the opposition having little hope of troubling the Britain team, it was decided to take the match to a small but highly active club. It was probably seen, too, as a reward for the club's benefactor, local solicitor Basil Hamilton-Whiteford, who had invested a considerable amount of his own money in promoting tennis, particularly among young people, in the area.

The choice of Carhullen might also have reflected the public's apathy towards the Davis Cup after years of failure by Britain. Less than ten years earlier, the nation that had helped to found the competition at the start of the century and won it four times in its first six years reached its nadir in the event. In 1922 a team of thirty-somethings plus the forty-four-year-old Frank Riseley won a tie against Italy but then conceded a walkover to Spain because the LTA decided that, if they had won that one too, they would have found it impossible to muster a team to go to the United States for the next round.

Not until Bunny Austin's selection in 1929 did things start to improve, although a photograph of the doubles against Monaco in 1931 that appeared on the front page of Plymouth's evening paper hardly portrayed an event that loomed large in the public consciousness. A few hundred spectators are seated down one side of the court, in front of a drystone wall of six or seven feet, with houses and countryside visible beyond. The club has not quite gone the way of the now-extinct Herga and Chiswick Park in London. The name has gone, rent hikes having proved too much for its survival, but at least the courts are still there, serving a nearby club.

Perry had secured Davis Cup selection first by featuring prominently in London's win in the annual match indoors against Paris at Dulwich Covered Courts Club in February and then at the trials at Queen's in early April. Despite losing to Austin in five sets in the trials final, Perry gave an intimation of the outstanding player he would become. A national newspaper reported that at the start Austin 'merely picked up an occasional crumb, almost, it seemed, by courtesy', before Perry faltered, partly because of the stamina problems that he would later address.

It was a sign of the amateur times that Perry's selection was facilitated by the fact that three contenders for places, Colin Gregory and Ian Collins, considered by Perry the finest doubles pair never to win Wimbledon, and Harry Lee, made themselves unavailable for professional reasons. Gregory was a doctor and Lee was taking accountancy exams and could not commit to the possibility – that became a shining reality – of a three-month Davis Cup campaign. For his part Perry was unencumbered by ambitions beyond tennis, and his single-mindedness almost certainly appealed to Herbert Roper Barrett, the autocratic non-playing captain of the Davis Cup team. Like Perry, Roper Barrett, singles runner-up at Wimbledon in 1911, was viewed by some in the establishment with a wary eye after he and Arthur Gore inflicted a heavy defeat on the Duke of York, the future George VI, and Sir Louis Greig, the chairman of the All England Club, in the first round of the 1926 Wimbledon doubles. (Others, though, saw the 6–1 6–3 6–2 score as much better than the defeated pair's talent deserved.)

The one match Perry played against Monaco, as the number two behind Austin, was over in straight sets but did take a physical toll. Austin himself dropped only one game in winning a rain-interrupted singles against Vladimir Landau, an exiled Russian, to give Britain the lead. Perry's opponent, René Gallepe, was large and bespectacled, and was described as playing like a professor demonstrating to a class. His main asset was a fast and tricky serve, and late in the match, when he introduced the lob with Perry struggling after a fall on the slippery surface, he opened a 5–3 lead. At this point Perry 'decided the third set must be won' and swept up the next four games for victory.

Perry hurt his back in the fall, an injury that would remain an annoying niggle for some weeks. He took no further part in the tie at Carhullen, his team-mates Austin, Pat Hughes and Charles Kingsley completing the 5–0 demolition. 'One swallow may not make a summer, but one new "star" may make all the difference in a lawn tennis season,' E.J. Sampson said in the *Manchester Guardian* after the win over Monaco. 'F.J. Perry may be the new performer who may make the 1931 season one to be remembered. If Austin has improved his stamina, and if Perry improves his backhand and steels his nerves in times of crisis, then we may shine in the Davis Cup competition . . . Other nations seem to be relying on old players; they have been unable to find new champions.'

The mood changed slightly when neither Austin nor Perry fared well at the British Hard Court Championships, their failures prompting pessimism ahead of the next Davis Cup tie in Brussels – misguidedly, as it turned out, with Belgium dispatched 5–0. More impressive still was the clean-sweep victory that followed against South Africa on the grass courts at Devonshire Park, the venue where only seven years before Perry had spied his future.

South Africa's Davis Cup team included Norman Farquharson, the Cambridge undergraduate who in due course, as we have seen, would be the last player to beat Perry in a Wimbledon singles. For reasons already described, Farquharson was one of those who developed a dislike for the Englishman's uncompromising approach to the game. He was not the first or last to be irked by Perry's efforts to destabilise opponents, which were well prepared and only occasionally transgressed the rules. Teddy Tinling wrote in his memoirs that in the locker room Perry had a sharp tongue and never missed an opportunity to make a penetrating comment, sometimes to the point of being extremely personal. 'On court,' Tinling added, 'he was never averse to using a caustic one-liner to distract an opponent.'

Nor was it was just varsity men such as Farquharson who resented this. Various players over the years did not always manage to hide their irritation. Don Budge, who became a great rival of Perry as an amateur and professional, reckoned, 'He could be brutally sarcastic when the mood hit him.' Another American, Jack Kramer, who won the 1947 Wimbledon title, recounted how Perry would say 'Very clevah' whenever an opponent played a particularly good shot against him. 'I never played Fred competitively,' Kramer said, 'but I heard enough from other guys that that "Very clevah" drove a lot of opponents crazy.'

Perry always said he learned the importance of using psychological ploys from another American, Bill Tilden. 'He never gave you what you wanted,' he said. 'One day he would talk to you, next day he would ignore you. He gave you the impression that he was doing you a favour by turning up. You couldn't take your eyes off him. That's important. On court they should be looking at you.' Some saw Perry's mind games as a manifestation of his mental toughness. A commentator who became a close friend of Perry's said, 'He was a very strong character and you could see how it was that opponents hated playing him, because he would make it very difficult for them. He did it by his technical ability, and made it worse – compounded it – by his attitude of aggression and total dominance.'

He would try to establish control right at the start of a match by being the one to spin his racket to decide who served, often throwing it ahead of him in an exaggerated gesture as he and his opponent came on court. During the knock-up he would call out loudly to his opponent, 'Any time you're ready.' In other words, he was the one making the decisions. 'If my opponent made a brilliant shot and regained the spotlight there was the fly-in-eye ploy. You make out you have something in your eye. It brings the focus back to you. Surreptitious gamesmanship I think you could call it.' Right at the end of a match his jumping the net was a premeditated demonstration of the energy he had in reserve. Even when play was not in progress, Perry had little ruses to steal an advantage. He liked to outshine opponents in terms of appearance, on occasions leaving the court and returning in an even smarter outfit than the one in which he started.

It said something else about Perry, though, that nearly all those who were brassed off by his many stratagems came around to admiring him and enjoying his company.

Farquharson's irritation normally failed to save him from defeat by Perry, in singles matches at least. In their only Davis Cup meeting, Perry was 'by far the better man' in the opinion of one commentator as he overwhelmed the South African on the first day of the match at Devonshire Park. His ability to take the ball early kept Farquharson away from the net, where he was known to be dangerous. At this stage, though, Farquharson might have been no more than 'a pretty volleyer', as one newspaper disparagingly put it, and Perry's fatal mistake in two years' time at Wimbledon might have been to underestimate the improvement in this shot. Earlier, Austin had been run close by the left-handed Bob Kirby, who failed with five match points, but it was the only time the home effort stuttered.

The Britain team stayed in Eastbourne for one more Davis Cup tie before Wimbledon, and this time Japan, allocated to the European zone because no other nation from Asia was taking part, were disposed of 5–0. For the first time Perry dropped a set in a live match, as opposed to one whose outcome could not affect who would win the tie, but he still felt he gave his best Davis Cup performance to date in his four-set win over Jiro Satoh, an awkward customer who would reach the 1932 and 1933 Wimbledon semi-finals before dying in 1934 after a bout of pneumonia.

A newspaper review of 1931 said Britain was indebted almost entirely to Austin and Perry for the revival in its tennis fortunes. 'There is practically nothing to choose between them,' it said. 'Austin is the more stylish, Perry the stronger and more reliable player. Considering what both did after Wimbledon, their failure at the championship meeting itself becomes "one of those things no fellah can understand".'

It was a measure of the expectation that now attached to the pair that Wimbledon was seen as a failure, even though Austin came within a point of reaching the semi-finals before going down to Frank Shields, and Perry lost in the semis, beaten by Sidney Wood, who went on to win the title.

At least they had little time to dwell on their perceived failure. The week after Wimbledon was taken up with travelling to Prague and adjusting back to a clay court for the European zone final against Czechoslovakia. Curiously, the game's international body did not drop the word 'lawn' from its title until 1977 despite the fact that long before Perry's day it had become a multi-surface sport. The International Tennis Federation's official history records that when the decision was taken it still caused 'those who revelled in the game's origins' to suffer heartburn. For Austin and Perry, forever having to recalibrate their games to the different surfaces was a constant cause of anxiety on their extended Davis Cup run.

The key to the 4–1 win in Prague was Austin's comeback to over-turn a two-sets-to-one deficit against the dangerous Roderick Menzel in the opening singles. Perry then dealt comfortably with Ladislav Hecht, and when he and Hughes dominated the doubles Britain had clinched their place in the penultimate stage of the competition, the inter-zone final, for the first time since 1919. They would play the Americans in Paris in a week's time. The winners of this match would then stay on in the French capital to take on France, who as holders received a bye straight into the title-deciding challenge round.

What a different world from Carhullen, where they had set out against Monaco in April, Perry and his team-mates entered when they gathered at Roland-Garros in the western suburbs of Paris. Instead of the shale court with its rough stone wall and vistas over the sodden Devon countryside, here was an 8,000-seat stadium rising steeply around a court of *terre battu*, a shrine to a nation's tennis mastery. In time the stadium would gain renown as the centrepiece of the French Open, but in 1931 it was the cockpit in which the Four Musketeers – Jean Borotra, Jacques 'Toto' Brugnon, Henri Cochet and René Lacoste – annually won the Davis Cup. In 1927 they had beaten the US 3–2 in Philadelphia to be crowned the first non-English-speaking winners of the trophy. The new stadium, named after a First World War flying ace and tennis enthusiast, shot up close to Porte d'Auteuil in a matter of months and was ready for the 1928 challenge round, in which France would again beat the Americans. By 1931 France against the US in the title match had become an eagerly awaited annual ritual that stretched back to 1925, and it was widely reckoned that the two nations were about to meet for the seventh year running – and for the fourth time at Roland-Garros, France having retained home advantage by holding on to the trophy since their 1927 success.

After two days of the inter-zone final, the likelihood of a US win over Britain had hardened to a near certainty. The Americans led 2–1, Perry, for what would be the only time in his career, having suffered two defeats in a Davis Cup tie, to Frank Shields in the first-day singles and then with Hughes in the doubles against George Lott and Johnny Van Ryn. Match number four was Wood against Perry, a repeat of the recently contested Wimbledon semi-final in which the love-struck American had beaten Perry in four sets.

This time, though, there was no Gertie Lawrence in the stand to elevate Wood's game.

After a scrappy match opinion was divided between whether Perry had won it or Wood lost it, although H.S. Scrivener, writing in the LTA's magazine, was in little doubt that Perry was lucky to win in four sets. 'He had made practically no impression on Shields on the first day; he had been pretty hopeless in the doubles match on the second and, if the truth must be told, when he started the safety-first game against Wood he was not playing it any too well. But it sufficed. It was not a very deep pit that he dug but Wood fell obligingly into it and played the safety-first game, too, and very much worse.' Maybe, but Britain now had an unexpected opportunity, and Austin seized it by playing what no one questioned was some of his very best tennis – 'neat' and 'flawless' were the adjectives Perry used – in winning the decider against Shields in straight sets.

The French crowd, delighted that the Americans had at last been ejected before the challenge round – the first time this had happened since 1919 – showered the court with cushions to mark Britain's 3–2 success. Chastened US officials, meanwhile, hurried off to fix up an earlier passage home, the decision to book the team on a ship leaving after the title decider now looking embarrassingly like overconfidence.

The telegrams had already started to pour in as Britain returned to their hotel in central Paris, where, in contrast to the American efforts to effect a retreat, British officials set about telegraphing home for more clothing and replacement rackets to tide the team over until after the challenge round at Roland-Garros the following weekend.

The Davis Cup, an event that for years had generated little interest in Britain, was now a matter of huge national importance, and to escape undue attention the players were sent for a short break to Fontainebleau, the picturesque area to the south-east of the French capital that is a favourite getaway destination for Parisians. The month of July had begun for Perry with the disappointment of losing to Wood at Wimbledon; now it would end with the chance to lift the Davis Cup, a prospect that had seemed highly unlikely at the start of the year.

The reaction in the US to the unthinkable outcome of the tie against Britain ranged from serious to whimsical, the latter response exemplified by the conclusion to John Kieran's column in the *New York Times*:

Try to consider it calmly. A chap goes to London and runs into a thick fog. Well, he expected it. That's all right. He goes into a British hotel and orders a meal. The service is poor. The meat is cold mutton. The coffee is evidently composed of three parts rainwater, one part leather scrapings and one part iron filings. The tourist says 'So this is England' and shrugs his shoulders. There can be no complaint. This is exactly as per schedule. But he doesn't expect Lord Nelson to jump down off his column and fetch him a crack on the skull. He doesn't expect the Lord Chief Justice to leap out of a brougham, grab his straw hat and kick it around Piccadilly Circus. He doesn't expect the Prince of Wales to climb up a cellarway and bite him on the ankle.

So it was with our unsuspecting tennis champions. The British are great people for custom and tradition. Our lads had romped through at Wimbledon. They had defeated Bunny Austin and Fred Perry here and abroad. They were going to defeat them again and then move on to wrestle with the French for the Davis Cup. It was all arranged. The program was set. And then – horror of horrors! – the ambush, the massacre! A betrayal of trust! Our faith in England will never be the same again. They did the unexpected!

The charged atmosphere of the draw on the afternoon before the challenge round alerted the Britain team to the excitement that was gathering around the three-day tie. Austin would play the first singles on the opening and closing days — Henri Cochet first and then Jean Borotra – and Perry would open against Borotra in the second singles before playing Cochet in the fifth, final and, potentially, deciding match (the doubles, as ever, having been played on the second day). This was not as Britain would have wanted it, the more experienced and phlegmatic Austin having shown his suitability for the stresses of a deciding match in the win over the Americans. Perry himself admitted that, at this stage of his career, his game was too carefree − a touch flash, even − for the crushing pressure of a contest to determine who won the Davis Cup.

Perry's predisposition to showmanship was rarely seen to better effect than in a singles he had played against Borotra, known as the 'Bounding Basque', in May when the pair met at Roland-Garros in the annual Britain v. France match. Borotra, nearly eleven years older than Perry, was renowned for putting on a display, partly for the crowd and partly to disconcert opponents. Perry was tipped off by Hughes that he could expect some theatricals from Borotra, particularly as this was their first meeting. Accordingly, Perry drew up some countermeasures.

Most probably he would have to cope with the Frenchman's favourite tricks of interacting with a member of the crowd, almost certainly a good-looking female, and a routine in which he interrupted play to choose which beret to wear out of a number he had brought on court. Perry pre-empted the first of these by putting his own plant in the crowd, a gorgeous model, and engineering a rally that ended with him chasing Borotra's winning smash to finish up in the young lady's lap. Then, later, when Borotra went to select his beret, he found himself upstaged again, this time Perry following him to the umpire's chair to put on a cap with a big peak. To top it off, Perry won the match to establish a supremacy over Borotra he never relinquished.

This supremacy enabled Britain to cancel out Austin's defeat by Cochet in the opening match of the challenge round. Perry won 4−6 10−8 6−0 4−6 6−4, a scoreline that told its own story of a dramatic contest in oppressive conditions. The many incidents included one in the third set that highlighted what has been a recurring issue in the history of the Davis Cup, the probity of officials. The LTA magazine reported:

> Perry drove wide and deep to Borotra's forehand and Borotra did not make a return. The linesman said nothing, but the crowd vociferated their opinion that the ball was out. Then the umpire, instead of calling the score as he should have done, asked the linesman not once but twice to give a decision.

On each occasion the linesman replied that the ball was in and the umpire reluctantly called the score in favour of Perry. It should be noted, however, that he did not take similar action on occasions when the crowd objected to decisions against our players.

Perry's own comment on this aspect of the Davis Cup was that in away ties the court always seemed to be much wider on the British side of the net than on the other.

The match took a heavy toll on both Perry and Borotra, more so on the Frenchman, who was hardly able to stand at the end of the five sets. In Perry's case, physical fatigue was exacerbated by his nervous reaction to the approaching thunderstorm that broke over Roland-Garros moments after the match ended. Despite this, Perry was expecting to play in the next day's doubles and, with the rest of the team, was surprised when Roper Barrett came into the dressing room to announce that Charles Kingsley would partner Hughes, who remained indignant for the rest of his life that Perry was not his partner for this particular match.

Whether it was the sight of Perry on the masseur's table that prompted Roper Barrett to rest him is impossible to tell; he was not the type to give explanations. Perry's own theory was that a combination of his having just played five hard sets and his poor practice form persuaded Roper Barrett to change the doubles pairing that had won four times out of five on the way to the challenge round. Perry was careful not to criticise directly the decision but did make the point that he was 'the worst practice player who ever walked a tennis court' and his true form should only ever be judged by how he played in competition.

France had no such selection problems. Cochet, who had not been overextended by Austin, and the well-rested Brugnon had performed well together in the 1930 win over the US and proved too strong for the British pair. But Hughes and Kingsley did at least win a set and Hughes's excellent form, which overshadowed Kingsley's shaky effort, roused another bout of soul-searching over Roper Barrett's selection. Still, France's 2–1 lead going into the final day was not yet decisive, and when Austin beat Borotra in four sets in the first of the remaining two singles, the outcome of the tie − and the destination of the trophy − rested on the match between the veteran Cochet, rising thirty, and the twenty-two-year-old Perry, whose Davis Cup career had begun just four months earlier.

The Frenchman could loosely be described as Fred Perry's mentor. If Perry had modelled his game on anyone's it was Cochet's, notably the early forehand. Cochet, too, was someone who knew the value of gamesmanship, and for once Perry reckoned he was outsmarted in this match both in terms of the tennis played and psychological fencing. One episode in particular stayed with him. At one set all and within two points of losing the third set, Perry served a fault, only for Cochet to whack the ball into the stands. Cochet then held up play, insisting the ball was returned before play resumed. After a considerable pause, a souvenir hunter reluctantly threw it back and Perry promptly double-faulted before losing the set. Perry's splendidly equivocal response was that he felt Cochet had conned him but he was willing to give him the benefit of the doubt.

Perry, who had not watched a ball hit in the Austin−Borotra match, preferring to sit in the dressing room under the stands and judge the course of the contest from the crowd noises, professed to not having been nervous against Cochet. He remained in contention until losing the third set, at which point the home favourite, lifted by the increasingly excited clamour from the stands, took charge to win 6−4 1−6 9−7 6−3 and retain the trophy for France. Respectful silence for the national anthems, played in a steady drizzle, quickly gave way to scenes of rejoicing as spectators spilled onto the court to carry their man triumphantly around the stadium.

As he looked on, Perry could ponder an extraordinarily successful first Davis Cup season in which he had played eighteen singles and doubles matches and lost only three times. In difficult conditions against Cochet, with the rain that held up play in the second set turning the red clay into a horrible goo and contributing to the strings in three of his rackets breaking, he had played as well as could have been expected. Sam Perry, among the spectators that day, commented, 'We looked on that tie as just the forerunner of a future one with a different result.' Britain's players returned to London for a dinner laid on by the LTA at the Savoy Hotel, after which Perry prepared to leave the next day for his second trip to the United States.

The excitement of Britain's run in the 1931 Davis Cup seemed likely to be sustained as the team won their first two ties of 1932, beating Romania 5–0 at the Abbey Park courts in Torquay and Poland 4–1 in Warsaw. Perry's victories in four singles and two doubles – for which he was reunited with Hughes – did not cost him a set.

The eccentricities of Romania's veteran player Nicolas Mishu at least made up for the lack of competitive entertainment. Mishu was renowned for thinking aloud on court and for his range of services, more than twenty in all, which included a couple delivered with his back to the net. The local Torquay paper said of his serving on this occasion, 'To meet anything more unorthodox in such a match would be quite inconceivable.' It reported that he concentrated on two types of delivery against Perry, an unusual version of the overarm serve, but chiefly 'an underhand service, drawing the racket sharply across the ball backhand fashion, so that the ball dropped over the net with little force behind it, but with a heavy spin'. Perry saw him off for the loss of two games. In the evenings, Mishu and Britain's Herman David, brought into the team because Austin was having an operation on his nose, maintained the light-hearted mood of the one-sided tie by playing the piano together at the teams' hotel.

At the Warsaw Lawn Tennis Club, Poland's fifth tie against Britain in eight years proved almost as unproductive for the hosts as the previous ones – but not quite. On this occasion they did manage to win a match, having previously not taken as much as a set off Britain, and such was the excitement that even though Ignacy Tloczynski's victory over Harry Lee came too late to make a differ-ence to the overall result the crowd chaired their man off court. Possibly because of this success, Tloczynski developed an affinity with Britain and ended up coaching in Edinburgh until his retirement in 1990 when he was seventy-nine.

The win over Poland put Britain into a European zone semi-final in Germany in early July, a contest that would be packed with drama in the best traditions of the Davis Cup – although perhaps not quite to the extent that Perry later made out. What was a big and indisputable surprise was that Germany won. Confidence that Britain would come through the tie at the Rot-Weiss Club in Berlin was based on Perry's rapidly established reliability in the competition and Austin's return after his operation, any question of his fitness apparently having been removed less than a week earlier when he reached the Wimbledon final.

As it turned out, Austin floundered — a reaction, presumably, to the effort of reaching the final the previous Saturday, the rushed journey to the German capital and his having to adjust to playing on a clay court — still known as a hard court in those days — for the first time since the 1931 challenge round. He lost both his singles, to Daniel Prenn on the first day and to Gottfried von Cramm on the third, defeats that Perry offset by crushing von Cramm for the loss of six games and teaming with Hughes for another comfortable doubles win. Now all Perry had to do was to beat Prenn and Britain's place in the zonal final against Italy would be secure.

Perry's account of the match against Prenn in his 1984 autobiography starts by saying that it took place 'right in front of Adolf Hitler'. It goes on to recount how he lost the first two sets on a treacherously damp court before his speed, negated early on by the slippery surface, became a factor once the court dried out. By winning the third set, he gained himself a break to reassess the match.

Perry's version of events then describes a dastardly piece of sharp practice when it was time to go back on court. A local official, on the pretext of avoiding the crush, took him on an alternative route that included going down some steep steps and then back up them after the gate at the bottom turned out to be locked. Passing by the clubhouse, Perry noticed that Prenn had been spared the courtesy of the supposedly easier route; instead, he had remained in the dressing room for an extended session on the massage table.

Incensed by this, Perry raced through the fourth set 6–0 and opened a 5–2 lead in the fifth. He even had a match point on Prenn's serve, which, according to Perry, was the cue for more skulduggery. The serve was good but the return was better, wrong-footing Prenn, and Perry moved forward to shake the German's hand at the end of the contest. But before he could reach the net, he was stopped in his tracks. Apparently Prenn had been foot-faulted for the first time in the match. Prenn won the point with his second serve and, inspired by this success, opted for a far more aggressive approach. Rushing to the net whenever possible, he swept to victory without the loss of another game. The result was marked by wild celebrations with Prenn being borne aloft from the stadium.

Home teams have always had scope to seek advantage in Davis Cup ties, most obviously by choosing the venue and surface, but Perry's version of how events unfolded seems to have been spiced up to make a better story. None of the shenanigans that he refers to has ever been reported elsewhere. Even taking into account there was no British press at the Rot-Weiss Club, it is unlikely that so much intrigue would have gone unreported either at the time or in the intervening years. Perhaps most tellingly, Perry himself failed to mention it two years later, in his first autobiography. His assessment then was: 'I will be candid about this match and admit that under the tremendous nerve strain, and in the hurricane [of] excitement over the court, I "cracked" and my game deteriorated very badly. To cap all, my nerve broke.'

Also, it was not the case that Hitler, who never showed the slightest interest in the exclusive sport of tennis, was present. A contemporary account of the match in the German journal *Tennis und Golf* gave a list of the VIPs who were watching. They included Franz von Papen, who had just started his brief spell as chancellor, the ministers Baron Wilhelm von Gayl and Dr Hermann Warmbold and the actors Lilian Harvey and Willy Fritsch. Hitler was not mentioned, which he most certainly would have been had he been there.

One piece of intrigue that does have a reliable source (Prenn's family) is that Perry's sluggish start may have been caused by a double portion of home-made apple pie served to him by Prenn's wife before the match. Even this story, though, is questionable, lacking as it does an explanation of how a rival's spouse managed to persuade Perry, so fastidious in preparing for matches, to tuck into a large dessert before such an important contest.

What is beyond doubt was Perry's distress at press reaction to the result. Although he had helped to secure both Britain's points in the 3–2 defeat — and come close to salvaging a third that would have won the tie — some newspapers singled him out for criticism because of his slump in the fifth set against Prenn. One did at least blame the whole team, dismissing them all as carthorses, and the *Daily Telegraph* attacked the selectors for choosing Austin less than a week after he had expended so much energy reaching the final of Wimbledon. The LTA responded furiously to the suggestion that Austin should have been left out, huffing, 'As an example of after-the-event fatuousness this is hard to beat and we consequently have much pleasure in giving it the coveted award of the usual biscuit.' It might perhaps have assuaged Perry's resentment if he had known that he would not lose another singles match before a tie was decided in the four years he remained on the team, and that Britain would win the trophy in each of these years.

Germany next beat Italy 5–0 before losing narrowly to the US one match short of the challenge round, but the nation's tennis was under threat from far more sinister forces than players from other countries. For the coming regime in Germany, tennis — like nearly everything else — was subject to close inspection, perhaps because of the scenes of patriotic fervour witnessed at the Rot-Weiss Club. In April 1933, less than a year after Britain played Germany and with Hitler now installed as chancellor of the Third Reich, this disturbing paragraph appeared in the LTA magazine under the heading NON-ARYANS: 'The German Lawn Tennis Association have announced the qualifications which will in future be necessary for their players in the representative tournaments and matches. "Non-Aryans" are to be debarred from committees nor will they be allowed to occupy any office in the Association. Clubs predominantly non-Aryan in character are to be excluded from membership of the Association. Non-Aryans are not to represent the clubs of the Association in matches.'

Two of Germany's best players were forbidden to compete because of their Jewish ancestry: Nelly Neppach, who had been the national women's champion, and Daniel Prenn, ranked number six in one

world list published in 1932. Neppach, depressed by the rise of
National Socialism, committed suicide; Prenn, whose family had fled
to Germany after the revolution in the Russian empire in 1917, now
moved on to England, the tennis-loving king of Sweden, Gustav V,
having advised him this would be the wise thing to do. The
International Lawn Tennis Federation shamefully took no action
against the German LTA, and the few people who emerged with
any credit from the episode included Austin and Perry, who
protested in a letter to the editor of *The Times*. The letter, published
on 15 April 1933, read in full:

> Sir,
>   We have read with considerable dismay the official statement
> which has appeared in the Press that Dr D.D. Prenn is not to
> represent Germany in the Davis Cup on the grounds that he
> is of Jewish origin.
>   We cannot but recall the scene when, less than 12 months
> ago, Dr Prenn before a large crowd at Berlin won for Germany
> against Great Britain the semi-final round of the European
> Zone of the Davis Cup, and was carried from the arena amidst
> spontaneous and tremendous enthusiasm.
>   We have always valued our participation in international
> sport, because we believed it to be a great opportunity for the
> promotion of better international understanding and because
> it was a human activity that countenanced no distinction of
> race, class, or creed. For this reason, if for none other, we view
> with great misgivings any action which may well undermine
> all that is most valuable in international competition.
>   Yours faithfully,
>   H.W. AUSTIN
>   FRED PERRY

So Perry did take some interest in politics although Austin, a religi-
ous man whose beliefs caused him to suffer high-handed treatment
by the establishment similar to that meted out to Perry, was almost
certainly the prime mover behind the letter.

Austin and his wife, the actress Phyllis Konstam, joined the

Christian organisation known as the Oxford Group – later Moral Re-Armament (MRA) – and according to the actor Peter Ustinov, a family friend, Austin was 'disgracefully ostracised by the All England Club because he was a conscientious objector'. Austin found his membership of the club had been cancelled when he returned to England from the US after the Second World War. He was first told it was because he had not paid his subscription but learned later it was because some members opposed his involvement with MRA. There was also a feeling in certain quarters that Austin, by leaving the country after the start of the war, had deserted his compatriots, despite the fact that the British government gave him its blessing to go to America to promote world peace. 'We were all of us faced with the possible end of civilisation,' he said. 'War threatened my wife, my daughter, my parents and all I cared about with destruction. It seemed uncanny to think of putting my baby daughter in a gas-proof tent.' Austin's belief was that Sir Louis Greig, chairman of the All England Club from 1937 to 1953, had cancelled his membership. Austin was black-balled until 1984. This same resentment would be felt by Perry after he took out US citizenship and stayed away from Britain during the war, even though, like Austin, he did wartime service with the US military.

Muttering over the defeat in Berlin continued until the start of the 1933 Davis Cup campaign, when some pundits called on the LTA to consider team changes for the match against Spain in Barcelona. The carthorses were now cabhorses, according to one newspaper, a description Austin adopted when signing letters to Perry 'The other cabhorse'. The LTA's decision to make Austin and Perry play unofficial Davis Cup tests in early April did little to promote an air of optimism before the tie against Spain, the matches reportedly being played in a lukewarm spirit that did not enthuse those who had paid to see them. When it came to the real action, though, the antipathy evaporated as the team rushed through the first four European zone ties of 1933 – against Spain, Finland, Italy and Czechoslovakia – for the loss of only two singles, in each case after the overall result was decided.

Roper Barrett's reputation as a flinty leader was underlined by this press dispatch from Barcelona, where, as expected, Britain disposed of Spain with an ease that by the end of the century would have been unthinkable: 'Every hospitality was accorded to the team, several invitations had to be refused by the non-playing captain, Mr H. Roper Barrett, who knows the value of early hours and insists on the elimination of any entertainments that may have an adverse effect on the players in his team.'

One of the two singles losses Britain suffered at the start of the 1933 campaign was an unfamiliar upset for Perry against a familiar foe, Giorgio De Stefani, when Britain held a winning 3–0 lead over Italy on the Devonshire Park grass courts in Eastbourne. Perry already knew De Stefani as an awkward customer, having lost to him two years earlier at the French Championships. Their rivalry would develop into something of a soap opera. On this particular occasion, though, Perry's performance almost certainly had less to do with De Stefani's ambidextrousness than it did with the fact that the tie had already been won. As one critic put it, Perry might have done better if he had exerted himself throughout the match rather than in parts of it. Roper Barrett saw to it that there was no such lapse from Perry during the potentially difficult match against Czechoslovakia, which took place a week after the victory over Italy, also at Devonshire Park. Britain won the tie 5–0, with Perry reaching his peak form of the summer with straight-set wins in his three matches.

Australia's geographical isolation from the rest of the tennis-playing world – as represented by those nations who entered the Davis Cup, that is – meant its team competed in the European zone. In 1933 the Australians were Britain's opponents in the zonal final, to be held at Wimbledon. Since the win over Czechoslovakia, Perry had suffered his unexpected defeat by Norman Farquharson at Wimbledon and with Australia's number one, Jack Crawford, having taken the men's title at the championships, the tie was accurately described by Perry as a toughie.

It became tougher when on an unimaginably bleak mid-July afternoon Crawford opened the tie by beating Austin. This increased the pressure on Perry to beat Vivian McGrath, a seventeen-year-old from New South Wales who was reckoned to possess exceptional promise. McGrath, one of the earliest exponents of the two-fisted backhand, would have some success against Perry, but never in the really big events, and on this occasion Perry won in straight sets. The conditions were such that one newspaper described Perry as 'a stormy petrel this Davis Cup day'.

Australia picked the two 'South Australian colts' Adrian Quist and Don Turnbull for the doubles, which suited Perry and Hughes, who faltered only in losing the third set. Austin then put the tie beyond Australia's reach when he gained the third point Britain needed to reach the inter-zone final in the first of the final-day singles. This meant that Perry, who had jarred his shoulder in the doubles, did not have to risk aggravating the injury by playing a decider against Crawford, who ended up featuring in what amounted to an exhibition match against Harry Lee.

Media reports reflected that this was not a victory for a nation used to tennis success; rather, it was seen as a triumph for a tired old beast whose international reputation amounted to not very much. 'Great Britain, that poor, despised back number of lawn tennis,' the *Daily Express* said, 'put the finishing touch to a great feat on Saturday. When Bunny Austin defeated the double-handed back-hand wonder from Australia, Vivian McGrath, our Davis Cup team had then eliminated all comers except the United States.' By this the newspaper meant that the US, winners of the American zone, were the last opponents Britain needed to beat to reach a second challenge round match in three years against France in Paris.

The French capital was also the venue for the meeting with the Americans, to be held the weekend after the win over Australia. While the rest of the team travelled straightaway, Perry stayed behind for treatment on his shoulder. He arrived in Paris for a final fitness test, hitting against Dan Maskell at Roland-Garros, less than forty-eight hours before the tie started. Having come through this satisfactorily, he and Maskell set off to join the rest of the team at the Hotel Crillon in the centre of town. What happened next was a favourite Perry story, which helps to illustrate the depth of interest in the Davis Cup in France at that time. He and Maskell passed a smart-looking restaurant that Perry liked the look of and he persuaded his colleague, who was worried it might be a bit pricey, that they should dine there rather than go to where the others were eating. The maître d'hôtel welcomed them warmly, the band played 'God Save the King' and when they tried to pay they were informed the meal was on the house.

Roper Barrett's concern that Perry's injury might still be a problem did not last long. Austin played magnificently in the opening singles to repel Ellsworth Vines, who had overpowered him in the 1932 Wimbledon final but on the much slower surface at Roland-Garros salvaged just six games – the same number Austin gleaned in the previous year's defeat. This success greatly increased Britain's hope of winning before Perry, with his suspect shoulder, met Vines on the last day in the final match of the tie. Overall victory was duly wrapped up when Austin's win over Wilmer Allison put Britain 3–1 in front.

There followed one of the most talked-about 'dead rubbers' in Davis Cup history when Perry stepped out to play Vines. Perry was supposed to be taking care of his shoulder, but when these two played each other, as they did on so many occasions, personal pride tended to supersede all other considerations. They would happily go on until the first man dropped, which in this case happened quite literally after Vines refused to stop despite turning his ankle in the fourth set.

Serving at 7–6 and match point down in the fifth set, Vines pitched forward headlong onto the court. Perry reacted quickest. He ran to the umpire's chair, grabbed a container of water and poured it over Vines's head, neck and shoulders. This failed to revive Vines, who was carried from the court by officials, with Perry, walking behind, given a rousing cheer by the French crowd.

Perry had reached match point courtesy of a couple of double faults from Vines, which some spectators applauded. Mercer Beasley, who coached Vines and was in the stands, said it was a combination of this unsporting reaction, the pain from his ankle and the intense heat that made Vines's 'whole being let go and his heart went out. He remembered nothing from the time he left the court till he was sitting under the stands in the shade, possibly for ten minutes.'

The incident became something of an issue, not because of the discourteous behaviour of the spectators – according to Beasley, the French cheered for the British because they did not fear them as much as the Americans – but because there was a feeling that US team officials had demanded too much of their players. With Allison's fitness also in question, the French press singled out Bernon Prentice, the American captain, for rebuke. Jean Augustin of *Paris Midi*, doyen of French tennis writers, asked, 'How can any country confide its sporting interests to a man who presented two players of great value resembling cadavers instead of athletes?' Didier Poulain of *L'Auto* reported that Vines had been bandaged like a mummy the day before playing Perry but had still been allowed to practise.

Vines countered by issuing a statement in defence of Prentice in which he said that an erroneous impression seemed to exist concerning his match with Perry. 'At the time I turned my ankle, Captain Prentice urgently requested me to discontinue play,' Vines added. 'Not only did he do so, but every time I passed his chair he repeated his request . . . It was only through my own insistence that he let me continue.' Beasley corroborated this, saying Prentice had repeatedly pleaded with Vines to quit. He said that the real story of the match was how well Perry played.

Perry had further medical problems of his own to resolve in the four days between the end of the match against the US and returning to Roland-Garros for the climactic meeting with France to decide the 1933 Davis Cup. Unlike the Americans, though, he was beyond reproach on fitness matters because the trouble he took over his physical conditioning was now widely recognised.

George Lott, an American player who was also an interesting writer on the game, published an essay about Perry in 1972 called 'The Finest Athlete I Ever Saw'. In it he remembered the second singles of the 1933 challenge round, a prodigious five-set contest between Perry and Cochet. What he wrote left little doubt about the state of Perry's readiness, and the article also found space for an unsubtle dig at French officiation.

To win the tie it was absolutely necessary for Perry to beat Henri Cochet, and in those days it was no easy matter. Cochet was the idol of 15,000 fans and had an equally high standing with all French linesmen. Six games to one in the fifth set was the margin by which Perry won, and a great accomplishment it was. At Forest Hills that year I asked Fred how he did it. Censorship forbids an exact quote, but the gist was that he ran Cochet into the ground until the Frenchman ran out of gas.

Perry vaulted the net at the end, but this, he admitted, was sheer bravado. If Cochet was out of gas, Perry had only a few drops left, and he passed out afterwards in the dressing room through a combination of mental and physical fatigue.

Anyone who imagines sporting crowds whipping themselves into a state of near-hysterical excitement as a phenomenon that arrived much later in the twentieth century – and certainly never happened in France, the epicentre of sophisticated behaviour – should read reports of Parisians cheering on the Four Musketeers when they were Davis Cup kings. The sense that the end might be near – after all, Cochet was to be thirty-two later in the year and Jean Borotra and Toto Brugnon, who played in the doubles in this tie, were thirty-four and thirty-seven – may have moved the crowd on this occasion to be even more enthusiastic in their support than usual. In the Cochet–Perry match any close call that went against France produced a din that lasted three or four minutes before play could resume, and Perry described the whole experience as nerve-racking.

Perry's win gave Britain a 2–0 lead, Austin having easily won the opening singles against André Merlin, a teenager France had felt compelled to introduce to counter their more youthful opponents. With only one more victory needed to win the cup, Roper Barrett decided to send out Harry Lee as Pat Hughes's partner in the doubles, and this time, unlike in 1931 when Kingsley was brought in, no one questioned the wisdom of breaking up the Perry–Hughes pairing. Although Lee and Hughes lost in three sets, the main thing was that Perry had more than a day in which to recover. He remained a little groggy, so much so that his practice hit with Austin after the doubles lasted only a few minutes before Roper Barrett ordered him back to the hotel for an early night. He woke on the Sunday morning still feeling jaded but ready for what would be a momentous forty-eight hours. Cochet, too, was rested and came through in five sets against Austin to pull the score back to 2−2.

Perry against Merlin would decide whether Britain regained the trophy they had last held in 1912 or France kept it for the seventh year in a row. In the estimation of a reporter from the *New York Times*, who had stayed behind in Paris despite American disappointment that it was not another France v. US challenge round, what followed was arguably the greatest match ever played at this stage of the competition in such tense circumstances.

Merlin struck the ball beautifully off the ground to win the first set and was dominant for much of the second. Austin had come straight out again after his match to watch from the front row of the stands with his wife Phyllis. 'I was chain-smoking cigarettes although I normally smoked only three a day,' he recalled. 'Phyll, normally a non-smoker, was smoking two at once because she felt it was luckier.' The atmosphere was electric with excitement, Austin said, after the crowd suddenly realised that a French victory was once more a possibility.

Merlin, who in Austin's words was performing feats of prodigious skill far beyond his normal form, twice came within a point of winning the second set. Perry saved one of these points with a shot that hit the line and caused the crowd to taunt the linesman who had signalled that the ball was good. Before Perry received the next serve he noticed the linesman had been replaced, the sort of summary removal that in another set of circumstances might have been followed by a rifle shot.

Perry's tenacity kept him in the match, the sense that he should win driving him on to take the initiative against an opponent whose game was better suited to the slow surface. It said a huge amount for Perry that despite being rattled by Merlin's immaculate start and the crowd's baying he managed to right his game from a position where many others would have been powerless to prevent theirs collapsing. Cushions showered onto the court as Perry came through to win in four sets. In the stands Borotra turned away. Reuters reported that as he did so he said, 'I can't watch this.'

There was an uneasy moment at the presentation ceremony, when the huge silver trophy, designed in America at the start of the century by an English-born craftsman, Rowland Rhodes, came away from its base. When the trophy finally found its way from Albert Lebrun, the president of France, into Roper Barrett's grasp, the captain of the Great Britain team 'hugged it tightly as though it were a baby', reported Associated Press, 'while the fans with lumps in their throats bade it godspeed'. Perry missed most of this after once again passing out in the dressing room, overwhelmed by effort and emotion. He came round in time for the open-top bus ride back into Paris, during which the sight of gloating Englishmen brandishing the cup that had been France's for the best part of a decade went down badly.

The brandishing went on all through the night, although to Perry's surprise it was Cochet's idea, once the official dinner was over, that the trophy should be taken on a farewell tour of the capital city of the country that had become its home. During the hours of darkness it visited a number of nightclubs. At nearly every stop the trophy was filled with champagne and the small group, gradually swelling as it collected hangers-on, was serenaded with renditions of the national anthems of the two teams. As the party, now a little bedraggled, made its way across the Place de la Concorde at first light, those in tow included members of an orchestra from one of the night spots. No wonder the Great Britain team were, in Perry's words, a haggard-looking bunch as they prepared to return home, although, as he also said at the time, this was not simply because of the celebratory carousing. It was partly the price that 'has to be paid for success in these days of intensive competition in sport'.

Cochet's insistence on accompanying Perry and his team-mates on a grand tour of Paris's finest after-dark haunts was one of two nice touches on the part of the vanquished hosts. The other was presenting Perry with a book, *Croisades pour la Coupe Davis*, a humorous account of the Four Musketeers' reign as champions. The inscription on the title page read, 'To Fred Perry – In memory of the victory, so well merited, of the splendid British team in the Challenge Round of 1933.' Borotra wrote these words and he, Lacoste, Cochet, Brugnon, Merlin and Pierre Gillou, president of the French Tennis Federation, all signed it. Perry noted that, when the time came, he hoped Britain would yield the cup with the same good grace. When that moment did come, which was not until 1937, Perry was no longer around, having turned professional.

In Britain hurried preparations were made to welcome the team home. When they landed at Dover on the evening of the day after the final, having endured a choppy Channel crossing − Austin said there was 'a gale of wind that turned us green' − they received a message from George V. This was originally sent to the British embassy in Paris but arrived after the team had left. The ambassador, Lord Tyrrell, promptly returned it so that it could be handed to Roper Barrett as he and his players set foot back in Britain. It was a masterpiece of patrician restraint: 'Please convey to the members of the British lawn tennis team my heartiest congratulations on their fine achievement in winning the Davis Cup for Britain. − George R.I.'

The *Golden Arrow*, the luxury train brought into service four years earlier, was waiting to take the team to Victoria station in London, and all the way along the route people turned out to wave and cheer. At the station a crowd estimated at over 6,000 filled the main concourse. Suzanne Lenglen, the greatest female player of her time, provided a vivid indication of the sense of loss France felt at having surrendered the trophy by mingling with the crowd at Victoria. She had flown to London after seeing off the British players from Paris because, it was said, she knew of no other way to overcome her sadness.

A group from Brentham reflected the mood of the British fans at the station when they lifted Perry and Austin onto their shoulders. Meanwhile Perry resigned himself to having lost all his belongings to souvenir hunters in the melee but was delighted to find that, rescued by a friend, they arrived home before he did. A dinner hosted by the LTA a few days later brought together the new champions and the 1912 Davis Cup players, Britain's last successful team in the competition.

In his first three years as a Davis Cup player, Perry appeared in all seventeen ties Britain contested. In the three more years that he was eligible to play − 1934, 1935 and 1936, which were also the years he won Wimbledon − he and Britain featured in only three more ties. The triumph of 1933 meant they did not defend the trophy until the challenge round the following July, and their continued success, inspired by Perry at the peak of his game, also gained them this exemption until the title deciders in 1935 and 1936. Perry played only singles in the four challenge round ties in which he took part and won all eight in Britain's historic domination of the men's team world championship from 1933 to 1936.

6

Foreign conquests: 1933–6

'The new champion from the tight little isle'

New York had never seen its like before. Or, as one British newspaper put it, 'A British Empire final at Forest Hills was unprecedented in the history of American lawn tennis and there were many who wondered whether the New York public would deem it more exciting on a fine Sunday afternoon than a visit to the coast.' Arthur Wallis Myers, a dedicated reporter and chronicler of tennis for most of the first half of the twentieth century, was referring to the men's singles final of the 1933 US Championships between Fred Perry and Australia's Jack Crawford. Any worries the tournament organisers might have had turned out to be misplaced. Myers, writing for the *Daily Telegraph*, went on, 'They came out in their coatless thousands to see the two invaders who, with increasing strength, had crushed every American challenger.'

Not only were all the stadium seats taken, temporary seating had to be installed to satisfy the unexpectedly high demand for tickets. This equalled, improbably in Myers' view, the clamour that had preceded the 1927 US final between those two great masters from the new and old worlds, the American Bill Tilden and France's René Lacoste – won by Lacoste 11–9 6–3 11–9.

By now, Perry was much changed from the callow youth who had visited the United States for the first time three years before. Urbane and thoroughly self-assured, he was subjected to close inspection by American sportswriters, who were struck by the English 'tennis player who dresses as well as he makes his shots'. One observed, 'Frederick John Perry has a sleek appearance, a bland cosmopolitan manner which belies the fact that he taught himself tennis on

London's public courts.' This fascination with Perry did not stop at journalists. He had started to acquire some influential friends in the US, including Bertram Weal, the manager of the Madison Hotel in New York. When Perry came ashore, Weal would join the welcoming press throng dressed in the journalist's uniform of raincoat and trilby, with a name sticker giving his publication as *Zit's Weekly*. Irving Squires was another friend. He was a businessman and a sheriff of Queen's County, whose borders encompassed Forest Hills. Perry needed no second invitation to do things with panache and readily accepted Squires' offer of police outriders to escort his car to the grounds.

For all his sense of being at home in America, which increased with each visit, Perry did not initially feel good about his fourth attempt at the US title. It had been a hard summer, and he was exhausted when he set sail for New York less than a week after helping Britain to regain the Davis Cup and the triumphal junketing that followed. Wisely, his masters at the LTA excused him from having to play in singles events immediately before the 1933 US Championships, and the recovery this facilitated, together with what he reckoned was a favourable draw, filled him with renewed hope.

The draw became even more favourable when quite unexpectedly Ellsworth Vines lost to the diminutive Bryan Grant, who was known for his doughtiness but should not have been a match for his far more accomplished compatriot. Perry was among those who felt Vines had been affected by the scathing press criticism for his defeat in the Wimbledon final by Jack Crawford and his two losses against Britain in the Davis Cup inter-zone final in Paris. Also bearing down on him had been an inquiry by the US LTA, just before the championships started, into his amateur status. Vines protested his innocence and said he wanted to jump for joy when the inquiry found in his favour. His true feelings are more likely to have been those set out in a letter to his wife, Verle, which he sent from London in June: 'My heart just isn't in my tennis anymore and all I can think of is you and how much I'll make by turning pro. Darling I know I'll be much happier doing that than just keeping on like I am.' Understandably, his play suffered, and Grant was just the kind of player to take advantage of a stricken foe.

Perry was worried that his game was a little flabby after he started with three comfortable wins. It needed to be more solid for his next match against the American Keith Gledhill, who had finished runner-up to Crawford in that year's Australian Championships and had just beaten the US boy wonder Frankie Parker. Knowing Gledhill could generate the kind of pace that he had not come up against for more than a month, Perry sought out the veteran American Vinnie Richards. He played four fast sets against Richards on an outside court straight after his easy third-round win and said he had no doubt this was why he scrambled past Gledhill after trailing by two sets to one.

He then raced through his quarter- and semi-finals, against Adrian Quist and Les Stoefen, without conceding more than four games in a set to make it to his first grand slam final. The victory over Stoefen was notable for its one-sidedness – the experienced American had never previously been restricted to as few as seven games in a best-of-five-sets match – and for a small incident that illustrated Perry's magisterial presence, when he declined a point that he thought had been awarded to him incorrectly.

Crawford was regarded as clear favourite to take the title, not least because he had arrived in the US from Europe having scored a brilliant title victory over Vines at Wimbledon to complete a sweep of the year's first three grand slams. If Crawford needed any more incentive to beat Perry he now had the additional spur of becoming the first player not only to win all four grand slams, but to do so in the same year.

Perry, who received many good-luck messages from Britain, had almost as big an incentive. His consuming competitiveness, which had singled him out for success, meant he wished nothing but disappointment on his rivals, especially in this case. The landmark that Crawford was closing in on was one he had in mind for himself. He busily started cooking up ideas to make life as difficult as possible for the Australian and comfortably won the preliminaries by arriving for the final in a Rolls-Royce surrounded by Irving Squires' police escort. Lest anyone should wonder, the blaring sirens announced, 'Here comes Fred Perry.' At least Perry knew Crawford was not going to overpower him as Vines could do. Also, he liked the fact that Crawford preferred to stay on the baseline, which gave him the chance to settle in to rallies and work for an opening.

Crawford was leading by two sets to one when the players took a break. The match seemed to be going his way although Perry did have grounds for optimism. He may not have known about one of them – the fact that the Australian's favourite racket was out of commission after a string broke at the end of the third set – but others were all too evident. Crawford was not serving particularly well in the gusting wind, and by concentrating his attacks on his opponent's backhand the Australian had nudged what was regarded as Perry's weakest shot into as secure a groove as it had ever been. Perry must also have gained encouragement from the fact that despite Crawford's advantage on the scoreboard, he was starting to slow down. One court-side scribe even dismissed Crawford as being in bad shape physically.

Nor did Crawford help his cause during the ten-minute interval. While Perry went off to change his clothes and have a rub down, Crawford wandered about, sat chatting with his wife and smoked a cigarette. The local press cold not resist one more jibe: 'With judicial composure Crawford strolled to the marquee where his plump wife was smiling.'

In his unchanged, sweaty clothes, Crawford took time to loosen up when the match resumed, and Perry pounced to establish a lead in the fourth set that the Australian seemed to decide was not worth trying to close. In the fifth set, Perry, to use his own term, went crazy, hardly missed a shot and ended up winning the last two sets for the loss of only one game. *Time* magazine, after mentioning that Crawford now kept patting his chest as though his heart or his lungs hurt him, described the closing moments: 'Perry, dancing around the court, barely able to wait for the ball-boys to furnish ammunition for his serve, smashed through four more games for set, match and title – the first an English player has won in the US since Hugh Laurence Doherty 30 years ago.'

The effect of his victory cannot be overemphasised. Even Perry's normally impregnable self-belief had been shaken by his shock defeat by Norman Farquharson at Wimbledon in high summer. Now it stood invincible once more, and in the twelve grand slams that Perry played between and including the 1933 and 1936 US Championships he failed to reach only two finals, injuries helping to account for this on each occasion.

The cables poured in from Britain, including one from Bunny Austin: 'Well done, old cabhorse.' The *Daily Telegraph* reported that Perry's father and stepmother had stayed at home all evening in England anxiously waiting for news. Sam Perry was then quoted as saying, 'I am naturally very proud that my son should be the first Englishman in 30 years to win the American Championship.' The LTA magazine linked what it called the greatest triumph of Perry's career with the Davis Cup victory and said it 'raised the prestige of English lawn tennis still higher in this year of triumph'.

A splendid contrast to the understandable outpouring of purple prose on one side of the Atlantic came from Bill Corum on the other. The American writer described a trip to the Madison Hotel to interview 'the new American champion from the tight little isle'. He said he finally located Perry on the roof surrounded by pretty girls and an Hawaiian band. 'The life of an international tennis star seems to have its points,' Corum wrote. 'And Perry appeared to be leading by at least fifteen love.' The author then owned up to not having elicited a great deal from Perry because 'you can't sit out under a big yellow pumpkin moon with Miss Great Britain at one elbow and Miss Scotland at the other, listening to moanin' music and talk tennis'.

After winning in New York and then retaining the Pacific Southwest title in Los Angeles, Perry made his first crossing of the Pacific to New Zealand and Australia. He was heading for a year of unprecedented achievement, during which he helped Britain retain the Davis Cup and helped himself to three grand slam titles – just as Crawford had in 1933, although in Perry's case he missed out on the French Championship.

If he tired of tennis from time to time, Perry never lost his love of travel in big ocean-going liners, which he found even more to his liking than the scenic railway journeys that also captivated him. His maiden trans-Pacific voyage made a lasting impression. 'I do not mind how often I repeat that glorious voyage across the Pacific,' he wrote. On the trip, he, Harry Lee, Frank Wilde and the Australian players Adrian Quist and Don Turnbull joined in cricket matches with the ship's crew, staging their own version of the Ashes.

The ports of call included Tahiti, where the governor of the French Polynesian island invited the British and Australians to take part in exhibition tennis matches at his palatial home. At Raratonga, the capital territory of the fifteen Cook Islands, the players were again in demand to demonstrate their sport. In New Zealand, where they arrived on a chilly morning in October, Perry was even more dazzled by the scenery – 'indescribably awe-inspiring' – than he had been in South America. The hospitality the players received was another feature of the visit and it persuaded them to give something in return, a series of impromptu one-day exhibitions, before crossing by sea to Sydney.

Perry found Australia almost as refreshing as America. He empathised immediately with the conscious effort of the majority of the population to cast off the stuffier aspects of life in Mother England – a parent from under whose starched skirts the country was happily emerging.

Except for one notable incident, he did not mind that occasionally he was roughed up by the omnipresent barrackers, who have long had a special place in Australia's sporting culture. The most famous at the time was a character called Yabba, whose cry to wayward bowlers at cricket matches, 'Your length's lousy but you bowl a good width,' was a national catchphrase. While generally receiving an excellent press, Perry was worldly enough by now to accept the inevitable criticisms. Very early on, he and Pat Hughes suffered a panning after they turned up at a reception in Melbourne wearing white dinner jackets they had had tailored in the US. It was a warning that anything seen as ostentatious was – and indeed remains – anathema to Aussies.

At another function the mayor of Sydney referred to the recent bodyline Test cricket series, which had caused a diplomatic crisis between Britain and Australia when the England fast bowler Harold Larwood, directed by his captain Douglas Jardine, targeted opposition batsmen rather than the stumps. The mayor asked Hughes, captain of the visiting tennis players, whether he too had arrived with a secret weapon. Hughes replied that he had, one that had no need of a hard cricket ball – his name was Fred Perry, who was going to bash them up with the destructive force of his tennis.

This looked a hollow boast when Perry suffered losses in the build-up to the 1934 Australian Championships. He started well enough by beating Jack Crawford in the singles final of the Victoria Championships, but in Test matches against Australia's best players, notably the teenager Vivian McGrath, his form was uneven. McGrath, described by one local sportswriter as 'Australia's Don Bradman of tennis', was still only seventeen. He had played in his first Australian Championships at the age of fourteen and at the 1933 championships, aged sixteen, had beaten Vines. He was a useful all-round sportsman who played cricket and golf left-handed, and although he was officially classified as a right-handed tennis player he used his left hand to produce the pace for his best shot, a previously little seen two-fisted backhand.

McGrath beat Perry twice in Australia's 4–1 triumph over Britain in the 1933–4 Test series, resulting in huge optimism in the Australian press. Crawford, who wrote for the local papers, warned against too much expectation, recalling that the Englishman had easily mastered McGrath only a few months before in the Davis Cup. He was right. Perry was biding his time. He had developed that telling virtue of being able to customise his play to the importance of the event.

Perry's most vivid memory of the Test series would not be his losses to McGrath but that during it he joined in the 'modern craze' of flying – and in some company. The Australia and Britain teams were chauffeured around Australia by Charles Kingsford Smith in *Southern Cross*, the plane in which six years before Kingsford Smith had made the first flight across the Pacific. It was not the smoothest of conveyances, and Perry said he had to press his back against the side of the plane to stop his teeth falling out. Maybe this alerted him to how rigorous travelling around Australia could be and was why he declined an invitation from the distinguished agriculturalist Sir Frederick McMaster, which was accepted by the other members of the British contingent, to visit the McMaster family's scenic station of Dalkeith. 'I preferred to remain in Sydney and practise,' Perry said. 'I had set my heart on the Australian Championship and wanted to do all I knew towards becoming acclimatised to the local playing conditions.'

The stadium at Rushcutters Bay in Sydney staged the 1934 championships. Big crowds came to cheer on Crawford, who was defending his title. The locals were optimistic. If he faltered there was always McGrath or another good Australian, Harry Hopman, to replace him as champion.

Moderate opposition in the first two rounds prompted Perry to do what he had done at the US Championships and recruit an experienced local to help him sharpen his strokes. In New York it had been Vinnie Richards; in Sydney it was Jack Clemenger, a former member of Australia's Davis Cup team. This, he said, put a keen edge on his game for what might have been a difficult quarter-final against Hopman. Playing imperiously, Perry conceded just ten games against Australia's number two. Hopman's plan to come to the net whenever possible was continually thwarted by Perry's controlled accuracy. He had learned his lesson when being hustled to defeat by the onrushing South African Norman Farquharson at Wimbledon six months before.

Perry lost his next two singles sets at the start of the semi-final against McGrath, who brought to the match confidence gained during his wins in the Test series. A combination of Perry's pride, stamina, ability and application, which was now as unwavering as any in the game, pulled him through. He displayed the champion's priceless assets of eradicating rather than multiplying errors in a crisis and of being emboldened by the prospect of elimination. By the end he was in total control. He won the fifth and deciding set 6–1, after which McGrath collapsed through sheer exhaustion.

Perry said after this match that there was something about McGrath's game that he found difficult to counter. He did not know what it was precisely, perhaps a pace slightly slower than that of others. 'I was in an awkward spot at the end of the second set,' Perry said, 'but lack of experience helped McGrath to lose. If he had rushed me off my feet perhaps I would not have met Crawford in the final. Perhaps next time we meet he'll adopt these tactics and I'll rue the day I ever told him what to do.' They would meet just once more in a big event, at the same stage of the 1935 Australian Championships, and Perry never gave McGrath the chance to adopt the tactics he prescribed.

In all, Perry played ten sets and ninety-eight games the day before the 1934 Australian final, winning the doubles final with Pat Hughes over the full distance in addition to his long semi-final against McGrath. And yet he beat Crawford, who had not been nearly so severely tested, in straight sets for the loss of only nine games. It was as if only a few minutes had elapsed, rather than nearly four months, since the closing two sets of the 1933 US final.

As ever, Perry had a theory to account for his domination. 'Put Jack and myself up against the world's top ten and Jack might get the better results, but Jack knows and I know that I have the type of game that must always worry him whereas he does not possess the type of game to incommode me.' On that Saturday Perry also reckoned that fatigue, brought on by twelve months of constant travel, had affected Crawford's concentration. This last remark might well have been an oblique dig or device to point up his own fitness. Perry arrived at the final in perfect condition despite having just as much reason as Crawford to feel tired. His travels had been no less arduous and his long Friday would have exhausted most players. He even found time after the ten sets of the previous day for a bit of scheming that would bring a dash of colour, markedly absent from the play, to the final – and would not go unnoticed by the barrackers.

In his 1985 history of the Australian Championships Bruce Matthews recorded a conversation with Perry in which, in the author's words, the gregarious Briton gave another reason why Crawford's concentration might have wandered. Perry and Jim Hines, Slazenger sales manager, met for dinner at the Australia Hotel on the eve of the final and hit on what they said was a light-hearted plan to unsettle Crawford. By painting Perry's racket white, they would upstage the champion's flat-topped racket. They even woke the stringer that night to get him to open up the factory and prepare the racket. On the day, although the racket caused the stir they hoped it would, the paint started coming off in Perry's hands because of his habit of constantly twiddling the racket through his fingers. He told Matthews, 'Late in the match Jim sent a message telling me to hurry up and win as I was running out of paint. Apparently with the marks on my forehead I looked more like a Red Indian on the warpath.'

The ploy led to a decision by Slazenger to market white Fred Perry rackets in Australia and Britain. Suspecting it would be a success, Slazenger floated a big box kite over the stadium when Perry and Crawford came off court. Emblazoned on it was, 'The white racket is a Slazenger.' In Britain the men's white racket came with a red stripe and the women's with a blue. Slazenger refused Perry's request for his own rackets to have a gold stripe because then everyone would have wanted the same. On the other hand, the white racket produced the same effect on the watching crowd as the white tuxedo.

Perry's inclination was always to interact with a crowd who liked to be involved, which was particularly the case in Australia. Evidently, as the self-confident Englishman with the painted racket came close to his crushing victory, some spectators needed to vent their irritation. Niggled by applause when he made a mistake, Perry turned to the gallery after Crawford hit a forehand into the net in the final game and asked, 'Why don't you applaud that one?' This was too much, and when Perry lost the next point on an error, the reaction from one section of the stands was of unrestrained glee. This prompted Perry to ask the umpire, 'Is this a cricket or a tennis match?' A spectator then called out, 'You asked for it and you got it.' The uproar this produced took a while for the umpire to quell. After quiet was restored the match finished without further incident, but this was another occasion when Perry had to face up to a poor press.

He apologised profusely the following day, his regrets being widely and prominently reported. He said he wished straightaway that he had not made the remark about cricket and tennis, which curiously seemed to cause the most offence. 'Perhaps I deserved all I got,' he added, before striking a slightly disingenuous note when he said that much of the time he talked to himself on court. 'It will land me in more trouble before my tennis career is finished, but I do not mean a thing by it. Upsetting my opponent is not my idea of winning a match.'

Overwhelmingly, though, Perry received generous acclaim for his title win. The *Sunday Sun and Guardian*'s lead story was fairly typical: 'Better tennis has never been seen in Australia than that of Fred Perry in his match against Jack Crawford yesterday afternoon.

He dominated the game from the beginning to the end of a very fine contest, one sided though it unquestionably proved to be.'

Crawford believed this was Perry's best performance against him, free of any weakness he could exploit. For his part, Perry did not believe that the month's break from competition that Crawford was granted before the championships, which included missing the second and third Test matches, had helped him. Strenuous practice was all very well, said Perry, but there was no practice like competitive play. He also felt Crawford had made the same technical mistake he had committed in the US final by not seeking permission to wear spiked shoes on the slippery surface, footwear that Perry opted for in both matches. Finally, Perry said that by studying a film of his play against Crawford in the first Test he had eliminated the mistake of running round the Australian's deep returns of serve, which opened up too much of the court.

In Britain Perry's success in Sydney received a great deal of attention. The heavyweight dailies even thought his second grand slam triumph, so soon after the first, worthy of a leader. 'We would be less than human if we did not welcome the break in the long years when a British victory in international tennis seemed the forlornest of hopes,' the *Daily Telegraph* said. The *Manchester Guardian* thought Perry's success 'should do much to explode the popular fallacy that England has degenerated athletically'.

Perry's own writings were a feature of his first trip to Australia. A series of essays in the *Sydney Morning Herald* dispensed advice on everything from training to practice to stroke execution to diet to smoking and drinking. On this last topic he wrote, 'You will find some players who play wonderful tennis and yet bend a very pretty elbow, and, by the same token, you will find players who smoke like chimneys.' He counselled that it was acceptable to smoke and drink in moderation and excused his own pipe, which people told him he smoked far too much, on the grounds that it stopped him eating pounds of chocolates and boiled sweets. His pipe, he said, was 'a vulcanite substitute for sweets'. As someone who hardly ever drank, he speculated that 'a little intoxicating liquor at the right time probably does one the world of good'. His food recommendations also promoted the idea that a little of what you fancied was the best policy. He was an unfussy eater himself, although careful before matches, and his experience in South America meant he never again touched crab or lobster and he avoided all seafood when eating inland. He also had a thing about cucumber, passing on this anecdote to his readers: 'I remember that a doctor once laid it down that the best way to have cucumber was to peel it, pour vinegar, salt and pepper over it, and then throw it out of the window.'

Throughout 1934 Perry produced tennis of a consistently impeccable standard. He suffered only one defeat of any consequence, at the French Championships – a setback that he would comprehensively avenge. Before Paris, though, there was a tortuous journey back from Australia to Europe that took in stop-offs to play exhibition matches in Sri Lanka and India. Perry had made friends with the tennis-playing maharaja of Cooch-Behar. On one of his visits he stayed in a vast residence belonging to the maharaja in west Bengal that was merely an annexe to an even vaster residence – the Victor Jubilee Palace, the design of which was based on Buckingham Palace – in which the maharaja lived. During his stay Perry and the maharaja entertained the staff by staging an exhibition match. The assembled workforce constituted one of the bigger crowds Perry played in front of outside the grand slams and Davis Cup, some 2,000 people.

In May 1934 Perry headed for France and his fourth tilt at the one grand slam that in those days was not played on grass. His first three tries had ended once in the fourth round and twice in the quarter-finals, but this visit to Roland-Garros was his first since he had so brilliantly demonstrated his mastery of the slower surface with his win over Henri Cochet in the challenge round of the previous year's Davis Cup. He would describe this as the hardest match of his career, certainly much harder than the first three matches he played in the 1934 French tournament, which he negotiated without dropping a set. This put him through to a quarter-final against Giorgio De Stefani, the ambidextrous Italian who had beaten him when they met before in Paris, in 1931, and who had inflicted the only singles defeat he suffered during Britain's triumphant Davis Cup campaign of 1933.

The next two Perry–De Stefani matches – the Italian's 1934 victory in Paris and Perry's revenge win at the Australian Championships in Melbourne in 1935 – should be taken as a piece because the one may, or may not, have had a dramatic bearing on the other, depending on which of Perry's two diametrically opposed versions of what happened in Paris in June 1934 is correct.

Version one appeared in an article signed by Perry for the Melbourne *Herald* in December 1934. In this he described De Stefani as a perfect tennis gentleman before giving the following account of events in France six months earlier:

> Personally I will never forget his [De Stefani's] consideration to me during a match in Paris last year [*sic*]. In the fourth set my ankle was severely strained during a fall. Giorgio was one of the first to help me up, and when he saw I was determined to carry on he took good care not to place any undue strain on my injured leg. He could have made it very agonising for me, but he did not take advantage of my plight. Giorgio won that match, but I am always thankful for his kindness on that occasion.

Version two, written fifty years later in his second autobiography, said that he had entered into a pact with De Stefani after injuring his ankle: he, Perry, would keep going if the Italian, on his way to inevitable victory, did not make him run around too much. De Stefani then reneged on the deal, manoeuvring him this way and that as he consigned Perry to his only grand slam loss of the year. In version two Perry said this treachery prompted him to tell De Stefani as they left court that he would beat him love, love and love next time they met. And this explained the 6–0 6–0 6–0 scoreline when they clashed in Melbourne in January 1935.

The first version, given it was written so soon after the event, seems more likely to be accurate. The second was probably the product of more than half a century of retelling, with bits and pieces brought in from elsewhere by an imaginative and inveterate yarner. What is beyond dispute is that the ankle injury did not stop Perry having a magnificent July, during which he won his first Wimbledon and played the major role in Britain's successful defence of the Davis Cup, triumphs that set him up nicely for his return to America for his first defence of a grand slam title.

Perry's victory twelve months before meant *Time* magazine, in keeping with its tradition before the US Championships, made him its cover story on 3 September 1934. The racy article said that dapper Fred Perry told newshawks when he arrived in Manhattan from Europe:

> I intend to fool around in Hollywood for a while. I don't know whether I'm going to be an actor or not. Universal approached me with an offer to make a picture but I don't think I could do it and remain an amateur . . . When you're a pro in England, you have to take the back door. I wouldn't consider it, now or ever . . . After Hollywood, I'm off for Australia. After Australia, I'm getting married, settle down and become sedate . . . I'm really tired of tennis, hang it. I like golf and I intend to master it . . . In the tennis world, there are five blokes who are as good as each other. In order to win, a bloke needs a bit of luck . . .*

To what extent any of this was verbatim is impossible to tell, but it is a fine example of the kind of joshing patter that Perry had developed since becoming an international celebrity to deal with the press's incessant questions. With a mixture of fact and fiction he sought to confuse and conquer his interrogators.

What was reasonably accurate was the suggestion that 'five blokes' were contenders, and Perry was wise enough to leave unsaid that of the five one, Perry himself, was now pre-eminent. Two were absent on this occasion – Jack Crawford and Bunny Austin had had enough for the year, but the field was still strong with Sidney Wood and Frank Shields the main hopes of the host nation. Ellsworth Vines, who was no longer a contender having turned professional, was escorted from the grounds by the grim-faced custodians of amateurism after he arrived at Forest Hills to commentate for a radio station.

---

* Ellipses in original article.

In its assessment of Perry as a player, the *Time* cover story detailed the more flamboyant aspects of his play, including the fact that he rolled on his back when he fell down, but added that critics who regarded his behaviour as an indication of frivolity were mistaken. They were 'the inevitable manifestations of a character in which the salient quality is solemn, almost neurotic determination to win'. The magazine passed on other helpful information about the title holder:

> Perry has been three times around the world. He has 50 tennis trophies, including spears and shields from Africa. He smokes a pipe, never drinks. He drives cautiously, avoids travel by plane. Slightly ashamed of his skill at table tennis, he now plays only onboard ship. He plays tennis eight months every year, does not practice before a match because it does his game no good. His fiancée is British Cinemactress Mary Lawson, a onetime tap dancer, who is 5ft tall, wears size 2 shoes, plays no tennis at all.

Perry won through the first five rounds without dropping a set. He was now in the semi-finals, where instead of the combative Shields he played his conqueror, the South African doubles specialist and son of a Boer War veteran, Bob Kirby, who did take a set off the champion but won only eight games in the other three. Perry's final opponent was Wilmer Allison, not quite in the front rank of the home challengers but evidently fired up by not having been picked for the Davis Cup. As if to prove a point, Allison put out 'the huge, handsome Lester Stoefen of California', crushed Wood in straight sets and surprised Perry, against whom he had previously been a submissive loser, by levelling at two sets all in the final and having two points for a 3–1 lead in the deciding set. In his own words, Perry squeaked home 8–6 in the fifth.

Close as the score was, Helen Jacobs, the American who won the women's singles that year, reckoned Perry's confidence was at such a pitch at this stage of his career that he was almost impossible to beat, even with the crowd supporting the home player. 'Perry's confidence inspires his brilliant attack and patience in long exchanges; it prevents the division of his attention in a crisis; out of it is born his indomitable courage in employing the most delicate strategy and to defy, rather than resent, the distracting behaviour of the gallery,' Jacobs said.

Champion for the second year running, Perry attempted to take the US trophy on the same sort of joyride as the Davis Cup the year before but was stopped from doing so by an officious security guard who told him he would have to win it three times if he wanted to keep it.

As winner of three of the four grand slams in 1934, Perry faced a renewed surge of interest in whether he was about to turn professional. Even the voyage to Australasia at the end of the year offered no respite. The media radioed him onboard and called him at every port at which the ship docked. In Auckland he went to the cinema and a journalist who just happened to be sitting next to him took the opportunity to ask whether he would turn professional. All the attention almost certainly helps to account for Perry's second visit to Australia being less successful than the first, although he still paced his challenge for the 1935 Australian title with such canniness that he came within one victory of retaining the championship.

Before Christmas, he lost to Jack Crawford in the final of the New South Wales Championships when the Australian used a new tactic against him, driving the ball straight at his body to cramp his ground-strokes. Perry served for the match at 5–4 in the fifth but did not win another game, and the crowd greeted Crawford's victory by 'cheering its head off for five minutes'. Next Perry suffered a much heavier defeat, one of his biggest as an amateur, taking only two games in three sets off Adrian Quist in a semi-final of the Victoria Championships. Perry gave a characteristically jaunty reaction to this loss. 'My troubles were over when I walked off the court,' he said. 'You can judge that for yourself when I tell you that at 4.30 p.m. I was hitting off from the first tee on the Metropolitan golf links.'

He then headed off for a holiday in the Blue Mountains of New South Wales, where Australia's colonial gentry liked to summer and just the place for a smart young tennis player to recharge before a major event. He arrived at Kooyong in Melbourne for the Australian Championships feeling grand, he told reporters, and ready to have a big smack at the singles title.

His passage to the final bore this out. The four comprehensive wins that took him there included the zeroing of De Stefani in the quarter-finals. The ubiquitous Wallis Myers, writing for the Melbourne *Argus*, had composed a brief profile of De Stefani for its readers early in the championships in which he referred to the Italian's 'great tenacity of purpose and unquenchable courage'. He also revealed that De Stefani used each hand in turn when he shaved. None of which was much good come his meeting with Perry, in which, said Myers, the champion 'was in one of those mad moods that have spelt disaster for opponents in the past' – perhaps De Stefani had upset him in Paris. Myers described Perry's hand as being 'so well controlled and so submissive to the brain that his opponent was forced to surrender the rally like a victim of a highway robbery, who has a pistol placed to his head'.

When Perry routed the dangerous McGrath in the semi-finals he really did seem poised to hold on to his crown. The final created huge excitement, a record crowd, put at 12,000-plus, attending on an oppressively hot day. Tickets were bartered outside the Kooyong stadium, providing, said one Melbourne newspaper, an echo of Wimbledon, although there was no mention of touts. Ticket holders simply sold on to those who did not have them.

The attraction of matches between Crawford and Perry was captured in something Quist said in an interview he gave in old age: 'The wonderful rallies sustained by the artistry of Crawford and the lightning-fast Perry will never be forgotten by those Australians who were privileged to see this beautiful tennis. The post-war champions were outstanding in ability and skill, but it is doubtful whether the public enjoyed their net-rushing tactics as much as they did the rallies and groundstroke skill displayed in the Perry–Crawford matches.'

Much later Perry said telephone calls from England about his future had badly disrupted his night's sleep before the 1935 Australian final, which was not something he mentioned straight after the match. 'Jack played marvellously,' Perry told reporters immediately after losing 2–6 6–4 6–4 6–4. 'I thought I had him when I led 3–1 and 30–15 in the third set. From that point he appeared to be gifted with the ability to put the ball on the line whenever he reached a vital point, and that proved too much for me.' Perhaps jamming up Perry with body shots had worked a second time, but it never would again. Perry would beat his persistent Australian rival in two grand slam semi-finals later in the year, at the French and Wimbledon, and in the Davis Cup in 1936 in his last match on Wimbledon's Centre Court.

While in Melbourne for the 1935 championships Perry wrote a series of columns for the *Herald* on the great tennis courts of the world. 'Electric Scoring Board At Roland-Garros' was the headline splashed over his long article on the venue for the French Championships, a passing detail that evidently caught the subeditor's eye as a notable example of European modernity. Perry's reference suggested he, too, had not seen it elsewhere. He also described the novelty of being ferried between central Paris and the courts at Auteuil in official cars. These were often terrifying rides with chauffeurs whose motto seemed to be 'Hit first, stop afterwards.'

In retrospect, though, his most interesting observation was how difficult it was to win at Roland-Garros, presaging as it did his feat six months later of gaining his one French title. With this he became the first player to hold each of the four grand slam crowns, although not at the same time, which was first achieved by Don Budge in 1938 – and more than seventy years later he was still the only Briton ever to have captured the clay-court game's premier prize.

It was not so much the slow clay surface that Perry found difficult. He had shown his skill on this in the 1933 challenge round of the Davis Cup, and as a shotmaker and tactician he liked the fact that the courts were more reliable than the grass surfaces in Britain. What he disliked was the scheduling at that time of the French Championships, the doubles being held in the first week and the singles in the second. All the top players took part in doubles in those days, which meant that Perry, who invariably had a good run in both competitions, would play virtually non-stop for a fortnight. He found this hard, partly because for 'a player of my temperament' Paris with its vibrant social life was not somewhere he liked to miss out on – even if tennis was the reason for doing so. The other difficulty was holding his form while having to play nearly every day for two weeks, often in the suffocating conditions of the 'bear pit', Perry's description of the sunken stadium court at Roland-Garros.

In 1935 Perry and Charles Tuckey made it to the semi-finals of the doubles, which kept him fully occupied for most of the first week. At least he than received a bye through the first round of the singles, and with a favourable draw reached the semi-finals – for the first time at Roland-Garros – without being taxed. His quarter-final win over France's Christian Boussus for the loss of five games awakened everyone, including Perry, to the possibility of an unprecedented triumph by an Englishman in the singles event of the French Championships.

Boussos was a left-hander with cracking groundstrokes who carried his nation's hopes of leading a new generation of Musketeers now that Henri Cochet and the others were no longer a force. Perry expertly dismantled his game, carried on confidently with a straight-sets win over Crawford in the semi-finals – so much for the British newspaper that had predicted his final loss to Crawford in Melbourne was a watershed result from which he would not recover – and 'slightly to my surprise' went on to win the final against Gottfried von Cramm of Germany. He dropped a set for the first time in the tournament but won the others easily, his only hesitation coming right at the end when he conceded two games at 5–1 and needed seven match points to finish off von Cramm.

The French press had seen plenty of Perry in the Davis Cup and now praised him generously for his play outside the team format. *Le Journal*, comparing him to the outstanding players of the 1930s, said, 'Perry is the best world champion of his time.' *Le Figaro* said of his performance in the final, 'His technique was excellent and his physical condition perfect. He is the complete player.'

With a second Wimbledon title and a second successful defence of the Davis Cup following in quick succession, Perry was seen as that ill-fated beast the racing certainty before the start of the 1935 US Championships. Wilmer Allison was the player who visited on the title holder the fate that inevitably befalls all such certainties, having confidently asserted beforehand, 'Nobody will give Perry a run.' Three easy wins and a testing four-setter in the quarter-finals against Frank Shields, who within a point of levelling at two sets all intercepted a Perry drive that everyone else agreed was going out, took Perry's run of wins at Forest Hills to eighteen. Allison, according to one American media description 'a weather-beaten, drawling, lantern-jawed Texan', then ended it in a semi-final that had dramatic consequences.

Allison won the match in straight sets after Perry had a nasty fall in the first when he landed sharply on the handle of his racket. He jumped straight up, not wanting Allison to know he was hurt, but was too badly injured to be competitive. 'I could not raise my arm properly and had to make all my shots with a round-arm stroke,' he said. 'I was in pain, too, but I could not give up, could I, with 15,000 people looking on?'

Perry had broken a rib and displaced a kidney, which also swelled up, and although publicly he gave Allison credit – 'I've had a licking coming to me for a long time' – his mood changed when he heard his conqueror coolly taking all the credit. Allison told the press that his victory was down to his having worked out how to counter the former champion's game. Perry and Allison were both travelling to Los Angeles straight after the tournament and Perry registered his disgust at what he saw as unwarranted boasting by withdrawing a promise to take some of Allison's bags with him on the train to the West Coast. Allison was flying and faced a luggage restriction. 'I never was a good loser,' Perry said.

His injuries ruled Perry out of the 1935 Pacific Southwest Championships, which he had won for the previous three years and had competed in since 1931. Although he fulfilled a commitment to go to Australia, he was there only briefly before leaving for England to rejoin his bride of a few weeks. He did play a match in the New South Wales Championships, but the pain from the rib and kidney damage while he struggled to a five-set win over 'some kid' (Simon Breakspear) persuaded him against staying on to try to regain the Australian title in January 1936.

A report of the match against Breakspear in the *Sydney Morning Herald* reckoned that Perry's injuries only partly explained what the paper called his very poor play. The crowd was noticeably silent and Perry himself conceded that at this point in his career he was fed up with tennis – had had it up to his hat brim, he said. Apart from having played for so long virtually non-stop, he was weary of all the shenanigans over the question of whether he turned professional. He felt trapped between what was almost certainly his own desire to join the pros and the continued promises of Sir Samuel Hoare and the LTA that, in consultation with his father, they would come up with some solution. This, he now realised, was 'all a lot of hogwash'.

Touchingly, one of the last things he did before boarding RMS *Strathnaver* to return home was go to the cinema in Adelaide to watch *The Wedding Night* – the one film featuring Helen Vinson, whom he had married three months earlier, that he had not seen.

He assured the press when he arrived back in London from Australia in January 1936 that however bronzed he might look he was little more than an invalid. He could not move his right side, he said, and would welcome a quiet time after playing tennis continually for nearly five years. He added that his wife, who had been filming in England and with whom he had been reunited at Dover, was looking out for a flat for them in London. 'I expect that we shall settle down very shortly.'

Perry did not feel well enough to undertake his first, tentative practice until late February, when he and Pat Hughes hit for three quarters of an hour at Wimbledon. He was still underweight and mentally drained. Not for the first time, the answer to his woes lay in the hands of his osteopath, Hugh Dempster, and the methods of Tom Whittaker, the Arsenal trainer. They restored him physically and the old eagerness started to return.

An outing in March to the Côte d'Azur, one of his favourite haunts, where he won an undemanding tournament in Cannes, signalled he was on the mend. By the time he arrived in Paris to defend his singles crown at the 1936 French Championships he had established he was back in peak condition by winning the British hard court title for the fifth year in a row. But fitness without match practice in international tournaments was not enough, and this time von Cramm, who had benefited from being coached by Bill Tilden, beat him in the final in five sets. The score in von Cramm's favour was a slightly curious 6–0 2–6 6–2 2–6 6–0.

One report of the match noted that Perry 'quite failed to give justice to his reputation as the best fifth-set player in the game today'. Perry conceded that for the first time in an important match he had failed to make any sort of fight of the fifth set. Stupidly, he admitted later, he said that he was bored, when he meant mentally flat, but it was too late and the press made much of his ennui.

If Perry ever needed inspiration, the British tennis establishment only had to give the impression they were down on him to provide it. He felt this keenly after his Paris loss, which left him with the Wimbledon crown as his only grand slam title. As Perry read the situation, the chiefs at the LTA and All England Club reckoned the defeat by von Cramm was evidence that his career had peaked, which was all that was required to spur him on. 'It seemed that I was dead and about to be buried and that a lot of people at the LTA were happy at the prospect,' he said, adding that this made up his mind that he would win Wimbledon a third time, which he duly did with a crushing win over von Cramm, help Britain defend the Davis Cup and then finish his amateur career in America. Nothing had happened in the nearly six months he had been back in Europe to dissuade him from turning professional and he set sail from Southampton knowing that the 1936 US Championships would be his last grand slam. It proved quite a finale with Perry becoming the first overseas player to win the singles title three times and so take permanent possession of the cup.

Perry did not meet any extended resistance until his semi-final against Bryan Grant, an American who was too small to be a consistent threat to the heavyweights but knew how to make a nuisance of himself. His practice of hitting slow, looped returns, a tactic now known as moonballing, disconcerted Perry sufficiently for him to drop his first set of the tournament on the way to an otherwise comfortable victory.

The final against Budge would be anything but comfortable, not least because of the overcast, humid weather that threatened rain throughout. They were not conditions in which to get steamed up, but Perry could not help himself when the umpire called a ten-minute break after he had gone ahead by two sets to one. Under the regulations the break after three sets had to be put back until after the fourth if there had been an interruption of more than ten minutes, which there had been when rain fell in the second set. The umpire ignored Perry's vehement protests and Budge, granted a reprieve in which to regroup after losing the third set, came back strongly to win the fourth.

Perry's mood during a see-sawing final set was also affected by his legal advisers, who included his friend George Leisure, having a little fun at his expense from the stands. Perry's guarantee for turning professional would be bigger if he beat Budge than if he lost and the advisers held up one of two contracts, big or small, depending on the score. It looked as though the small one would be needed when Budge led 5–3 and served for the match. Crucially, though, Budge was by now totally worn out. He called his serve in the fifth set a dishrag. 'I was so exhausted in reaching up to hit my serve that I felt as if I were leaning on the ball.' Perry pulled back to 5–5 and looked the more likely winner although it took him eight more games to secure his third title after breaking for a 9–8 lead. Perry would recall that in that eighteenth game he kept a ball in his pocket from before the first point, ready to be used in a warmed-up state if he reached match point. When he did, he produced the ball and barely gave Budge a moment to compose himself before sending down a serve that he followed quickly to the net. He did not stop when the service close to a line was a winner, hurdling the net to shake Budge's hand before anyone could object.

Years afterwards Budge said this match, which forced him to realise the need for better conditioning, and another involving Perry were the two most important matches in the later stages of his tennis development. The other took place four months later, in January 1937, with Budge sitting in the umpire's chair. As a gimmick, he officiated at the Vines–Perry match held at the Chicago Arena early in their first professional tour. Budge said that he fully expected Vines, with his harder shots, to overwhelm Perry, and to start with he could not understand why it was that Vines was having to run around just as much as his opponent. 'Then I saw it,' he said. 'Perry was taking the ball on the rise, hardly six or eight inches after it had bounced – "on the short hop", as they call it in baseball. Vines, on the other hand, was waiting in a leisurely fashion and letting the ball bounce.' There is a suggestion here that Perry, whose game after all must have been pretty familiar to Budge at this stage, found room to make his forehand an even more dynamic shot as a professional than it had been when he was an amateur. Certainly, having noted it, Budge made full use of his prior knowledge when he came to face Perry as a professional.

After the 1936 US Championships, Perry's legal team still had some haggling to do over his professional contract, which left him with enough time to finish his amateur career by playing in his favourite tournament, the Pacific Southwest Championships in Los Angeles. His journey across America by train, no longer quite the adventure it had been when he first did it five years earlier, did have one big surprise when he was presented with a Ford convertible after visiting the motor manufacturer's assembly line during a stop-off in Detroit. In a scene that might have been taken from a knockabout road movie, Perry set off in the blue convertible with whitewall tyres to complete the journey by road only for all sorts of things to go wrong with it. He decided to abandon the car after putting in a call to Ford to tell them where he had left it. Word quickly came back to his hotel to take the car to a certain garage. When he presented the car there a mechanic, primed personally by Edsel Ford, the president of the Ford Motor Company, was waiting to fix it, and the convertible did after all carry Perry to his West Coast destination.

At the Los Angeles Tennis Club Perry's amateur career ended on Sunday 27 September 1936, when Budge avenged his defeat at Forest Hills two weeks before. The house had been packed for some time when the two men stepped on court for the final, which Budge, serving with the force of a carpenter driving six-inch nails into hardwood, won in four sets. Perry would have liked to go out with a win but still found time for some banter as the match slipped away from him. He asked Budge whether a line judge involved in a minor dispute was his brother. 'Yes,' said Budge. It could have been Budge's brother, Lloyd, who was a decent player, but Perry would probably have known him and more likely it was a playful interchange.

In a symbolic motion, intended or otherwise, Perry's last point before joining the pros was accompanied by a gesture of farewell. 'Budge's vicious serving took him to 40–0,' reported *Western Tennis* magazine, 'and Fred merely waved at the screaming ace that ended the match.'

The end of Perry's amateur career in 1936 also brought to a close the influence that his father had over his tennis. Up until then Perry was answerable to the LTA, whose officers took at least as much notice of what Sam Perry had to say as his son's views. Now Perry was directing his own affairs, in the first instance signing up to a professional tour with Ellsworth Vines that would start early in 1937. There is plenty of evidence, though, that Perry never lost his warm and sincere regard for his father's guidance. This had been particularly helpful during the formative years of his sporting career; less helpful perhaps, but just as forthcoming, when he was trying to assess the blandishments of the professional promoters. The dedication in his 1934 autobiography was: 'To My Father who gave me my chance in lawn tennis'. His esteem lasted and might even have grown. In his later autobiography, he wrote, 'I had a deep affection for him and a great respect for the way he had overcome poverty and lack of education to become a much-admired man.' Long after his father died in October 1954 Fred gave an interview to the local newspaper in Ealing, in which he said, 'My father was a great man, psychologist and great speaker.'

If there was grit in their relationship it formed as a result of the death of Hannah Perry, for which Fred imputed so much of the blame to his father's political career, and because of Sam Perry's second marriage barely a year later, which Fred seemed to treat more and more as if it never happened. It is just possible that this is why Sam Perry's death from a cerebral thrombosis, brought on by diabetes and raised blood pressure, did not receive a mention in his son's second autobiography, which contained an emotional response to his mother's death.

When Sam Perry died, a columnist in the *Stockport Advertiser* commented, 'Mr Perry was proud of his son's achievement in the lawn tennis world, but there is no reason why he should be remembered merely in relation to Fred's prowess. To start life as a half timer and to climb to two parliamentary private secretaryships, as he did, betokens qualities of character and perseverance which must be admired.'

7

The wonder of Wimbledon: 1934–6

'It is a lucky nation that owns a Perry'

If Fred Perry embodied the more egalitarian age that was on its way, Raymond Tuckey personified, in tennis at least, the one that was starting to pass. Tuckey would show that it was still possible to win a Wimbledon title while serving as an officer in the armed forces with only limited opportunities to play competitively. He came from a tennis-mad family. Charles, his father, was a housemaster at Charterhouse, who with his wife Agnes formed a fiendishly competitive pair on the tournament circuit. Charles Tuckey would have competed at Wimbledon if the tournament had not been played during termtime, but Agnes did play and won the mixed doubles title in 1913 with Hope Crisp. Her career was so long that in her fifties she partnered Raymond in the mixed doubles, the only recorded instance of parent and child teaming up at Wimbledon. Raymond Tuckey's greatest success came in 1936, when, a serving lieutenant in the Royal Engineers, he nevertheless won the Wimbledon men's doubles with Pat Hughes, whose two other grand slam doubles titles were as Perry's partner in Paris in 1933 and Sydney in 1934.

Tuckey was the first man Perry beat in 1934 to start the sequence of twenty-seven singles victories that would embrace his three Wimbledon titles and Britain's three successful defences of the Davis Cup – all of these matches played at the All England Club in the months of June and July, twenty of them on Centre Court. During these three summers of omnipotence Perry reached a place in the estimation of the British public that was probably as exalted as any domestic sportsman or woman has achieved, before or since. Even those prejudice-encrusted old diehards who regarded Perry's presence at Wimbledon as a latter-day equivalent of the Vandals arriving at the gates of Rome would eventually be won round. Tuckey, who played with soldierly uprightness, was also the only British opponent among those Perry beat in his twenty-one successive wins in the Gentlemen's Singles Championship, a sign of how widely tennis was now played to a very high standard. Wimbledon could no longer be characterised as an outpost of empire, a far-flung possession at the end of the District Line.

The shift had begun after 1909, the year of Perry's birth, when the Englishman Arthur Gore, at the age of forty-one, won for the third and final time. Until then British players, along with Norman Brookes, the first of the great Australians, who became champion in 1907, had monopolised Wimbledon, but Britain had failed to produce another male champion since Gore. The fact that Perry played only one compatriot during his last three Wimbledons, having played eight in twenty matches at his first five championships, had another significance: it was just one more sign of how the domestic game was no longer managing to keep up.

Perry, on the other hand, now stepped onto that elevated plain occupied by only the greatest players – those with exceptional ability and impregnable temperaments. The two are not always compatible, but in Perry they coexisted like soulmates. His weaknesses were only relative. Most opponents would have been happy to own the backhand that in Perry was seen as a blemish, just as Roger Federer's was more than sixty years later.

Like every exceptional player, Perry possessed an all-round game that was as good as any of his rivals' and had in addition one weapon of rare quality. His running forehand was as devastating a stroke as any in the 1930s, and these included two of the very finest: the bullet serve of Ellsworth Vines, who had won the 1932 Wimbledon final with an ace that Bunny Austin never saw, and Don Budge's brutal backhand. Jack Kramer believed Perry's forehand was a stroke of such idiosyncratic brilliance that it 'screwed up men's tennis in England for generations to come. The way he could hit a forehand – snap it off like a ping-pong shot – Perry was a physical freak. Even after he had faded out of the picture, the coaches must have kept using him as a model, because the British boys always come out on the court stamped like Perry – until they try to hit like Perry.'

Dan Maskell knew better than anyone that the Perry forehand had been as finely tuned as a concert piano for the Wimbledon championships of 1934. In the week before the tournament he practised four times with Perry, on the last occasion playing 'three sets of absolutely tip-top tennis'. Nor did Maskell have any doubts about Perry's fitness. In a newspaper article he provided balm for the nation's fears over the ankle injury Perry had sustained barely two weeks earlier at the French Championships. He knew the injury might play on Perry's mind, but the overwhelming evidence of the practice sessions was that he was physically sound, his game razor-edged. Maskell recorded that a tournament official who had watched him hit with Perry passed on that he had never seen such fast tennis, and was sure that Perry would not face a sterner examination during the two weeks of competition that lay ahead.

It was typical of Perry to subject himself to such a thorough examination, another example of the rigorous work ethic that he liked to keep hidden behind an air of insouciance. Expert at identifying and exploiting the weaknesses and injuries of others, he needed to play those three grinding sets with Maskell to ensure that he would not give opponents any encouragement by showing the merest hint of a limp.

Throughout his career Perry never left anything to chance. He stopped driving just before big tournaments because he felt it affected the focus of his eyes. During Wimbledon a friend, Sandy Thompson, a soft-drinks salesman, took unpaid leave to chauffeur him around. Thompson's other task was to ward off well-wishers who wanted to shake Perry's hand before a match. This was something Perry would never do because he claimed it made him lose the feeling in his fingers. Often he would stand with his right hand deep in his jacket pocket to avoid unthinking, reflex handshakes. The gauze strip he devised for keeping the palm of his racket hand dry was the forerunner of the wrist sweatbands that nearly all tennis players now wear.

In the unlikely event that Perry watched another match before he went on court, which he insisted was a stupid thing to do, he did so from ground level, 'which is the position you are going to play from'. He never had a massage in the first week of major championships, reasoning that if he needed one he was already clapped out. At Wimbledon he relaxed before matches by pottering around on a putting green opposite the All England Club. Dan Maskell would summon him when the time came to prepare for action.

Perry did not need obvious signals to home in on an opponent's weakness – his antennae picked up the smallest sign. He observed Jack Crawford's nervous habit of wiping his sweaty hand on his shirt; he rubbed it on his trousers when he was relaxed. Perry reasoned that Crawford's sweat-drenched shirt left the Australian's hand wet, making it difficult for him to grip his racket. So Crawford's use of his shirt front was always the moment to apply added pressure. He attacked Gottfried von Cramm when the normally inscrutable German baron gave off the subtlest of distress signals – a slight draining of blood from his cheeks revealing pale pink spots. Also, he worked on von Cramm's obsession with tidiness by leaving the lining of one of his trouser pockets hanging out during a match, knowing how much it would irritate his opponent. Bunny Austin's nervous tic was to walk round in little circles, which Perry played on by delaying his serve.

But for the injury that accounted for his quarter-final defeat in Paris, Perry might have been going for a grand slam of the four major championships when he played Wimbledon in 1934. He had won the US title in September and the Australian in January, on both occasions beating Jack Crawford in the final. Crawford had been having health problems and Perry disposed of the Australian in a final yet again when in early May he won the British hard court title at the West Hants club in Bournemouth for the third year running.

Perry and Tuckey were third match on Centre Court when Wimbledon opened in grey, sultry conditions that by the end of the week had given way to the sunshine that illuminated the last, triumphant strides of Perry's march to the title. The sense of excitement was unusually high for the start of the tournament, elevated not so much by the prospect of a great match but by the chance to catch a first glimpse of the young Englishman since his reputation had spiralled. In the past nine months, not only had he won grand slams in New York and Sydney, but had guided Britain from their long years in the wilderness of failure to Davis Cup glory.

There was something else: a slight air of edginess. Perry had become accustomed to it by now, even enjoyed it a little. It hung over any match he played in front of a home audience against a fellow Englishman, particularly at Wimbledon, where the crowd had a keen sense of how a person fitted into the intricate warp of social class. Their relationship with Perry was still ambivalent, even a little uneasy. They admired Perry's rise from what most of them regarded as a disadvantaged background. But wasn't he a little gauche? A bit overkeen? A slight chip, perhaps? Young Tuckey was the right stuff. With a bit of luck maybe he could upset the, well, upstart.

From the opening points, Perry banished any possibility of this happening. Cool, concentrated and moving with feline grace, he won the first two sets comfortably. No matter that there were flaws – 'More errors on the baseline and more foozled volleys than should be there in the potential Wimbledon champion,' one commentator observed – this was his first match since the French Championships and his return to skiddy, low-bouncing grass.

Tuckey knew that if he kept the ball away from his opponent's forehand for too long he would play Perry's backhand into form. He chanced one wide to the right, but Perry snapped the ball back, wrist breaking, racket head accelerating and the ball gathering pace as if propelled by an explosive charge. With some players, a rally lives off the speed of the serve, the ball losing velocity like a spent meteor. Perry could summon startling extra pace from nowhere, a seemingly magical ability, the racket suddenly becoming a blur of exaggerated violence while his head remained steady. More than forty years later, in the 1975 Wimbledon final, Arthur Ashe was to exploit a great champion's inability to generate his own pace when he drove the counter-punching Jimmy Connors to distraction – and one of the most unexpected defeats in the tournament's history – by patting the ball over the net. Tuckey tried a similar tactic and also went down the middle to restrict his opponent's room to swing, but Perry's feet moved as fast as his racket hand and within an instant he had created the small amount of space that a man of his strength needed to gain the necessary leverage.

Eventually Perry overran the young officer, whose doughty resistance however earned him the prize of the third set. One commentator reckoned that the number two seed was 'taking liberties' in the set he lost, adding, 'We had to await the fourth for reassurance.' Trifling with opponents in these circumstances was not Perry's way, though. Once satisfied with a few necessary adjustments and that he was in shape for a long match, he abruptly terminated the match by winning the fourth set 6–0.

Perry conceded a mere four games in beating his next opponent, Dick Williams, a forty-three-year-old American whose dramatic story was by now much more interesting than his tennis. The scion of a wealthy Philadelphia family, he had first competed at Wimbledon in 1913, a year after he survived the sinking of the *Titanic*, in which his father was killed by a falling funnel. Dick Williams suffered terrible hypothermia in his legs after diving into the icy waters. The doctors wanted to amputate because of the danger of gangrene, but Williams refused to let them. He brought the stricken limbs back to life by forcing himself to walk around the deck of the rescue vessel. He was back playing tennis within three months, and in 1914 and 1916 won the US singles title. At Wimbledon in 1920 he won the doubles with Chuck Garland and was making a sentimental return to the championships in 1934. He played Perry on Court 4 in the spirit of an exhibition, given the certainty that surrounded the result. The *Daily Telegraph*'s Arthur Wallis Myers summed up the mood with a quote from Alexander Pope – both players were out 'to make men happy and keep them so'.

It was different in the third round, when Perry was back on Centre Court for a match against an old adversary that was to be the first of only two five-setters he would play during his three years of Wimbledon hegemony. The thunder that growled around the skies of south-west London was inspired accompaniment. In Perry's own words, Roderick Menzel was 'a giant, with a service that kicks as high as a house'. But the percussion that characterised the Czech's game was more impressive than his precision. Menzel's was old-fashioned ordnance of the point-and-hope variety.

In the first set everything Menzel tried worked. Perry looked frustrated as his opponent's thunderous strokes drowned out anything he attempted, his virtuosity counting for little. Menzel pocketed the opener 6–0, and although Perry won the second 6–3 he had not yet quelled the storm raging on the other side of the net. The third went to Menzel, and the crowd, feeling for their home champion, fidgeted uneasily in their seats.

Perry's first severe test of the tournament had planted doubt in his mind about the state of his ankle. Before the match, Perry's osteopath, Hugh Dempster, had told him to go for the wide forehand. There was no point in holding back; if his ankle gave way, too bad. The ferocity of Menzel's game had closed Perry's mind to this instruction, and in the stands Dempster scribbled a note to be delivered to Perry during the first changeover in the fourth set: 'Either you go for the wide ones or I pull you off court.' The effect was electric. Putting the injury to the back of his mind, Perry found that his ankle could withstand even the most awkward movement. In control of his game again, he comfortably won the last two sets as the tiring Menzel reverted to type, spraying the ball around as haphazardly as a novice.

King George V and Queen Mary, the most devoted of all British monarchs in attending the championships – they missed only two years between 1919 and 1934 – visited on the first Saturday. Wearing a bowler hat and heavy jacket whatever the weather, the king would lean forward keenly assessing the play as the statuesque queen gazed out from behind dark glasses. They found Perry restored to his regal best against the twenty-year-old Australian Adrian Quist, a player whose immense promise was never wholly fulfilled except in doubles. For Perry he was the ideal antidote to the force of Menzel: good but not good enough to be threatening. Unburdened of his ankle worries, Perry had time to run through his repertoire of shots, checking them as a mechanic might the engine of a racing car to ensure the parts were pristine. If he was to win the title, he would face three big races in the second week and there could be no grit in the works.

On the second Monday Perry needed four sets to subdue the combative American George Lott, who three years later would raise his fists and take a swing at Perry before a professional doubles match in Hartford, Connecticut. On this particular afternoon the American's best chance may well have been to plant one on the Englishman, although he did make Perry go thirty punishing games to win the third and fourth sets and the match. Perry then moved on to a semi-final against Sidney Wood.

Perry liked Wood. They were already familiar with each other's games from three previous meetings: in the 1931 Davis Cup, which Perry won, their semi-final encounter at Wimbledon in the same year and a fourth-round match at the 1932 US Championships. Wood had won these last two. On the day of their latest semi-final a column by Perry appeared in a London evening newspaper. He wrote warmly about the 'happy-go-lucky American', telling the story of a day in 1928 when they had both played at the Herga club in Harrow and Wood had left first. As he walked towards his car, Wood spotted Perry in earnest combat in a handicap singles on an outside court and blithely interrupted the action. 'Sidney passed complete with goods and chattels,' Perry wrote. 'He just dropped them where he was, walked over to me, stopped the game, held out his hand and said: "Well, so long. Hope to see you again some time" – a great fellow this Wood.'

But Perry's soft spot for Wood hardened to granite on court, particularly with the prize of his first Wimbledon final so tantalisingly close. While Perry stalked and stared, the American was jaunty and apparently carefree – so casual in manner, *The Times* reported, that he 'often walked to the net when he came in, as if to suggest he could win the match how and when he would. No one could have lost the first five games of such an important match so coolly.' Although he would never admit it, Perry was almost certainly unnerved by Wood's nonchalance, maddened even that his own strenuous endeavour was being answered quite so casually. It was perhaps why he never played his best against the American.

On this occasion Wood made up for his slow start by taking the second and fourth sets. In the fifth, the Centre Court crowd sensed that Perry's place in the final might even be snatched from him. The hush before each of his serves became deeper and more intense, the cheers for each point he won more rousing. To their credit neither player showed any sign of flinching. Wood finally seemed to be taking the whole thing seriously; Perry remained totally absorbed, looking for any sign of weakness that would betray his opponent. In the end it was simple tennis mastery that did it for Perry. Two backhands aimed with crack-shot precision whistled past Wood to break his serve and, with a 5-3 lead, Perry served out the match. Now only one man, Jack Crawford, the reigning champion, stood between Perry and his first Wimbledon title.

Crawford had learned to play on his parents' 1,200-acre farm, which according to the Australian's biographer was in 'the middle of nowhere'. In fact it was near the small town of Urangeline in the Riverina district of New South Wales. A tennis court on the farm and five siblings to play against gave Crawford advantages of a sort, but what he did with them was as remarkable, in its way, as what Perry managed, having started playing when he was much older than Crawford with no advantages whatsoever.

When Crawford first appeared in a tournament in Sydney aged twelve he had never played competitive tennis before, had never had a lesson and had never seen a good player in action, and yet, according to one account, 'he was already a fluent and graceful strokemaker with a maturity far beyond his years'. From a tennis point of view, he seemed 'to have sprung into being, like the goddess Athene, fully formed and ready for battle'. In the late 1960s, during a period of high achievement for Australia's male tennis players, the authoritative writer Paul Metzler said the way they played the game bore the stamp of Crawford's free and classic style, which he had developed on his own more than forty years earlier.

Crawford was ruddy-faced and more thickset than Perry, although his legs were spindly. He weighed around 180 pounds when he was young and had gone way past 200 by the time his long playing career ended. An American writer contrasted Crawford with 'the tall, somewhat languid youths of whom the US first ten is largely composed' and the top English players, whose obsession with style meant they played 'as though the net were a mirror'. Crawford evoked an earlier age, almost always wearing a long-sleeved shirt done up at the wrists, and using a flat-topped racket, slightly thicker-framed than had become conventional. This reflected the influence that Norman Brookes, who was in his fifties and still played with a flat-top, retained over the game in Australia. Crawford took little else from Brookes, being as open and good-natured as the older man was withdrawn.

He was not the sort to make a fuss or excuses. This he might have done at Wimbledon in 1934, when he suffered a throat infection that affected him particularly badly during his quarter-final against the American Les Stoefen four days before the final. 'During the second set, which he lost 6–2, it seemed impossible that Crawford could go on at all, but in some miraculous way he seemed to recover his strength,' one newspaper reported.

Crawford was not alone in suffering from a sore throat in the unusually dry and dusty conditions. Several other players had the same thing, forcing a high number of withdrawals. It even led to throat specialists being brought to Wimbledon each day to examine and spray players' throats. Crawford, whose condition cannot have been helped by his heavy smoking and asthma, almost certainly felt unwell for the rest of the tournament but kept quiet about it.

Such stoicism played particularly well with audiences at that time and added to the Australian's popularity, which was already high after his stirring final victory against Ellsworth Vines twelve months before. He leapt the net, Perry style, after that triumph and years later commented drily, 'I didn't realise I could clear such a high barrier. It was the first and only time in my life I attempted such a feat.' Queen Mary was one of Crawford's many admirers, to the extent that she had been known to abandon the royal box to go to watch him play on an outside court. When the king asked Crawford how old he was, at the presentation ceremony after the 1933 final, the new champion was said to have been beaten to the answer by the queen, who piped up, 'He was twenty-five on the twenty-second of March.' With such royal patronage, it was hardly surprising that Crawford was at least as much a favourite with the crowd as Perry when the pair walked out for the 1934 final.

Underfoot, the court had been seared almost white by the sun, which on this day beat down more ferociously than it had on any other. Even towards the back of the stands spectators fanned themselves as the heat reflected off the court's surface. Only Perry seemed unaffected by the conditions. His dress and bearing were meticulously planned. Not for him – nor Crawford, for that matter – the shorts that were now becoming fashionable among male players but that Perry did not think looked as classy as long trousers. Perry strove to outdo his opponent in every way: outdress him, outpsyche him, then outplay him.

Ticket touts had their own reasons for being psyched up now that an Englishman was back in the final. A correspondent of one national newspaper reported a conversation that in all probability he did hear even if the dialogue did not quite ring true. 'From a conversation I overheard yesterday the touts are prospering by the resale of their tickets,' he wrote. 'At a café near Wimbledon Common two men were talking near me: "That makes £15 we have cleared in the past two days," said one. "Yes," said the other, "and with the finals tomorrow and on Saturday we should clear another £20."' The report explained that nobody could buy more than two tickets as the All England Club tried to prevent them getting into touts' hands. 'The men I overheard speaking, therefore, could buy only four tickets, which cost them in all 32s [shillings], so they made more than £11 profit in two days.'

The Englishman played magnificently, producing tennis that Crawford would surely have been unable to resist even if his health had been good. Perry said after the match, 'I don't think I have played better and I don't think I ever will again.' George Lott wrote some years later, 'On that particular day, in that particular match, I had seen the perfectly conditioned athlete play the perfect match . . . He reached the peak of his effectiveness.' From 3–1 down in the first set, Perry won twelve consecutive games to kill the match as a contest. 'For a Wimbledon final there was a strange lack of excitement in the crowded galleries,' *The Times* said. 'Much of the match was too nearly perfect for that.'

Perry's forehand was merely the deadliest weapon in an armoury full of menace. He executed his backhand – distinguished by its short backswing – with the powerful efficiency of a butcher laying into a carcass. He trusted it so completely that he surprised Crawford throughout by moving in behind it. When he did come to the net, Perry would often try out the latest of his stratagems. He would position himself so that his white clothing provided the background for his opponent's next shot, making it difficult for him to see the ball – a trick that was pure Perry and that only Bill Tilden rumbled. The quality of his volleys, E.J. Sampson reported in the *Manchester Guardian*, at least gave the crowd something to enthuse about once the result was no longer in doubt. It drew such roars of applause that the umpire primly called 'for "Quiet please" as he would to naughty children and, in the Wimbledon tradition, the crowd was promptly quiet'.

Nearing the fulfilment of a life that for the past five years had been devoted to tennis, Perry combined technical dexterity of the highest order with a mental toughness that in other walks of life turns men into tyrants. He closed his mind to all possibilities bar the one that he would win, and do so comfortably. He took the second set to love, losing only eight points. At the end of the set Crawford refused the opportunity to reward himself either with a wipe of his towel or a sip of water (sitting down between sets and games was not introduced at Wimbledon until 1975). He stood ruefully on the baseline apparently trying to devise a plan to challenge Perry's superiority when the match resumed.

For a while he managed it as he started to pass Perry with his backhand. He even broke for a 5–4 lead with a return off a fierce forehand that toppled off the tape and dropped dead on Perry's side of the net. Perry gave the ball such a glare it would not have been surprising if it had gone up in a puff of smoke. It was Crawford's last success. His forehand went to pieces and so did his nerve. He failed to serve out the set and, after falling behind 6–5 when Perry held, he was faced with having to hold his own serve to stay in the match. He gambled all on his volley and opened a 40–0 lead before Perry deftly drew him into a series of rallies, sensing his opponent was now too taut to survive beyond more than three or four shots.

The final point provided one of the few unsatisfactory moments of the match. Crawford double-faulted after his first serve was ruled a foot fault, a call by the line judge that reverberated around the world. *Time* reported, 'Linesmen at Wimbledon last week discovered a new and ingenious method of detecting foot faults: looking through the reverse end of a pair of opera glasses.' Crawford, added the magazine, and the thousands in the stands had thought it was a clean ace, and after a second serve that fell lamely into the net to bring an end to the match Crawford aimed an unsubtle bow at the offending linesman.

Perry emerged from the thrall of combat into the perverse reality that among the Wimbledon faithful he was, if not exactly unpopular, a champion more admired than loved. The sympathies of the Centre Court were divided between loser and winner, perhaps not even equally. In the dressing room, he said, he was shamefully treated by an All England official, Commander George Hillyard, who informed Crawford that the better man had lost.

Unpleasant though this episode was, however, Perry knew that beyond Wimbledon's uncompromising hierarchy and its most intransigent spectators he was held in high esteem by the vast majority of the nation. He had seen plenty of evidence of this after the previous year's Davis Cup success and his popularity was confirmed by the scenes of celebration he drove past on the way home from beating Crawford. The affection in which he was held was perhaps best expressed by the evening paper stands that proclaimed his triumph in one word – 'Fred'.

No wonder he refused to allow what had happened in the dressing room to spoil the occasion for him completely. Having summoned an official to apologise for the remark, which he set as a condition for playing in the upcoming Davis Cup tie against the United States, Perry chatted happily with Crawford and swigged from the bottle of champagne presented to the Australian runner-up while he had been left empty-handed. Anthony Sabelli, secretary of the Lawn Tennis Association, duly arrived to deliver the apology and this effectively was the end of the matter. Perry said his mood at the time was such that if someone had handed him a contract to turn professional he would have signed it on the spot, and what happened that day left a rawness that never completely healed. But he also said he never had another dispute with the authorities of the All England Club and would later describe Wimbledon as 'the greatest place in the world'.

If Perry needed further reassurance that away from Wimbledon's rarefied atmosphere he was held in much higher regard, it came from a top-hatted doorman at the Savoy Hotel where he went to celebrate. As Perry left, he mentioned that he was heading for Eastbourne to join the Davis Cup squad for training. The doorman insisted on discarding his top hat and frock coat and driving him there. Nor did the king and queen endorse the Wimbledon view of Perry, registering their approval by asking him to return to the All England Club the next day – Saturday – to watch the Ladies' Final from the royal box. Perry received news of the royal summons from a police inspector as he stepped into the Grand Hotel in Eastbourne in the early hours of Saturday morning. A police escort returned him to London. Crowds were already gathering to cheer Their Majesties and 'there I was', Perry said, 'doffing my cap because I didn't really know what was going on'. At Wimbledon, he shaved and bathed, scrambled into a fresh outfit that his father rushed to the grounds and staggered – his word – into the royal box. The King apologised for not having been present to see an Englishman win Wimbledon for the first time during his reign, 'but I do hope you'll appreciate that there are a few other things I have to do'. Perry recalled that by now fatigue and confusion had so taken control that he muttered, 'Oh, don't bother about it.'

At the dinner that followed the championships, a double celebra-tion for Britain with Dorothy Round having won the women's title – a feat not achieved since Gore and Dora Boothby in 1909 – Perry displayed no sense of the injustice he may have felt over the reaction to his triumph. Modesty was most definitely de rigueur on these occasions, and Perry, who had been known to dispense with conven-tional niceties, behaved impeccably. He said that when 'my time comes to be beaten, which will probably be next year, I hope I lose in the same charming manner as Jack did'. Crawford, still refusing to mention that part of the reason for his disappointing perform-ance in the final might have been that he was off colour, was just as magnanimous. 'Perry played magnificently,' he said, 'and England could not have found a better champion.'

In 1934 Britain celebrated another victory, Henry Cotton winning the Open Golf Championship at Royal St George's, Sandwich.

The Times took this as its cue to run a folksy editorial. It advised those Englishmen who ascribed decadence to their country whenever an international contest was lost to 'recover their balance and remember that a game is a game, and that neither the interests nor the honour of the nation hangs upon the result'. It was an Olympian view that hardly chimed with Perry's attitude.

Fifty years later the celebrated journalist Ian Wooldridge brought Perry and Cotton together to reminisce about making 1934 an *annus mirabilis* for British sport. Paradoxically, at the time of their successes, the public-school-educated Cotton was a professional player while Perry was still more than two years away from playing for money. Cotton alluded to this when he said to Wooldridge, 'I was full of nothing but admiration for Fred.' To which Perry shot back, 'Hell, I was consumed by jealousy. There was Henry swanning around in a Rolls-Royce while I was driving an Austin Seven.' Wooldridge finessed something else typically quirky out of Perry when he asked what made a great champion. Perry immediately thrust out a hand and Wooldridge reported, 'The inside of the fingers, from the top knuckle upwards, were as smooth and soft as satin.' Perry told him, 'The secret is the sensitivity of grip. Pianists and violinists have it. It is called the gift of touch. Without it there is every chance you'll never be good at sport.'

Three weeks after beating Crawford in the final at Wimbledon, Perry returned there to lead Britain's defence of the Davis Cup. The British had gained exemption until the title-deciding contest with their thrilling victory in Paris a year earlier over France, who having gone straight through as defending champions for the previous five years now found themselves having to qualify. This they failed to do, losing in a European zone match to Australia. The US then beat Australia to go forward to play Britain in the challenge round on Centre Court.

The tie started on Saturday 28 July. Austin opened with a comfortable win over Frank Shields and then Perry came through in five sets against Wood, his superior fitness the deciding factor over the closing two sets. It was partly because he was so fit that Perry managed to conceal from the Americans that during the match he damaged his back, so much so that after dinner that evening he was unable to get up from the table.

The British tradition of not playing major sporting events on Sundays – it was many more years before television changed this – could not have been more welcome on this occasion. With Pat Hughes and Harry Lee playing the doubles on the Monday, which they lost, Perry had more than forty-eight hours to rest his back before facing Shields in a contest that could decide the tie. With three hours to go before the match started, Perry was again on the treatment table at the central London practice of Hugh Dempster. Dempster prodded and tweaked the Perry back, produced a couple of noises from it that Perry said sounded like banjo strings snapping and gave instructions that the player should wrap up warm until the match.

One British newspaper evidently knew that Perry had a problem and reported that, beneath his shirt, his back was strapped with sticking plaster, which even with the help of alcohol applied to the skin came off with the greatest difficulty after the match. But not all journalists were so well informed and another correspondent saw the fact that Perry wore two sweaters for the first set as pure cockiness. 'Perry was so confident at the start,' he wrote, 'he did not even remove his sweater.' Perry discarded the sweaters after winning the set, and as his muscles eased he gradually lost the apprehension that had slightly cramped his shots at the start. He trusted his back so completely in the end that he clinched Britain's victory in a magnificent twenty-eight-game fourth set.

Shields, who refused to be rattled by a stream of foot faults against him in this set – England were as capable as France of producing patriotic line judges – saved two match points in the final game before Perry outfoxed him by squeezing two identical shots down the line, the first to take the score to deuce, the second to secure the victory. Perry jumped the net in customary fashion to shake hands as the 17,000 crowd erupted as if a late winner had been scored by England at Wembley. Perry expected Shields to be crestfallen but the ever-chipper American grinned and said, 'You son of a gun, right in the same goddam place.'

The American press also reacted graciously. The headline 'Bully for John Bull' appeared over the piece by *New York Times* columnist

John Kieran, who wrote that there was nothing to do except doff the bowler to the fat guy in the Union flag waistcoat. 'It's about time they declared an extra bank holiday over there to celebrate the comeback of Great Britain in sports.' Kieran linked Davis Cup success to Perry's Wimbledon triumph and Henry Cotton's victory in the Open and also mentioned the Ashes win over Australia at Lords, adding – to help out his American readers – that this took place on their 'favourite field, cricket' (England would, though, lose the series 2–1).

By the time Perry returned to defend his singles title at Wimbledon in 1935, he had held on to the US Championship and, despite losing in the 1935 Australian final to Jack Crawford, his victory over Gottfried von Cramm in the French final had made him the first player ever to win all four grand slam titles. He had also fallen in love with an American film actress, Helen Vinson, whom he would marry later in the year. Their liaison aroused frantic interest on both sides of the Atlantic. In April they sailed together on the RMS *Berengaria* to England, where Vinson was due to shoot the film *The Tunnel*. The couple had eluded the media when they left New York, but were met at Cherbourg by the vanguard of the British press and disembarked at Southampton into a blizzard of flashbulbs.

There were still nearly two months until Wimbledon. During this time Perry retained the British hard court title in Bournemouth, beating Bunny Austin in the final on an afternoon that was so cold he arrived on court wearing a scarf, gloves and a fashionable yellow cashmere coat buttoned up as high as it would go. Then he went to Paris to win the French. The eight weeks also allowed the excitement to abate, just a little, over Perry's homecoming with an American beauty on his arm. In the circumstances he was as ready as he could expect to be for the defence of his Wimbledon title, his preparation for the tournament having taken its now familiar course of representing his club, Chiswick Park, in the county championship rather than playing at Queen's.

The takings for the first day of Wimbledon were donated by the All England Club to the King's Jubilee Trust – a poignant gesture, as it turned out, for George V would be dead in six months and the country then confronted with the abdication crisis. Perry's contribution to the day was a one-sided win over the Canadian champion Marcel Rainville, which he followed two days later with another three-setter against the young American Wilmer Hines. Once again he took the opportunity of unexacting early matches to tweak his game for the special demands of grass. Never a great stylist, Perry's unique collection of strokes – ingenious, quirky and highly effective – demanded greater attention than the more classical games of von Cramm or Crawford. While others had the uncomplicated pendulum swing of a grandfather clock, Perry's shots had as many interlocking movements as in the latest Swiss watch. Enormous energy, too. The first week allowed Perry to stoke the furnaces that would power him through the championship fortnight with gathering momentum.

Johnny Van Ryn, another American, was one of the few men who could match Perry for pace around the court, and he tested the champion's mettle in the third round by winning the first set and rescuing a match point at 5–3 in the fourth before losing the set, and the contest, 10–8. The Yugoslav Josip Pallada won only twelve games against Perry in the fourth round and yet still took the third set to love. Perry abandoned hope of winning this set after Pallada's immaculate baseline game won him the first three games, but he soon fathomed how to reassert his superiority and did just that. Pallada's problem was that his baseline play, while beautifully polished – one commentator reckoned, 'It would be envied by many an Englishman' – was of a type that Perry knew too well.

The final of a tournament is often not the most difficult match, and the looming presence in the 1935 quarter-finals of Menzel, beaten by Perry in the third round the year before, was the sort of hazard that could bring disaster. Playing on Court 1, Perry came through a ferocious first-set tussle that must have confirmed in his mind that nothing could stop him now in his quest for a second title. Wimbledon's own record of the tournament reported, 'Menzel's big serve and devastating volleying in this set would have subdued anyone in the game today except Perry.' At 6–5 down, Perry saved a set point. He then went behind again 7–6 to Menzel's bullying play, before producing one of those overwhelming surges that destroyed an opponent's will to keep fighting. Six out of the next seven games went to Perry for the loss of a mere seven points.

Any watching rival must have been dispirited not just by the way he could suddenly dictate the course of a match, but by the invincibility of his defence, an often-overlooked aspect of the Perry game that sprang from the cussed nature of the man. On the practice court he would work compulsively to eliminate frailties. He was never going to deliver the same winners with his backhand as he was with his forehand, but this did not mean it could be easily exploited. Against Menzel his backhand proved unyielding when under attack, as important in eroding his opponent's resistance as his explosive forehand.

By the end of the twentieth century, lawn tennis had become simply tennis. The grass-court game was in retreat, the surface surviving on the tournament circuit only in north-west Europe and on the East Coast of the United States. Wimbledon is the only grand slam now played on grass. The US Open in 1978, and the Australian Open a decade later, had moved to new homes with more easily maintained hard courts. In 1935, though, grass was still widely used, and Perry's match against Crawford in the Wimbledon semi-finals was the fourth time that year the pair had played each other on the surface.

Anyone who had tracked Perry's progress through to the semi-finals knew that his losses to Crawford in their first three grass-court encounters – all in Australia – were a redundant statistic. By midsummer he was playing with great confidence and reliability. From Perry's endless practice sessions with Dan Maskell he knew instinctively the best response to all but the most unexpected situations. He rolled past Crawford, not effortlessly, but leaving the Australian in no doubt from about the midpoint of the contest that he was chasing nothing more substantial than honourable defeat. With his four-set victory, Perry was now poised to become the first man to retain the men's title since the abolition in 1922 of the challenge round, the old tournament structure in which the defending champion only had to play the final round.

Baron Gottfried von Cramm, one of seven sons of an Oxford-educated *Junker*, was Perry's final opponent. He had spent his formative years in a social sphere far removed from the one that Perry had known. Before he was old enough to play, von Cramm used to roll the courts for his father and brothers on the family estate near Hanover. Once considered ready to handle a racket, the boy showed immediate promise and, when asked by a relation what he was going to be, replied sombrely, 'The world's tennis champion.' The family wanted him to be a diplomat, to which end he was sent to Berlin to study law, but the young von Cramm remained steadfast in his ambition to be the world's best at tennis. When his father found out that his son was using the funds he sent him not on his studies but on playing tennis, he finally accepted that Gottfried would never settle for the world of diplomacy. He not only granted him his wish to pursue a career in the game but also gave him permission to marry his childhood friend, the dark, vivacious Baroness Lisa von Dobeneck.

Von Cramm was intelligent, gracious and always impeccably turned out. He was almost impossible to dislike. According to an American writer, von Cramm 'speaks some French and Swedish and a reasonably fluent English – and is equally amiable in any of them'. His sense of fair play was such that on match point in the doubles match of a Davis Cup tie against the US he admitted that the ball had brushed his racket, despite knowing it was something only he was aware of and that it meant the point would go to the other pair. A British commentator declared, with spectacularly misplaced optimism, that he was 'the type of player who encourages many to think that international sport may lead to international understanding and goodwill'. He was also a homosexual, although the fact that his marriage to von Dobeneck was short-lived was said to have more to do with his long absences playing tennis than his being partial to male company. His sexuality did, however, lead to a series of run-ins with the Third Reich, and a story that he was inspired to one of his greatest victories by a telephone conversation with Adolf Hitler was entirely concocted.

The conversation was said to have taken place in 1937, the year in which von Cramm, who had lost the previous two Wimbledon title matches to Perry, went down heavily for the third final running, this time vanquished by Don Budge. When von Cramm came up against Budge again shortly afterwards in the Davis Cup inter-zone final, also played at Wimbledon, he gave the American a much closer match. The story went that a telephone call von Cramm received from Hitler just before he was due on court, during which he was overheard to say '*Ja, mein Führer*', was what motivated him to raise his game. In fact this was as false as the other Hitler story, the one about him watching Perry's Davis Cup match against Daniel Prenn in Berlin in 1932. Budge fabricated the tale of the phone call to liven up his account of the Davis Cup contest, and admitted as much when confronted by von Cramm about it after the war. Von Cramm never had anything except an uneasy relationship with the Nazi regime, who took a dim view of his sexual orientation and his heretical view of their mission.

The Nazis jailed him for five months in 1938 on the pretext of an affair with a male German-Jewish actor. In fact the sentence was a punishment for something quite different. Von Cramm had pointedly failed to promote the National Socialists after being sent on a world tour by the party expressly for that purpose. A Reuters report from Berlin in March 1938 said von Cramm was in custody having been detained by the criminal police. The report added, 'It is semi-officially stated he is suspected of moral delinquency.' It also quoted 'the official tennis board in Berlin' as saying, 'He is in hospital, where he is suffering from neurosis of the heart and may not be visited.'

Some time later, the British player John Olliff, a great admirer of von Cramm who sought to clear the German's name of the trumped-up charge, said he was told by an official in Germany that a file on the case was 'annotated with instructions to both prosecuting and defending counsels that the defendant would be found guilty'.

By 1939 Von Cramm was free again, and if he had been allowed to play at Wimbledon that year might well have fulfilled his ambition to win the tournament. Thanks to Oliff's intervention, Queen's voted 12–11 in favour of accepting von Cramm's entry for the London Championships, which he won by overwhelming the American Bobby Riggs in the final. Wimbledon, though, refused to let von Cramm play and Riggs, a self-confessed hustler, claimed he walked away from the championships with more than $100,000 dollars in winning bets, having won the singles, doubles and mixed doubles.

War broke out soon afterwards and von Cramm proved a loyal German without attempting to ingratiate himself with the Nazis. He received the Iron Cross for his services in Russia.

After the war von Cramm returned to tennis, but, although he won the German singles title in 1949 at the age of forty, was no longer a contender for the major honours. He attended Wimbledon in 1949 and 1950 as a reporter for the newspaper *Die Welt*, but was unable to play there again until the International Lawn Tennis Federation readmitted Germany in 1950, four days after the championships ended. In 1951 von Cramm, still wearing long trousers, returned for what turned out to be a farewell Centre Court appearance, losing in the first round to the future champion Jaroslav Drobny. Not everyone, though, who had sided with the enemy was allowed back. The Czechoslovak Menzel, who had become 'an ardent Nazi' and took part in English-language propaganda broadcasts from Berlin, was permanently barred.

Von Cramm also had a second go at matrimony, but it was no more successful than the first. A loveless marriage to the Woolworth heiress Barbara Hutton lasted only briefly, and his unsettled life ended in a road accident in Egypt in 1976. Von Cramm's greatest triumphs had been on the slow clay of Roland-Garros, where he reached three consecutive French finals, winning in 1934 and 1936 and losing to Perry in 1935. In the 1936 final he gained his revenge over Perry, using a backhand that had been transformed into a respectable shot by Bill Tilden, another homosexual who was never happier than when devising ways of bringing down the red-blooded Englishman with cranky strokes.

When he lost heavily to Perry in the 1935 Paris final, von Cramm was still operating with the dysfunctional backhand that Tilden was about to put right and very few doubted that he would lose again to the Englishman in the Wimbledon final a month later. 'Perry would appear to have reached the happy condition when he cannot play badly enough to lose,' *The Times* said, 'and to see him at his best is to feel that he will go on winning for ever.' Certainly Perry felt confident he would retain the title he had won the year before against Crawford. Duncan Macaulay, secretary of the All England Club, recalled bumping into Perry coming out of the players' dining room just before he went on court for his second singles final. 'Are you fixed up as regards your practice with Maskell?' Macaulay asked. 'Yes, thank you,' Perry replied, 'but I don't need it, you know. I shall beat this fellow 6–2 6–3 6–4. That will be a nice-looking score, don't you think?' Visualisation as a way of preparing for sporting contests was something that would be widely recognised much later, but Perry evidently was already on to it.

In its precision and parsimony in handing easy points to von Cramm, Perry's performance in the 1935 Wimbledon final was arguably even closer to perfection than the one he produced to beat Crawford a year earlier. He won in straight sets for the loss of only ten games. Not only did his all-round strokeplay have a sharp, clinical edge, but he positioned himself with a prescience that confounded the German. 'What the match really amounted to,' one newspaper report said, 'was that Perry usually knew where von Cramm would send the ball, whereas von Cramm was never quite sure about Perry.' So much at one was he with his game, Perry played as if in a trance. When he came to, the Centre Court reception confirmed that Wimbledon had finally accepted Fred Perry as worthy of something warmer than mere admiration.

There was no let-up in Perry's form when, come the end of July, he stepped out again on Centre Court in the Davis Cup challenge round. Once more Britain was up against the US and the feeling that the visitors were on a doomed mission was again colourfully expressed, this time by the American journalist Henry McLemore. He said that if Perry, whose presence virtually guaranteed Britain two points, could not be stopped, the US's chances of winning were not only null and void but nux vomica – possibly the only time that the plant whose seeds are a source of strychnine has been invoked in sports copy.

Two different (from 1934) singles players, the veteran Wilmer Allison and America's new young champion Don Budge, a twenty-year-old flame-haired Californian whose Scottish father had played football for Glasgow Rangers, faced Britain this time – and if McLemore was right about the certainty of two points coming from Perry, Austin needed to win just one of his singles to secure an overall home victory. This he did in the opening match. McLemore described Austin as the finest stylist in the world and said he saved his top game for when the royal standard flew above Wimbledon, signifying the presence of the king and queen. On this occasion the royals were absent and Austin triumphed despite playing below his best. Leading 5–4 in the fifth set, Allison smacked the net so hard with his racket when he missed a simple volley, which would have given him two match points, that the umpire asked for the net to be remeasured. It was the American's last act of defiance.

'Young Budge is a fine player, but Perry showed the crowd a finer,' the *Manchester Guardian* said. Perry's six years' seniority had much to do with this, and Budge, who by the end of the decade would be comfortably the world's best player, showed ample evidence of the strengths that were lying in wait until he gained more experience. For the moment Perry was too good for him and coolly attacked Budge's feared backhand in order to prepare the way to strike down the forehand line. His relatively comfortable four-set win put Britain 2–0 ahead at the end of the first day.

McLemore had reckoned the doubles the only match 'the Americans can feel fairly sure of' and disparaged the British pair – Hughes for being a veteran who was past his prime and Raymond Tuckey for not having proved he even had a prime. It was good, caustic stuff, but turned out to be ruder than it was accurate with Hughes and Tuckey coming back from two sets to one down to beat Allison and Johnny Van Ryn. Three–nil up, Britain had achieved three Davis Cup wins in a row, and celebrated by cleaning up 5–0, the first whitewash in the challenge round since the US had beaten France ten years before.

Von Cramm would again be Perry's opponent in the 1936 Wimbledon final, the German buoyed this time by having beaten Perry five weeks before in the title match in Paris. All year Perry had been waiting for something to galvanise him. He had found it a struggle to regain his fitness and appetite for the game after the bad injury to his ribs and kidney that had played such a big part in his defeat in the US final the previous September and prevented him from competing in the Australian Championships in January.

In May he had looked in good trim, beating Austin in straight sets to win the British hard court title for the fifth time. Austin was on edge that day, asking the umpire to do something about the whirring cameras – pointed mostly at his opponent – while Perry, said one report, looked 'fit, lean and hard-bitten . . . a picture of a great and graceful athlete ready and eager to win'. This made the let-down that followed in Paris all the more upsetting for Perry. He was particularly mortified that von Cramm had dominated the deciding fifth set, which was the time in a match that Perry usually stepped on an opponent, crushing him with his superior speed and fitness.

Perry's own account of what changed his mood in time for Wimbledon mentioned two specific things: a letter from his father urging him to pull himself together and the feeling that the English game's condescending ruling class, judging he was washed up, was 'giving me the treatment'. He felt the Establishment was no longer concerned whether he remained an amateur or turned professional. He said, 'I had been back in England since April and nothing had been done to encourage me to stay in the amateur game.' This decided him: he would win Wimbledon to prove the doubters wrong, and then, having re-established his value to the domestic game, he would join the professionals in America.

In his approach to winning tennis matches Perry had been far ahead of his rivals, except the leading Americans, for some time. Now, spurred on to win the 1936 Wimbledon title, he seemed to develop a compulsion to do so that verged on a disorder. He prepared even more keenly than he had for his first two finals. Pat Hughes and Dan Maskell played against him in relays to help build up his stamina and refine his timing on grass, and he called in David Jones, an American with a huge serve, to sharpen his reflexes for any big-serving rivals he might encounter in the coming fortnight. This prudence was rewarded in his semi-final against Budge, who used a heavy seventeen-ounce racket and at one point looked capable of crushing Perry's title defence through the sheer weight of his game.

Perry had quickly cut his way through the opening two rounds, honing his game against Gerald Stratford, a Californian without Budge's power, and Kasom Chartikavanji, from Siam. The twenty-five games it had taken to dispose of Chartikavanji were not nearly enough and Perry had hurried off to find Maskell to give him the exacting workout that had proved beyond the Siamese.

His third-round win over Van Ryn was to be the first proper test of how well he was playing. The seventeen out of nineteen games he won from 3–1 down in the first set against one of the better players on the circuit provided the answer. 'He can never have displayed such world-beating tennis in an early round at Wimbledon,' the tournament's journal recorded, adding that Van Ryn 'could only stand and admire the precision with which his opponent was hitting to the lines, on the drive and in the air'. Cam Malfroy, a New Zealander whose sound volley was desperately in need of a good supporting act, took just eight games off Perry in the fourth round to complete an opening week in which the champion had played his most formidable tennis on the practice court.

Perry had no truck with Bryan Grant's antics in the quarter-final on the second Monday. A five-foot four-inch American who weighed barely nine stone, Grant was one of the game's great retrievers and had beaten Budge and Vines on grass, upsets that earned him the nickname 'Itsy Bitsy the Giant Killer', or 'Bitsy' for short. If things were going badly for Bitsy, he would hit great looping shots; if he had no chance of reaching a return he would fall flat on his face, unashamed slapstick that brought cheers from the crowd. Perry, who regarded playing to the gallery as part of his repertoire, was unamused. 'I would never even look at him,' he said. 'I just ignored him completely, so he stopped trying to pull that one on me.' Like Malfroy, Grant scrimped a miserable eight games.

Budge was Grant's polar opposite, in build, temperament and style of play. No trickery from him, particularly on the backhand side, from where the ball flew like a tracer. It was said that he was the first player to use the backhand – including a rolled version that changed tennis technique – as an attacking shot. As in the Davis Cup the previous year, Perry's tactic was not necessarily to keep the ball away from this shot. This time his tactic was to await the right moment to take it on and then deliver the ball so quickly that Budge had no time to set himself. So, on the Tuesday before the match, Perry worked harder than ever on striking the ball as early as he possibly could with a view to disabling the Budge backhand. Perry always maintained he had no fear on the other wing. He ridiculed Budge's forehand, saying it was delivered with a backswing that looked as though he was preparing to beat a carpet. This was no more than another Perry ploy, for he knew only too well that Budge could apply real pressure from either side.

Unquestionably Budge discomfited the title holder in their semi-final. Perry was tense and agitated throughout, conceding his only set of the championship when he lost the first having been two points from winning it. At 4–1, 40–0 ahead in the second, he again faltered against the wrecking-ball power of Budge's play. He managed to steady himself to win the last four games from 4–2 down in the fourth set. It was by far the most difficult match he had played that year – and would be surpassed as such only by the US final he played two months later, also against Budge.

Apart from the ferocity of that Wimbledon semi-final, Budge also liked to recall an incident in which Perry tested his own ability to turn off and then reapply his concentration in the middle of an important match. It happened when a piece of newspaper blew across the court just as Perry was about to make a simple return. Instead of going through with the shot, Perry let the ball go and casually strolled over to pick up the paper. He then started to read it and burst out laughing, at which point Budge decided to join in the pantomime. As Budge approached, Perry told him to laugh too even though the item was something as dull as a weather report or stock market prices. Perry then played the next point 'as violently as if nothing at all peculiar had happened', which Budge construed as a lesson 'in the matter of management of the competitive instincts'.

At the time it was supposed that von Cramm suffered his leg injury, which spoiled the 1936 final as a contest, at the start of the match. Perry subsequently revealed that an indiscreet masseur giving him a rub-down shortly beforehand had told him that von Cramm had hurt his groin while practising that morning, even adding that the challenger would be most inconvenienced when reaching to his right.

Under the guidance of the faithful Pops Summers, the Perry camp had already been doing intelligence work on von Cramm. Waiters, chambermaids and other helpers at the Savoy, where the German was staying, were among a network of spies who reported back on everything from what he ate to how he slept. Now, with the fresh information supplied by the masseur, Summers advised Perry that in the knock-up before the final he should feed straightforward balls to von Cramm's backhand, but force him wide on the forehand.

Newspapers subsequently reported that von Cramm injured his right thigh in the tight opening game, when he forced Perry to nine deuces on his serve, but Perry knew his opponent was struggling from the off and said later he saw von Cramm wince as he stretched for a forehand. 'I immediately looked up in the stands and Summers gave me the "go".' Von Cramm held to 30 to make the score 1–1, but would win only one more game as the leg injury of the morning restricted, then eliminated, his ability to make quick movements.

The score, 6–1 6–1 6–0, gave it equal status with the 1881 final as the most one-sided men's title match in Wimbledon history. Peter Wilson of the *Daily Mirror* reported that Perry had asked von Cramm midway through the second set if he wanted a masseur, to which von Cramm replied it was no good and he must carry on. But the challenger made no mention of this afterwards, all part of the code of not falling back on excuses.

Many years later Perry would play up his ruthless streak, saying if he could have beaten Von Cramm 6– –1 instead of 6–0 he would have done. In fact, at the time he was sympathetic. The next evening at the Wimbledon Ball at the Grosvenor House Hotel he described his victory as being by the back door and said, 'I am very sorry that yesterday's match should have ended as it did. I sympathise with Gottfried, and I must admit that an injured man is very much easier to beat than a fit one.' There were cries of 'No' when he made the remark about the back door and there was even more of an outcry when he said, 'It is possibly my last win – I am getting old.'

Perry would return one more time as a player to Centre Court, for the Davis Cup final three weeks later, but his days of competing in the Wimbledon championships were over. While he had gained greater acceptance from stuffier elements of the public, he was still at odds with the British tennis establishment, particularly the LTA president Sir Samuel Hoare and some of those at the top of the All

England Club. Although being stripped of his membership of the club when he turned professional was a matter of course given the oil-and-water nature of amateurism and professionalism at the time, Perry still felt a small jar of resentment when it happened. After he left the UK in the late summer of 1936, he stayed away for more than a decade.

If Perry disliked the Wimbledon hierarchy, he loved the tournament itself unconditionally from the moment he first played there. He did not play his most thrilling matches at the championships because at the time he had put himself beyond the reach of even his sternest rival. The Centre Court was his gladiatorial space as surely as Madison Square Garden was Jake La Motta's or Epsom Downs Lester Piggott's. His three-year reign as champion was a monumental three-year embrace. Once Fred Perry had claimed the title, no one came close to prising it from his grasp.

Perry marked his very last appearance as a competitor on Centre Court with a performance of extraordinary brusqueness. The score in the 1936 Davis Cup final against Australia stood at 2–2 after Austin lost to Adrian Quist in a match that went on for so long that LTA officials started fussing about the possibility of the deciding singles between Perry and Jack Crawford having to be suspended because of the approaching darkness. The officials then irritated Perry by advising him how to handle the situation so as not to lose any advantage if the match did have to be finished the next day. It was coming up to 6 p.m. and Perry abruptly ended the unwanted counselling by announcing he would be off court by 7.15. He then charged the net whenever possible and even told Crawford at one changeover that he was going to come in no matter whether he played the ball off strings, handle or frame. The match was over in barely an hour, Perry winning 6–2 6–3 6–3.

Although by now Perry had made up his mind that he would turn professional before the year was out, he was not letting on to the outside world. The day after beating Gottfried von Cramm in the 1936 Wimbledon final, Perry dismissed as 'the usual baloney' a report from New York that the promoter Bill O'Brien had offered him $50,000 to give up being an amateur. The truth was a little different, and Dan Maskell was possibly the only other person who understood this. Maskell was with his great friend on Tuesday 28 July 1936 when, moments after he had clinched Britain's 3–2 win over Australia, Perry turned back without saying a word and had a final look around Centre Court as an amateur player. 'Maskell knew I was gone from Wimbledon and the Davis Cup.'

'So we hold the Davis Cup for the fourth successive year,' E.J. Sampson said in the *Manchester Guardian*. 'France before us held it for six years and the United States before France held it for seven. Let us be thankful to hold it and realise what it takes to do so in the face of the growing strength of the United States, Australia and Germany. It takes an Austin and the world's best. It is a lucky nation that owns a Perry.'

In 1937, with Perry now a professional living in America, Britain lost 4–1 to the US in the challenge round at Wimbledon. It was the end of a Davis Cup reign that has never been resumed.

8

Mixed doubles

'Women fall for him like nine pins'

A person in Britain probably reckons to have achieved celebrity status when his or her private life becomes a matter of concern for the media. Fred Perry's fame started to grow in the early 1930s, spread well beyond tennis in 1933, when he followed up playing a lead role in Britain's Davis Cup victory by winning a grand slam title, and blossomed into fully formed celebrity in 1934, when he won his first Wimbledon. A month after this victory at the All England Club, the *Daily Mail* claimed an exclusive when it announced Perry was to marry the English actress Mary Lawson. The script might have been written by the playwright of the moment, Noël Coward, who would later put the romance into railway stations with his play *Still Life* that was made into the film *Brief Encounter*. In a scene fore-shadowing the film, Perry and Lawson agreed on their engagement during a romantic parting at a London train terminal.

From 1934 Fred Perry's liaisons were firmly in the public domain even if they did not receive quite the attention they would have done had he had such a rompingly good time half a century later. This had less to do with the manners of the press, who even then were perfectly capable of ruthless intrusion, than with sportsmen and women not yet being as prominent as they are now. Also Perry led a will-o'-the-wisp life that made him difficult for the most assiduous of newshounds to keep up with, given communications and travel were far slower than today. There was, too, the distrac-tion of a world preparing to go to war. And yet, despite all this, once Perry was a fully qualified celebrity his *affaires d'amour* did not go unnoticed.

He was left alone by the media in the early days of his adventuring, during which he showed that his forwardness was not confined to racket sports. A letter written by Ellsworth Vines to his fiancée from Philadelphia in August 1931, soon after Perry arrived for his second visit to the US, makes a caustic reference to 'waiting for the Great Perry to put in an appearance' after he had gone off with 'some girl he met at Rye he is quite enamoured with'. On another occasion, an escapade in a hotel in Boston involved Perry and the American player Bill Fiebleman tying sheets together to form a rope so they could make a social call on two female players on the floor below. 'I shiver when I think of that climb,' Perry said in due course.

As Perry's reputation spread, he no longer needed to undertake such dangerous and furtive adventures. Access was by the front door, willingly opened, particularly in Hollywood, where it did not take him long to make an impact. An American columnist wrote of Perry, 'He is six feet tall, weighs around twelve stone; sculptors declare his physique perfect . . . women fall for him like nine pins. When he goes to Hollywood, male film stars go and sulk in Nevada.' And there is evidence that in time Sam Perry grew to take some satisfaction from the fact that his son's conquests were not confined to the tennis court. Jean Webster, a neighbour of the Perrys in Brentham, recalled being taken by an aunt to see 'the ribboned medal in its mauve, silk-padded case' that Fred received for one of his Wimbledon victories. 'Being eleven years old,' she said, 'I quite thought I was going to see the great man himself, but he was already in the USA courting a film star.' She added that the film star's photograph was proudly displayed on a sideboard.

Perry enjoyed the company of a number of leading actresses. Most memorably perhaps there was a night out with Jean Harlow when he first arrived in Los Angeles in 1931. Harlow had appeared in the 1930 film *Hell's Angels*, in which the assets that gained her high marks did not include her acting. 'It doesn't matter what degree of talent she possesses . . . nobody ever starved possessing what she's got,' said *Variety* magazine. She must have been quite a vision, enough to have frightened the life out of a coy young Englishman, but not Perry. According to Perry's version of events, his date with Harlow took place on his first evening in LA. He and Pat Hughes, waiting at their hotel for a car to take them to a dinner at the Los Angeles Tennis Club, were surprised when separate limos turned up for them. Perry said his headed for Beverly Hills, where it stopped in the driveway of a grand colonial mansion. A maid let him in and moments later he was greeted by Harlow – the meeting he had jestingly requested in New York some weeks earlier as a prerequisite for playing on the West Coast. They spent the night on the town, giving the dinner a miss, an idea that was entirely Harlow's, Perry said, and one that only a fool would have dismissed. When the car dropped him back at the hotel he compared notes with Hughes. He, too, had been escorted round town by a partner who answered the requirements he had stipulated.

Perry's friendships with other stars were a little more lasting than the brief fling with Harlow. His charms would find favour with Bette Davis, Loretta Young and Marlene Dietrich. The last two developed a frosty disregard for one another, although there is no record of this having anything to do with their common interest in the English tennis star. 'Every time she sins,' Dietrich said of Young, 'she builds a church. That's why there are so many Catholic churches in Hollywood.'

In Perry's own phrase, he and Davis became firm, fast friends after an unlikely boy–meets–girl episode. The encounter took place when Perry visited the Warner Brothers studios with an actor acquaintance. There on set was Davis in bed with a dog sitting on the bedclothes alongside her. Perry remembered he made some wisecrack about lucky dogs, which apparently did it for the queen of one-liners, whose aphorisms included, 'When a man gives his opinion he's a man; when a woman gives hers she's a bitch.' Davis was already familiar with some of tennis's young bucks, including the dashing American newcomer Gene Mako, and came to watch Perry play soon after that first meeting. She arrived dressed in a pair of shorts designed to turn heads. Perry jokingly objected and she went home to change. From this promising start, a long-term friendship developed. 'We were always easy and natural in each other's company,' he would say. 'Not exactly family, but almost.'

Perry made little effort to conceal his admiration for Loretta Young, whom he also got to know in Hollywood. In 1935 he caused quite a stir by turning up during the championships at Wimbledon with Young on his arm. Stories of a romantic link abounded, and each was undoubtedly smitten by the other. But there may have been a subplot to Young's willingness to go with Perry to the All England Club that even he was unaware of at the time. Young was expecting a child, the result of an affair with Clarke Gable while they co-starred in *Call of the Wild*, and being seen out and about with Perry on vacation in England was almost certainly an attempt to avoid and mislead the Hollywood press during her pregnancy. When asked, though, she did play down her relationship with Perry, saying on one occasion, 'I like Frederick very much, but the fact is there isn't any love life for me now;' and on another, 'You can bank on it that I'm not going back to America as Mrs Perry.' She also denied that she had had anything to do with the termination earlier that year of Perry's engagement to Mary Lawson.

Evidence of Perry's liaison with Dietrich appears in a biography of the German-born actress and chanteuse written by her daughter Maria Riva. She said that it had become fashionable in Hollywood to mix with the tennis set, and while the great Bill Tilden was a sought-after dinner guest, even better than him was Perry, who was 'a charmer both on and off court. Jet-black hair, slicked down close to the head, an aquiline, handsome face, an athlete's body.' Riva went on, 'Fred Perry taught my mother to play tennis with great patience and lots of little passionate hugs, punctuated with rapid kissing between flying balls. I sort of hoped the smitten Spaniard might arrive and witness the smitten Englishman at work, but my mother was very skilful in keeping her admirers from overlapping.'

The 'smitten Spaniard' was Mercedes de Acosta, the Cuban-American poet, playwright, costume designer and energetic lesbian – much more so than Dietrich, who enjoyed affairs with either sex but whose commitment to homosexuality is hard to gauge. One theory, advanced by a curator of Dietrich memorabilia in Berlin, was that 'she simply wanted to know everything'. De Acosta would sometimes write to Dietrich four or five times a day. The letters, delivered by messenger, would be addressed to 'Darling One' or 'Golden One' and contained lines such as, 'It is one week today since your beautiful naughty hand opened a white rose.' She would sign herself 'White Prince' or 'Raphael'. Riva commented that de Acosta was so smitten that she was boring. 'Maybe this suited Greta Garbo, but I knew my mother would soon find it suffocating.'

Regardless of whether Perry ever knew his love rival was a female poet, he can have had no doubt about the strength of Dietrich's feelings for him. A photograph exists of the two of them at the screen star's home in Santa Monica. They are seated on a low garden wall as part of a foursome that also includes Rudi Sieber, the Czechoslovak casting director to whom Dietrich was married for fifty-two years until his death in 1976. But in this particular photograph Dietrich has eyes only for Perry, who is wearing bathing trunks and baring his very striking athlete's torso, which is held up against Dietrich's raised right leg. They are, as the celebrity magazines say, sharing a joke. In one of the books in which it appears Riva's caption refers to it as a family photo and says the famous Wimbledon champion is sitting 'next to his latest conquest'.

The photograph was taken in October 1934, shortly before Perry set sail to defend his Australian title. While he was in Australia Perry wrote a letter to 'the great Marlene Dietrich' which was a curious mixture. Written in a neat hand and with only one grammatical blemish, the misspelling 'definately', it was no rip-roaring love missive. He used the headed notepaper of the Menzies Hotel, Melbourne, and signed off, 'Auf Wiedersehen – and good luck! Fred Perry'. On the other hand, he spoke of his longing to be back in Los Angeles and not wanting to go on 'dashing around the old world playing lawn tennis', a remark that sounds like a veiled declaration that he would consider settling down if requested. He referred to a charm, which Dietrich obviously knew about, that was 'doing yeoman service', and told her three times that his ship from Australia docked in Los Angeles on 23 February. Finally, he asked her to write to him, sending her letter by return to Auckland, where it could still reach him before the final leg of the voyage back to America, 'to let me know how you are getting on in the great film city these days'.

Stanley Doust's exclusive appeared on an inside page of the *Daily Mail* in August 1934. It began, 'I am able to announce the engagement of F.J. Perry, the world's champion lawn tennis player, to

Miss Mary Lawson, the actress and film star.' The reporter had called Perry in Newcastle, where he was playing exhibition matches. Perry told him that he and Lawson had been friends for a few weeks and had become officially engaged when she saw him off from King's Cross station two days before. Lawson, twenty-three – two years younger than Perry – had stayed behind in London, where she was filming with Cecily Courtneidge.

The relationship was pretty much doomed from the start, with Perry setting off less than a week later for America – and into the way of sweet-scented temptation, which he found so hard to resist – while Lawson remained in Britain to pursue her acting career. This was no fleeting separation. Perry was heading for New York, from where he would go to Hollywood and then on to Australia and not return to Britain until the spring. Another problem was referred to by Lawson's sister, who said, 'Apart from a natural interest in Fred's tennis she does not care much for the game.'

Lawson, likened to the American actress Janet Gaynor because she, too, was only five feet tall and was usually cast in nice-girl roles, had been in serious relationships before she met Perry. There had been an engagement to a London businessman three years before and a more recent one to a cameraman at Shepperton studios. The cameraman was said to be terribly upset when his fiancée deserted him for Perry, but Lawson's father, a retired Darlington railwayman, told the press that his daughter had given him back the ring a few weeks before she agreed to become Perry's wife. The date for the marriage to Perry was tentatively set for March 1935 in a register office. Lawson told her local newspaper in north-east England that she had a dread of big weddings 'with orange blossom and all the other trappings'.

In Perry's continued absence, the romance quickly withered. 'Fred, I know, likes America and wants to live there. I don't,' Lawson said in April 1935 after news broke that the engagement was over. 'I do not blame him for that but my work, in which I am naturally greatly interested, and my interests are in England. In the past I have had offers from Hollywood. I have refused them. I intend to remain here.' The strain of constant press enquiries also played its part in ending the engagement. 'Publicity has killed our romance,' Lawson told the

Darlington and Stockton Times. 'I am sick and tired of the ridiculous rumours which have been going about and of being rung up time after time about some story or other. Somehow or other everything seems to have gone wrong from the start.'

Perry, it was said, had spent £200 – the equivalent today of well into four figures – on the telephone call from Los Angeles in which he and Lawson had agreed to cancel their wedding plans. Lawson, who was appearing at the London Palladium in *Life Begins at Oxford Circus* with Bud Flanagan and Chesney Allen at the time, was reportedly so distraught that between scenes she stayed in the wings rather than return to her dressing room to avoid having to put up with people staring at her.

Lawson's desire for a married life in England rather than go to the US had a tragic conclusion. In May 1941, while appearing in a stage play in Liverpool, she died when the house in which she was staying with her husband, the film producer F.W.L.C. Beaumont, was destroyed by a bomb dropped by the Luftwaffe. She was thirty and had never quite made it to the front rank of her profession although not all of her fourteen films were so-called 'quota quickies' – movies made in haste to try to reverse America's domination of British cinemas at that time. Films in which she was the lead included *Radio Pirates* and *Can You Hear Me Mother?*, both made in 1935, and *To Catch a Thief*.

Before the end of his engagement to Lawson, Perry had already begun his liaison with Dietrich and had fallen for divorcee Helen Vinson, an actress from Beaumont, Texas who now lived in Hollywood. Born Helen Rulfs, the daughter of an oil company executive, Vinson was quite tall and was described as a chic, elegant beauty with a tinge of a southern drawl. Like Lawson, Vinson fell short of being a major star; unlike Lawson, she tended to land roles as the femme fatale or scarlet woman.

When Perry crossed the Pacific back to Los Angeles early in 1935, after losing in the Australian final to Jack Crawford, he purposely encouraged speculation that his mission was to finalise the terms on which he would turn professional. This provided a smokescreen for the story he wanted to remain secret, that the main reason for his return to the US was to see Vinson. The actress's first marriage, to the carpet manufacturer Harry Vickerman, with whom she had eloped at the age of eighteen in 1926, had ended in 1934. It was said he disapproved of her show-business friends and, complained Vinson, would not allow 'people of the theatre' into their home.

The friendship with Perry would not stay a secret for long because the couple decided to travel together to England, where Vinson was due to make a film and Fred needed to start preparing for the European season. They managed to avoid the press during their transatlantic crossing, after Perry's friend the hotelier Bertram Weal switched them from the *Georgic* to the *Berengaria*, but by the time they reached the French port of Cherbourg the word was out and the couple were joined on board by two members of the British press. Their stories ensured that Fleet Street was waiting en masse when they docked at Southampton.

Perry's tennis certainly did not suffer from having Vinson with him in Europe during the summer of 1935, even if he did say that in the early weeks of their being together in England he found it difficult to concentrate on his playing. Her attendance was clearly no longer a distraction come high summer, with Perry having a bountiful June and July, during which he won the French title for the only time, collected a second Wimbledon singles title and helped Britain to rout the US 5–0 in the Davis Cup on Centre Court. He told Associated Press that he hoped to be a married man before he sailed to the US in early August.

In fact, the marriage did not take place until September. Originally the couple wanted it to be the second part of a double celebration on Saturday 14 September, after Perry had won his third US title at Forest Hills in New York. Wilmer Allison ruined this idea when he beat Perry in the semi-finals on the Thursday. The result depressed Perry not just for the obvious reason, but because, he said, it dropped his value if he were to turn professional from a boat to a dinghy. He was demoralised, too, by the injury to his ribs and kidneys that he received in a fall early in the match and by what he regarded as Allison's triumphal bragging afterwards.

Later that evening over dinner at the Madison Hotel, Perry's friend Irving Squires, the businessman and sheriff of Queen's County, broached the idea of bringing the wedding ceremony forward by forty-eight hours as a way of lifting his mood. 'Why not marry now?' he challenged the couple. Vinson, who at twenty-seven was one year older than the groom, was certainly game. 'The fact is that we are so happy that we are simply silly,' she said at the time. A frantic scramble then took place to do the deed before midnight on Thursday 12 September so as to avoid a Friday the thirteenth ceremony. Harrison, thirty miles away and a version of Gretna Green in Scotland, was the only place that waived the rule demanding twenty-four hours' notice that could be reached in time.

'The streets were dimly lighted,' Perry said of their arrival in Harrison. 'There was hardly anybody about, but we managed to find the house of the magistrate, where our friends had arranged for the ceremony. You don't need quite as many marriage formalities here in the States as you do at home in England.' Vinson's account of what happened, given to a British newspaper, was more colourful than Perry's. It detailed how all the officials had gone home when they arrived, so they went to a police station, where she asked an officer sitting behind a big desk, 'How can I get married?' Having overcome his surprise, the officer telephoned the town clerk, who in turn summoned a judge, who promised to be with them before the midnight deadline. Vinson had no time to prink for the nuptials, but she looked marvellous, said Perry, in what he called an ordinary day costume and what she said was a brown, tailor-made suit.

Apart from Perry and Vinson, the wedding party included Irving Squires, Bertram Weal and his wife, and Lawrence and Cathleen Lowman, friends of the couple who lived in Harrison. They all went on to the Westchester Country Club, where they were joined by other friends rounded up at the last minute for an impromptu wedding feast of champagne and hamburgers. In view of what lay ahead for the marriage, the fact that the celebrations did spill over into Friday the thirteenth is worth recording. For those who prefer less fanciful reasons for things not working out, Vinson perhaps inadvertently provided them herself when she announced, 'Our marriage will be thoroughly successful because I am an American woman and exercise my prerogative of being independent.'

The couple received messages of congratulations from Perry's father and stepmother and Bunny Austin. Perry had sent his father a cable that read, 'Helen and I just married. Send love. Injury not serious, but no tennis eight weeks.' Sam Perry, who told the papers he was not in the least surprised by the news, said, 'Mrs Perry and I naturally hope that they will be very happy.' Austin described it as a splendid development. 'I have met the new Mrs Perry,' he added. 'She is a charming girl, very beautiful.' If Fleet Street was expecting something sparky from Mary Lawson, they were to be disappointed. 'I have read about Fred and Miss Vinson in the papers,' she said, 'and I was expecting to hear of their marriage. I have no regrets. I wish Fred all the luck in the world.'

None of Perry's other marriages stirred the same amount of interest as the first, which was the only one he undertook as a British citizen, Wimbledon champion and the towering presence in Britain's world-beating Davis Cup team.

At least the early weeks of Perry's marriage to Vinson went well. They left for California within forty-eight hours of the wedding, and the LA papers carried photographs of the happy couple as they stepped off the train on the West Coast. With Perry unable to play because of his injuries, they honeymooned at leisure at the Chateau Elysee outside Los Angeles. Friends staged a lavish welcome for them there, which the social columns eagerly reported. 'Fred Perrys entertained at elaborate reception attended by cinema and Los Angeles society leaders' ran the headline over one account of the party. 'The reception which Al Kaufman and Myron Selznick sponsored Tuesday night at the Chateau Elysee for Mr and Mrs Fred Perry was one of the most brilliant parties given for the tennis stars. The party was the first to welcome the Perrys, who arrived here from the East on that day. It also happened to be Mrs Perry's birthday.' The actor Carl Brisson also entertained them at a dinner party for luminaries of the film world at his Bel Air home.

Within barely a month, though, they were separated by the demands of their careers, when Perry sailed on the SS *Lurline* to Australia while Vinson stayed in Los Angeles to finish some studio work. They would be apart for nearly three months, reuniting in the New Year in England, where Vinson would arrive first to make a film. The travelling, often separately, was what very soon put a strain on their relationship, something that Perry himself admitted when he called theirs a Hollywood marriage. This, he explained, was one doomed to failure. In fact the travelling merely exposed the weaknesses in their partnership. Neither seemed remotely interested in trying to avoid constantly heading off without the other, which indicated a far deeper devotion to what they were doing outside their marriage than to what was going on inside it.

Their relationship quickly became a mess – Perry's words – and so began a legal process of disengagement that lasted three years, which contradicted another of Perry's observations in old age, 'We married in haste and repented the same way.' In December 1938 the newspapers, particularly those on the West Coast, eagerly lapped up the lurid details that emanated from the Superior Court of Los Angeles County.

Few of the papers could resist pointing up the irony that the couple separated, according to the divorce documents, on Armistice Day, 11 November; nor was there much effort to avoid some very obvious puns. The *LA Times* report of 8 December started, 'Frederick J. Perry, former world's tennis champion, suffered a love-game defeat yesterday when his wife, Helen Vinson, stately blond film actress, sued him for divorce in Superior Court. Miss Vinson charges the British athlete, who got his tennis start on the London public courts, with extreme cruelty, and complains that on several occasions he gave way to temperamental outbursts.'

It was obviously an unpleasant situation, but 'extreme cruelty' was used here – and in Perry's future matrimonial wrangles – in a legal sense and should not be understood as it would in a general context. When it comes to divorce, especially in California, all sorts of minor domestic transgressions qualify as cruelty, and most probably Perry could have come up with as much nastiness directed against him as his wife did against her.

The specific instances of cruelty that Vinson alleged were in fact little more than everyday spats. These had begun as early as May and June 1936, when, Vinson said, Perry neglected her and refused to accompany her to parties. She charged as well that in July 1936, when they were in London, she became ill and asked Perry if she could return to the US, a request he angrily refused, ordering her to stay for his tennis matches 'so people won't talk'; that in September

1938, when they were in New York, Perry used violent and offensive language when she told him she was going for an interview for a radio contract; and that later the same month she was compelled to eat alone after Perry flew into a violent rage when she asked him to take her out to dinner. Vinson also claimed a division of property that she valued at $74,400. Included in this sum were $20,000 of stock in the Beverly Hills Tennis Club, $10,000 for 'War Loan Bonds of English Government', $4,000 for household furniture from 718 N. Linden Drive, Beverly Hills, and $2,400 for two Buick cars.

For his part, Perry's main concern seemed to be the financial implications of their divorce. They clearly occupied his mind more fully than any other aspect. He maintained that many of the items listed as shared property were owned separately by him and threatened to dispose of them. This resulted in Vinson's lawyers seeking a restraining order, which was granted. The surprise next development in the saga almost certainly stemmed from Perry's worries over money, because there was nothing else to account for the announcement of a reconciliation. In March 1939 the *Los Angeles Examiner* carried a photograph of the couple walking side by side. Below it, a story quoted Vinson's attorney as saying that the actress and the dashing athlete 'had mended their differences and decided to renew their "perfect romance" in another try at married life'.

The paper's scepticism, neatly captured by the inverted commas, was borne out early in 1940, when Vinson renewed her action against Perry. A summons issued on 20 February directed him to appear before a Los Angeles court – something that he did his best to avoid doing, presumably a stalling tactic recommended by his lawyers. On 8 March Vinson's lawyers reported to the court that Perry, having been told he would be served the summons at the Beverly House Hotel on 5 March, asked for this to be delayed until the following day, when he would be at the Beverly Hills Tennis Club to receive it at 10.30 in the morning. He did not show up. Perry's lawyers claimed he had been unexpectedly called out of town; Vinson's countered that they believed he had left California to avoid being served the summons and so delay the divorce proceedings. As part of the legal procedure, the summons now started to appear in the *Los Angeles News* on a weekly basis, and eventually Perry did receive it, but this still failed to bring the case to court. On one occasion Vinson was called away to New York and on another Perry's lawyers said they were far too busy to prepare their client's case in time for a hearing. Perry's professional playing commitments then became a factor, with his legal team claiming that if he missed a couple of events he was entered for it would affect his earnings and reputation.

In the end time was called, and on 7 November 1940 Vinson was granted an interlocutory decree after the revelation of more intimate allegations. Vinson said Perry had an uncontrollable temper and that his outbursts, which always occurred at night, were followed by his yelling, slamming doors and pushing around furniture, sometimes until five in the morning. She said that as a result she had lost her appetite and weight, became very nervous and her movie career was put in jeopardy. As the court papers made clear, though, the interlocutory decree was not a judgment of divorce, and Perry and Vinson would remain husband and wife until a final judgment in a year's time. This took place on 17 November 1941.

Perry did not comment at the time on why his first marriage failed. Much later he put it down to their both being famous and Vinson resenting the fact that his fame generally overshadowed hers. He said she hated it when letters arrived at their house addressed to Mrs Frederick J. Perry. The announcement 'Fred Perry and his wife Helen Vinson', which invariably signalled their arrival at functions, also caused friction. She contained herself until they returned home when, he said, the pots would fly again.

Perry's recollected account of the years – 1938–41 – it took for the marriage ties to be severed was a masterly piece of compression, making it seem a much snappier process than it was. One thing he did make clear was why he had been so concerned over the money side of the divorce. According to Perry, Vinson's 'high-priced Hollywood lawyers really clobbered me', tying up his bank accounts and having the locks on the marital house changed so that he was left with just the clothes he had been wearing on tour. Having started to make money as a professional player, he reckoned the divorce set him back three or four years. Another money-related consequence of the marriage, according to Perry, was that because of tax bills run up in England by Vinson he could not afford to go back there. He said that she owed the Inland

Revenue a tidy sum for her well-paid roles in films made in 1936 and 1937, which might have become his responsibility had he pitched up in London – or anywhere else in the UK – to play tennis.

In time, Vinson and Perry both settled into long-lasting marriages. Vinson did so with Donald Hardenbrook, a stockbroker, who persuaded her to give up acting when in 1945 he became her third husband. Although she had worked almost continuously throughout the 1930s, Vinson never moved out of the second division, and complying with Hardenbrook's wish was probably an acknowledgement that she never would. Their childless marriage lasted until he died in 1976. Vinson lived for a further twenty-three years before dying at the age of ninety-two.

Perry still had to work his way through two more unsatisfactory marriages before the fourth and enduring one. He was in Mexico when he met his second wife, Sandra Breaux, whom he described as a beautiful American model. Breaux had arrived in Hollywod from San Diego in 1934, after a photograph taken by her brother-in-law attracted the attention of moviemakers. She enjoyed the social scene in Los Angeles and was soon sufficiently well known for her name to be worthy of mention by gossip columnists. Marshall Kester recorded her presence at a glitzy party given by the director W.S. 'Woody' Van Dyke at his home in Brentwood Heights in August 1935. The invitation read, 'No husbands, wives, girl friends or escorts allowed. Come alone. If you're lucky, you won't go home alone.' It sounds the sort of party Perry would have enjoyed, but it was too early in the year for him to have arrived in California.

Like so many hopeful beauties, Breaux's film ambitions were eventually traded in for a career as a model – or mannequin, as one report unflatteringly described her – and early in 1941, while appearing in a fashion show in Mexico City, she met Perry, who had moved south after leaving Vinson. On 30 March that year the *Los Angeles Times* carried a photograph of a smiling Breaux above the caption 'Is It Love? – Newest romance in Tenniser Fred Perry's life is Santa Ana's Sandra Breaux, actress and model, slated to become his bride when his divorce from Helen Vinson becomes final.' Impetuosity, it seems, took over, and they were married two days later on Tuesday 1 April 1941. No effort was made on this occasion to avoid an inauspicious date. Nor did it seem to matter to Perry that he was still technically married to Helen Vinson, and would be until 17 November. A judge conducted Perry's marriage to Breaux – the second for both of them – at a civil ceremony at the home in Cuernavaca of the society couple Irving and Rosie Netcher – Irving being the wealthy part-owner of a Chicago department store and Rosie a former dancer who had made her name as Roszika Dolly.

At a ceremony in Elkton, Maryland in January 1942 Perry and Breaux solemnised their status as husband and wife, almost certainly to make sure they were seen as a legal couple in the US given the initial overlap with Perry's first marriage, but by the summer of 1945 the two were living apart. In August that year Breaux submitted to a divorce court in California that she had been subjected, wilfully and wrongfully, to a course of extreme and grievous mental suffering, an allegation Perry denied. Once again, the language was more technical than literal, legalese to bring the marriage to an end as quickly as possible.

Reflecting on a second marital failure, Perry confined himself to comments such as 'Everyone makes mistakes'; on another occasion he described marriage as being like a very slippery diving board. In reality the combination of his gregarious nature, living life at full tilt for most of his first thirty years and the incompatibility with long-term bonding of constantly being on the road made it unsurprising that he took time to settle into a lasting relationship.

Perry married a third time when he was into his late thirties and with his greatest achievements more than a decade in the past. Still the gossip writers of California found space for him. Lucille Leimert's 'Confidentially' column in the Los Angeles Times ran this on 24 January 1947: 'Purely personal . . . Lorraine Walsh and tennis-playing Fred Perry a twosome at the Beverly Hills Tennis Club prior to Fred's taking off for Florida. Looks serious!' Like Perry, Walsh had been married twice before and in common with her new husband's previous two wives she had Hollywood connections. Before meeting Perry she was married to Raoul Walsh, a distinguished and highly original film director, while her sister, Ruth Walker, was the second wife of the actor Walter Pidgeon – a keen sportsman who played tennis regularly at the Beverly Wilshire Hotel. Pidgeon was a friend of Perry and when he was in England in the late 1940s presented the prizes at a professional coaches' tournament in Cheltenham at which Perry played the winner in a challenge match. In his 1984 autobiography Perry gave just under two lines to his marriage to Walsh, even fewer than the three he devoted to his attachment to Breaux.

The couple married in Covington, Kentucky in April 1947, before settling in Florida. They split six years later after a turbulent time together with Walsh's problems with alcohol almost certainly contributing to their difficulties. A family friend recalled that drunk or sober Walsh was entertaining company but 'she probably wasn't someone who would be comfortable to live with.' She met and fell deeply in love with Perry during a sober period after divorcing Raoul but at some point in their marriage started drinking again. Their relationship also suffered when they were sued over whiplash injuries received in a car accident by an actress, Barbara Bliss. The widely reported case, involving damages of $50,000, was settled in Bliss's favour in May 1949. The unhappiness of the marriage became clear during the divorce proceedings in Palm Beach. Perry alleged that she nagged him, had once turned on the lawn sprinklers on all his clothes and was guilty of extreme cruelty. Walsh countered that on their fifth wedding anniversary in 1952, after she had given him his present, she happened to look into his dresser and found all his clothes gone. At this, she alleged, he lost his temper and was aggressive towards her. The decree granting the divorce, which gave Perry's net annual income as $12,000, incorporated a settlement that allowed him to keep the house he had bought in Boca Raton and her to take the Cadillac coupe. In addition, he had to pay her, starting straightaway, $525 a month for the next two years, then $325 monthly until 1958 and thereafter $275 a month.

In a typically bold rebuff to Oscar Wilde's aphorism about hope triumphing over experience, Perry soon married again. Barbara Riese Friedman, his fourth wife, had led a life whose trajectory had certain aspects in common with his own. These included coming to the United States from Britain and marrying unsuccessfully into the Hollywood set. The couple went through three marriage ceremonies in their first few weeks together, and although this was not a conscious effort to strengthen their union, it had this effect. They stayed together until Perry's death more than forty years later.

Given that Perry and Sandra Breaux had a second ceremony, Perry racked up an impressive aggregate of seven weddings with four wives.

9

A professional man

'Is it my patriotic duty to remain an amateur for
the glory of England?'

For three years the bubble was always about to burst. These were
Fred Perry's own words shortly after the bubble did burst in 1936,
when it could no longer withstand the pressure that had built up
inexorably from the moment he won his first grand slam title at
Forest Hills in 1933. 'Will Perry turn professional?' was the question
that hung over him for longer than it took him to fall in and out
of love with each of his first three wives.

In Perry's own mind the question soon changed, probably even
before the win at Forest Hills, from 'Will I turn professional?' to
'When?' Once he had committed himself to a life in tennis in 1929
he quickly realised that if the game were to sustain him he would
have no other option. Unlike his contemporaries in Britain's Davis
Cup team, he was not qualified for any other profession nor did he
have private means. The idea gained momentum after he made his
first visit to the US in 1930. The fact that this was the home of
professional tennis soon became one more reason for liking the place.
He already admired the can-do attitude, the absence of secret old-
school-tie connections, the year-round tennis-playing climate, which
he encountered first in California and then in Florida, and pretty
women who spoke with American accents. On top of all this here
was a place where he could make himself a very comfortable living
by continuing to do what he did rather well.

A range of reasons lay behind his taking until the mid-winter of
1936 to announce he was turning professional. Prominent among
them was the shibboleth held dear by the tennis establishment in

Britain that a chap did not play tennis for money. Given the strength of this belief, it is hardly surprising that it affected Perry's way of thinking in his early playing days. The Americans might have embraced professional tennis, but no leading British player had ever swapped 'glory for gold', as one newspaper put it when Perry did commit himself to this particular New World heresy.

Although professionalism was common by the 1930s in British sport, it was riddled with class prejudices. In the first instance, as early as the seventeenth century, it had been the very class that now abhorred it that had promoted it. The aristocracy were prominent among those who sponsored sportsmen to compete against each other, notably in prizefights and as jockeys in horse racing, to entertain them as a spectacle and as a vehicle for gambling. The growth of team sports, which stemmed from their popularity at public schools in the nineteenth century, exposed Britain's pious and duplicitous attitude towards professional sport. In football, professional teams were made up of overwhelmingly working-class players while the amateurs, if they wanted, had their own leagues and the Football Association catered for them with a separate cup competition. In cricket, professionals and amateurs, who played alongside each other, were referred to as players and gentlemen and had separate dressing rooms. Annual Gentlemen v. Players matches survived until 1962. Rugby split in two over the issue, with rugby league being regarded by the middle and upper classes as rugby union's rarely discussed, working-class cousin.

Between the two World Wars the Lawn Tennis Association held a generally dim view of professionalism. Promises to Perry that they would sort something out that would make it worth his while to stay amateur were largely prevarication. They knew that, without Perry, Britain would soon relinquish the Davis Cup. One of their stalling efforts was their hopeless pursuit of a relaxation in the code that forbade him from making a profit from films.

While Perry eventually saw through all this, he was nevertheless in a difficult position. His father's support for the LTA's efforts made it harder for him to distance himself from the association. There was also the emotional upheaval that any national goes through when switching allegiance to another country, which Perry made up his mind he would have to do when he turned professional. His father was mindful of this, and it may well have been the prospect of his son's emigration rather than a high-minded belief in amateurism that lay behind his support for the LTA's stance. The wrench for Perry was made all the greater by the deep satisfaction he gained from being part of the highly successful Davis Cup team, whose 1933 triumph preceded any of his great individual honours.

His marriage to Helen Vinson in 1935 was what hastened the need to secure his financial future. 'Since my marriage my first duty is to see that Helen Vinson is taken care of in a fitting manner and one to which she has been accustomed,' he said on the day he started his first professional tour in January 1937.

Professional tennis tours, which dated from 1926, were the brain-child of the American Charles C. 'Cash and Carry' Pyle, a theatre owner from Illinois. He had recognised the commercial possibilities of promoting sport in the same way as show business and saw no reason why sportsmen and women should not benefit financially just as actors and other entertainers did. Before he turned his attention to tennis, he had already introduced six-day cycling races, dance marathons and roller-skating derbies in which the performers shared in the profits. He also launched a 3,485-mile foot race across the United States known as the Bunion Derby. This was not his best idea – it temporarily bankrupted him – although the upside was it inspired the award-winning dramatist Michael Cristofer to write a play of his life, *C.C. Pyle and the Bunion Derby*.

Tennis attracted Pyle because, despite the depression in the late 1920s and 1930s, attendances remained buoyant, with players such as Bill Tilden, Helen Wills, Ellsworth Vines and Perry giving the sport a glamour no other possessed. And Pyle, stung by the lesson of the Bunion Derby, had done his sums. He had also worked out that the only way these sums would add up was if he were bold from the outset. So, in one of the great sporting coups of the twentieth century, he engaged the French tennis player Suzanne Lenglen for that inaugural tour in 1926 for the eye-popping sum of $50,000 plus a share of the profits. Lenglen was arguably the earliest female sporting superstar, and when Pyle signed her the fact that his first capture from the amateur game was such a high-profile and glamorous figure, and that he was prepared to pay her such a vast amount, showed just how serious he was about professional tennis.

With Lenglen on board, others were easily persuaded to follow, including Mary K. Browne, the greatest draw in American women's tennis. On the men's side, Vinnie Richards, Howard Kinsey and Harvey Snodgrass, all big names in the US, and Paul Feret, a French player signed to keep Lenglen company, were added to the troupe. The tour opened at Madison Square Garden in New York with around $40,000 taken at the gate.

By the end of the first Lenglen tour everyone had made a profit, and Pyle had proved what was blindingly obvious from the crowds that the game attracted: tennis had a professional future. Even so, the amateur bodies, with their control of the four major championships, effectively ran tennis for another forty-two-years, retaining their grip despite the fact that the United States Lawn Tennis Association proposed an open championship as early as February 1933. And the USLTA was not alone. Throughout the 1930s some persuasive voices, including prominent ones in Britain, spoke up in favour of the concept. Perry's was one such voice. He said it was all very well for tennis legislators around the world to bemoan the fact that tennis had turned into a business when it was they who were helping to make it a business and a very profitable one too.

In an article for the *New York Times* in 1937 Perry also pointed out that every leading amateur of the previous five years had turned professional and 'these men are still the same fellows they always were, even though they are paid to play'. In other words, no hell and damnation had been visited on those who had dared to challenge the supposed sanctity of amateur sport. As the amateurs could learn from the professionals, Perry said, it made sense for them to join together. He waxed quite evangelical: 'Let us then get together on this thing for a change, and, instead of the amateurs taking great pleasure in running down the professionals, and the professionals, in their turn, taking equal delight in telling the world how bad the amateurs are, there is no reason why we cannot band together to aid the amateur game by giving its players the benefit of our experience and attempting to teach them something by means of exhibitions and other games.' Nevertheless, he thought, this was unlikely to be achieved for at least fifteen more years – a figure that he should have doubled.

The interest stimulated by Pyle's first professional tour was not maintained in the short term, mainly because there were no male players of sufficient stature to excite the public. When Vinnie Richards took over the organising from Pyle, he signed Karel Kozeluh, a Czechoslvak with a fine reputation but who had not taken part in the major championships and so lacked a popular following. Other recruits included players such as Ramon Najuch of Germany, Frenchmen Paul and Edmund Burke and the American Emmet Pare, all relative nondescripts.

Bill Tilden, tennis player and showman extraordinaire, was just the man to restore professional tours as commercially viable popular spectacles. Tilden bickered endlessly with the USLTA over rules governing amateurism, to the extent that he was barred from the 1928 US Championships. After he came back, at the age of thirty-six, to win the US singles title for the seventh time in 1929, he took up a career as a professional tour organiser and player, performing with considerable distinction well into his forties. But without box-office players to join him in the enterprise, even Tilden was unable to keep the tours going indefinitely.

Interest again dwindled until Tilden and Bill O'Brien, an entrepreneur who had played professional baseball and trained as an accountant and osteopath, persuaded Ellsworth Vines and Henri Cochet to come over from the amateurs for a 1934 tour. They straightaway pulled in a bumper crowd at Madison Square Garden, and their appeal gained the promoters a breathing space to devise a winning format. This was an annual tour across the US to find a professional champion, with the cast replenished on a regular basis, every year if possible, by a top amateur who would re-engage the public. Perry was a perfect fit, a brilliant player who loved to interact with audiences and was a known Yankophile. Even before he married a Hollywood actress in 1935 it was strongly rumoured that he might take out US citizenship.

★   ★   ★

In Britain the question of whether Perry would turn professional became a matter of national interest from the time he returned to London in 1934. He was now a well-known figure who transcended sport. He had led Britain to victory in the Davis Cup the previous summer and in his time away since August had won the US and Australian Championships. He was still onboard ship returning to Southampton when he received a wireless message from the LTA urging him not to talk to anyone about his plans. Confused himself at this stage about what direction his career should take, he happily acceded to their wish. When asked about his future, he spoke airily about his loyalty to the LTA and his desire to keep Britain on the top of the lawn tennis world.

It was left for others to address his dilemma openly. Press comment tended to divide predictably, with right-wing newspapers opposed to his defection from the amateur ranks while the *Manchester Guardian* thought otherwise. Arthur Wallis Myers of the *Daily Telegraph* referred to professional tennis as pie crust with no steak and kidney underneath and said, 'American promoters bid frantically for Perry's body, forgetting he has a soul of his own.' The *Manchester Guardian* noted that tempting offers to turn pro came inevitably from the United States because this was the only country where professional tennis had been really lucrative. 'It is Tilden's own greatness and his clever sense of showmanship (he was a wonder showman on court!) that has been the reason for this success,' the paper added. 'To remain attractive his team wants ever fresh and notable additions. Thus Cochet and Vines were invaluable. So would Perry be, not for long perhaps, for once he had gone the round fighting Tilden, Cochet, Vines, Nusslein, &c. the novelty would have gone. In a comparatively short time, however, big money can be made, and Perry certainly could not be blamed if he were to help himself to some of it while the going is good.'

In August 1934 it was reported that Perry had refused an offer of $50,000 from O'Brien to join the Tilden troupe. In fact, the telegram making the offer had been handed to Perry at Wimbledon the day after he won his first singles title there a month earlier. He said it was visible, sticking out of a suit pocket, in photographs of him taken that afternoon.

At times during these early days of speculation Perry said he came close to resolving to take the money. When he felt this way, though, he was nearly always reacting spontaneously to an incident that had frustrated him rather than carefully considering the implications, and the feeling soon passed. For example, he said that the time he was ignored by the All England Club official after winning his first Wimbledon title was one occasion when he would have grabbed a fistful of dollars if it had been offered, and yet by the time he received O'Brien's telegram the very next day he had lost the urge. The reasons he gave for turning this offer down included the prospect of having to pay out half the money in taxes, of being ostracised from every tennis club in London and of it being unfair to his fiancée Mary Lawson.

At other times he made out he was on the brink of going pro seemingly to create muddle in order to hide his own confusion. In October 1934, just before he set off from Hollywood to defend the Australian title, he said he was twenty-four hours away from making up his mind. 'I must consider my future livelihood,' he said. 'I'm in a tough spot over these professional offers, and as I'm due to sail for Australia I have very little time in which to decide. I can earn £20,000 by touring the United States playing exhibition matches with Ellsworth Vines and I can be £10,000 richer at the end of five months. If I turn professional I shall not return to England.' The most significant line here was the one that caused the least interest at the time. The last sentence was probably Perry's first public pronouncement that he was thinking of moving to the US, but this was lost because it was tagged on to the totally false suggestion that he was about make up his mind about whether he would soon be playing for money.

Pressed a day later to state what he had decided, Perry merely replied with questions of his own: 'If you were in my place what would you do? Is it my patriotic duty to remain an amateur for the glory of England, thereby discarding the opportunity to make myself financially independent for the rest of my life?' He then carried on packing his trunk for the voyage to Australia.

Another story from around this time illustrates the extent to which the question of loyalty to England occupied Perry's mind. It involved a chance conversation he had with Harpo Marx, the supposedly mute member of the Marx Brothers, at the Beverly Hills Tennis Club. Milton Holmes recorded the conversation in an article in *Liberty* magazine. Harpo to Perry: 'You can't buy groceries with glory. Why don't you turn professional now and cash in? There's your opponent [pointing out of the window at Ellsworth Vines, who was giving a lesson]. You and Vines could clean up. It's your greatest chance. Why not grab it?' Perry to Harpo: 'I can't let England down.'

Some, but not all, commercial deals went begging as Perry agonised over what to do next. Agents were not yet part of the sporting scene, although even the most tigerish of this burning-eyed breed that emerged in the second half of the twentieth century might have had difficulty turning Perry's marketability into cash given the suffocating rules that governed amateur sportsmen and women. One of the biggest opportunities that Perry felt obliged to turn down came from Alec Simpson, whose company made the Daks tennis trousers that Perry wore. After Perry won his first Wimbledon, Simpson showed him the mock-up of an advertisement that was due to appear in the *Daily Mail*. It featured Perry playing a smash with the catch line 'Fred Wins Wimbledon in Daks'. In return, Simpson proposed a lifetime payment of one shilling (5p) for every pair of Daks trousers sold anywhere in the world. Perry said that from then on whenever he spotted a pair of Daks trousers in the street he thought, There goes another shilling.

One commercial deal Perry did manage to cut was with Albert Slazenger, whose company manufactured tennis equipment. It was one of the reasons Perry survived for as long as he did on an amateur's slender pickings. Perry's use of Slazenger rackets meant he was a huge asset to the company and one it was desperate to retain. Strictly speaking, the arrangement Slazenger and he worked out amounted to sponsorship that contravened the amateur code, but they got away with it through the technicality of paying him through the company's Australian operation. This way Perry was paid officially only in Australia and could receive money from the deal outside that country. It was the sort of crackpot thinking that an ideal as nebulous as sporting amateurism was able to accommodate.

The charade was maintained during the lunch in London at which the Slazenger deal was officially announced just before the 1935 Wimbledon championships. Fatuously, Perry had to make out that he was no longer simply a tennis player. 'I shall be a businessman with a black coat and striped trousers and I shall not be placing all my eggs in one basket,' he said. 'I managed to get to the top of one tree, and I shall try to get to the top of the other.' In their desperation not to lose Perry from the British Davis Cup team, the LTA went along with an arrangement that they would have taken a dim view of had it involved anyone else. Anthony Sabelli, secretary of the LTA, said limply, 'Other prominent amateurs hold similar positions with other lawn tennis firms.'

Every so often there were other attempts to make life a little easier for players such as Perry who had no private resources. In 1938, too late for Perry, the LTA flirted with the idea of adopting the so-called 'eight weeks' rule', common in certain European countries, whereby amateur players were allowed to receive travelling and living expenses for this number of weeks each year. The more zealous of the amateur purists harrumphed that this was like trying to wipe out burglary by legalising it for a couple of months a year.

No such relief came Perry's way, and he was left to evade and trim to get by. In October 1935 he went even further than he had at the lunch in London four months earlier, saying that he would be working for Slazenger full time and tennis would be relegated to a pastime. This was soon after he had suffered the serious injury when losing to Wilmer Allison in the semi-finals of the US championships and so was doubly uncertain about his future. He told the international news agency Associated Press that he had abandoned the idea he had had the previous April of turning professional. 'From now on tennis will be just a hobby with me,' he added. 'I'm going into business [with Slazenger] and you really can't make lawn tennis your business, you know. Of course, a man must have a hobby, so mine will be tennis.' This was nonsense, and maybe Perry was simply having a bit of fun at the expense of the AP reporter, but this in itself indicated a mind in a certain amount of turmoil.

Albert Slazenger's other big idea to save Perry as an amateur for his company and the country was not so successful. The plan, which Perry learned about much later, was to sell him a house in Wimbledon, which Slazenger owned, for £500, and then with a consortium of like-minded businessmen to buy it back for £100,000. The trouble was that not as many of these like-minded people existed as Slazenger imagined. The general view was that playing for his country should be reward enough, and the Save Fred Perry Fund died from lack of funds.

The bubble might have burst early in 1935, when Perry felt the pressure rise during the Australian Championships with renewed speculation that he was about to desert the amateurs. Phone calls from London kept being put through to his room throughout the night before the final against Jack Crawford, the last one just before daybreak. When he lost the final, one headline translated the defeat as 'Bang goes £20,000'.

After he rallied from this rare loss to Crawford to win the French Championship, retain his Wimbledon title and then provide the hammer blows that crushed the Americans 5–0 in the Davis Cup challenge round, Perry finally knew that, with little left to prove as an amateur, it was just a matter of time before he moved on from what he could glean from the Slazenger deal, his journalism and LTA allowances to earning big bucks as a professional. Still, though, when precisely this would be required a little more anxious effort.

'Cunning old Bill Tilden', as Perry put it, ratcheted up the stakes by goading him. Tilden said he was not sure whether Perry was 'the worst best player or the best worst player' he had ever seen, and although he was a formidable opponent he hit every shot wrong. 'If I tried to make a forehand drive the way he does,' said Tilden, 'I'd either hit the middle of the net or somebody sitting up in the top row of the stands.' Perry knew what Tilden was up to and remarked that although he was supposed to have only one shot, the forehand drive, it was apparently worth $100,000.

Perry said it was during the summer months he spent in England in 1936 that he realised he could delay no more. During this time it became clear to him that the LTA's promises about something turning up were pure Micawberism. Word had also reached him by now of the failed attempt by Albert Slazenger to interest the business community in keeping him in Britain. He said he was still smarting when he set off for America, and as soon as he arrived in

New York he told his lawyers to negotiate the best possible professional terms.

Armed with this instruction, Perry's lawyers went to Frank Hunter,
a former Davis Cup player who was part-owner of the exclusive
21 Club in New York, and his business partner Howard Voshell, who
were known to be working on a professional tour. Hunter and Voshell
were described by Associated Press as 'a pair of former "first ten"
luminaries', and with Perry now on board for their promotional
debut they managed to persuade a syndicate of his New York contacts,
including Jack Kriendler, who ran the 21 Club, the songwriter and
film producer Buddy De Sylva and William Seaman, a tea merchant,
to support the project. If any of them hesitated before signing up it
was hardly surprising, given that O'Brien's promotion the previous
winter, which featured Vines and Tilden, had lost around $22,000.

Vines knew as well as anyone the importance of recruiting Perry.
For the previous two years he had been trying to entice him away
from the amateurs. Evidence of his efforts can be found in the
many letters he wrote to his wife, Verle, when he was on the road.
As early as August 1934, Vines told her, 'We're going to try and
get Perry signed up', the 'we' referring to Lloyd Icely, president of
the Wilson sports equipment company. Soon afterwards, he followed
this with 'Talked to Icely and he tells me they'll put $5,000 on the
line to get Fred Perry. I'm sure going to talk turkey to Fred when
I see him.'

When Perry proved elusive in 1934 and again in 1935, Vines
showed his frustration: 'Today I talked with [promoter Jack] Curley
and it looks like Perry after all those negotiations has given him the
big run around . . . Guess with Fred being hurt [in the 1935 US
Championships] and getting married he just couldn't stand it all, but
he sure gave Jack a lousy deal after everything was set and I hope
he has to come back crawling on his knees one of these days.' Vines
finally sounded confident that Perry would switch to the pros in
late August 1936: 'Had a talk with Perry this a.m. and I believe he's
a certainty.'

Perry liked to recall that one of the more reluctant members of
the syndicate put together by Hunter and Voshell told a fellow
member that if they made money out of the deal he would give

him a 'horse's ass in diamonds'. When they did make money, the doubting member presented his colleague with a gold cigarette case encrusted with diamonds shaped like a horse's backside with a ruby set right in the middle.

Perry signed the contract making him a professional on 9 November 1936. AP told newspapers around the globe, 'The world's outstanding amateur tennis player for the past three years quit simon-pure ranks cold for a salaried career.' At home, a British national said Perry's decision 'ends one of the greatest controversies concerning the plans of any famous British athlete in which his right to make such a move has been hotly debated'.

All the signatories to the contract met at Perry's lawyers, Donovan, Leisure, Newton & Lombard, on Wall Street. The deal was for a tour of North America with Perry committed from 5 January to 13 May 1937, the tour opening at Madison Square Garden on Wednesday 6 January. At the time, Hunter predicted Perry would make between $75,000 and $100,000, a figure that some observers regarded as optimistic given O'Brien's losses a few months earlier. Perry's account years later was that he was guaranteed $100,000 and ended up earning even more, but that the break-up of his first marriage meant he was not subsequently left with a great deal.

Vines was playing professional matches against Tilden in Japan at the time Perry agreed to the contract. It took a little while to track him down to where he was staying, and Perry related what happened when he made the long-distance call. Vines started by protesting at being woken at six in the morning but was immediately wide awake when Perry himself told him that he had signed away his amateur status. He agreed eagerly to the terms of the contract. Another of Perry's memories from the day of the signing was that on the way to a celebratory lunch he hesitated before crossing the street, only to be told by George Leisure not to worry because he was insured with Lloyds of London so everyone was looked after.

After lunch Perry packed his bags and caught a train to Los Angeles to spend Christmas with Helen Vinson at their home there. 'There is nothing more for me to win,' he said in a farewell to his amateur career. 'Why should I put myself up as a target for all these fellows? Tournament tennis is hard work with nothing to gain and everything to lose. From now on I am playing tennis for my health.' This last sentence was one of those Perry curiosities. Perhaps, having lived in London so long, health was rhyming slang for wealth.

Opinion in Britain again split in an entirely predictable way with the LTA president Sir Samuel Hoare summarising the organisation's attitude in a cable that asked, 'Why did you do it?' Perry was told he would lose his honorary membership of Wimbledon and the tie that went with it, which prompted him to make the wry observation 'After all the trouble they'd gone to presenting it to me.' Perry also said he received a letter from an official of the International Lawn Tennis Club of Great Britain telling him to never again wear the club sweater. 'I made sure he wouldn't have to worry about that – I sent a sleeve to him as a present,' Perry claimed.

At the LTA's annual meeting in December the mood was more conciliatory. Hoare, who chaired the meeting, was an MP and arrived straight from the Houses of Parliament, where he said in his opening remarks he had just witnessed 'the last act of a great tragedy' – a reference not to Perry but the abdication of Edward VIII. He then spoke about Perry's decision to turn professional, noting, 'He has abandoned – for reasons good or bad, into which none of us need enter – the amateur world of lawn tennis. Whether his decision is right or wrong, it is not for us to say, but it is for us to thank him for his services . . . and give him our best wishes for the future.' His words drew applause.

The LTA's official magazine spoke haughtily of Perry's decision 'to seek his fortune in the ranks of the exhibition player', but it did commend him for all the titles he had won and 'above all, his physical condition, which played so great part in his many successes'. *The Times* had no great objection to his decision to play for money but moaned about tennis generally becoming 'so grim and strenuous' that 'never again are we likely to find men leaving their offices and going down to Wimbledon to win the championship'.

Once more, the *Manchester Guardian* came closest to giving Perry unconditional support: 'His decision will almost certainly mean that Great Britain will lose the Davis Cup (and with it, in the minds of the gossips, a great deal of international prestige), but no fair-minded person will upbraid him. It is hard enough in all conscience for many of us to obtain jobs these days, and to object to a man's doing for money the one job he can do supremely well is curious conduct.'

A footnote from Australia provided evidence, hardly earth-shattering but revealing, of the global interest in Perry's new status and that its effect would be felt worldwide. The New South Wales LTA, who had been expecting him in Australia for the 1936–7 season, reported that they would lose £1,000 at the very least as a result of his absence from the state championships and would suffer a significant reduction in their cut from the gate money taken at the national event that followed.

At about the time Perry would have arrived in Australia had he stayed amateur he capitalised on his new professional status by signing up to a venture that gave him as much pleasure, if not the same financial rewards, as his later participation in the clothing industry. His tie-up with the Beverly Hills Tennis Club, a favourite meeting place of the stars, began a few weeks after he turned professional in November 1936, when he announced at a lunch that he was buying into the club. Later he was joined in the venture by Ellsworth Vines, the pair securing co-ownership with their earnings from the professional tours of 1937. They would retain an interest in the club until the 1950s.

The Beverly Hills club had existed since 1929. A co-founder, Larry Bachmann, wrote, 'There was a pertinent reason for starting the Club. At that time the only tennis club was the Los Angeles Tennis Club, which had a rule that excluded those in the film industry and Jews.' One of Bachmann's fellow founders was the former fourth-ranked US player Fred Alexander, who came from the so-called four hundred families – New York's social elite whose number was dictated by the capacity of Mrs Caroline Astor's ballroom.

All Alexander wanted to do was play tennis; Bachmann was about to start at university; while Milton Holmes, the third co-founder, was an actor. Each had his role: Alexander's to put up the money to buy the lots on North Maple Drive, where the club has been ever since; Bachmann's to persuade people to pay to join the club even though the negotiations to buy the land were not yet complete; and Holmes's to supervise construction and manage the club. 'I got some seventeen people to pay for joining a club that did not yet exist,' Bachmann said. 'I was successful not due to my salesmanship but because my father was a producer at Paramount. Among those I recruited were Ernest Pascal, Ralph Block, Edwin Knopf and Robert Montgomery.'

Even so, against the background of the Great Depression and the US economy's slow recovery from it, the club struggled to make a profit. Holmes, who took over from Bachmann as schmoozer-in-chief, was responsible for introducing Perry and Vines to the club, inviting them to practise there during the Pacific Southwest tournament. Eventually he had to go further and try to persuade them to buy into it – their names, foremost, and their money being the club's best hopes of pulling back from the brink of financial disaster. He succeeded first with Perry, whose enthusiasm for the project persuaded Vines to come aboard. As a close friend of Perry, Holmes stayed on as an associate and manager of the club.

Work on revamping the club began the day after Perry announced his involvement. This included rebuilding the clubhouse to the striking design of Millard Sheets, a young Californian artist who was the protégé of Dal Hatfield, an art dealer and club member. A swimming pool was dug out, at the expense of one of the six courts, and the new co-owners saw to it that the 'swimming members' of the club included a selection of pretty things prepared to hang around the pool while they awaited Tinseltown's more substantial rewards. This, according to Perry, helped business to boom, although the club's slightly expanded membership was still confined to the world of entertainment.

The club continued to be a haven for stars seeking refuge from their admirers – 'once they rub off their greasepaint and sally forth for exercise' – in an even more intimate environment once the refurbishment was finished. Without betraying any confidences, Perry reported that 'a lot of crazy things' went on at the club. The British contingent was particularly strong. It included Ronald Colman, David Niven, C. Aubrey Smith, an actor and former Test cricketer (one cap as captain in 1888) and Charlie Chaplin. Errol Flynn, the buccaneering Australian actor, was also a member of this group.

Perry loved all the glitz and glamour, and fitted effortlessly into a social scene markedly different from the one in which he had grown up. On 11 July 1937 he partnered Chaplin against Vines and Groucho Marx in a celebrity doubles, umpired by Fred Alexander, to mark the change in ownership of the club. As *Western Tennis* noted, 'The foursome would have cost producers a tidy fortune to lure onto stage or screen.' The match was knockabout stuff with the players at one point eating lunch on court after Groucho produced a picnic hamper and tablecloth. The spectacle ended with Groucho thinking about jumping the net before crawling underneath it to congratulate the British expats on their victory. The next day's headline in the *Los Angeles Times* read, 'Charlie Chaplin, Perry win screwy tennis match'. The doubles that followed was far more earnest, with Vines and Perry just managing to beat their old amateur foes Sidney Wood and Frank Shields. To avoid a wrathful response from the custodians of the amateur game, who kept a close eye on such things even in America, no admission fee was charged, which somehow made it all right for Wood and Shields to play against the pros.

In the end, Perry's matches at the Beverly Hill Tennis Club were as close as he got to playing regularly alongside the big names of Hollywood. At one stage his ambition was to do this on the silver screen as well, a dream that never quite turned to reality. Others, too, thought he might have a future as an actor. He certainly had the face, figure and poise to be a film idol, and by 1934, when he won Wimbledon for the first time to become as well known as any international sportsman, some of his friends in Hollywood suggested he should give the movies a go. The problem, as ever before he turned professional two years later, was whether he might compromise his amateur status, and the plan, initially, was to perpetrate another of those charades designed to avoid this happening. As a small first step, it was suggested he played just enough tennis to establish his identity in a film without either coaching or speaking.

The British press, always eager for Perry stories, picked up on these early moves to launch him in films. The *Daily Mail* quoted a conversation one of its reporters had with Perry shortly before he sailed from Southampton to America in August 1934. The newspaper said Perry had been asked to appear in a movie called *At Your*

Service, and the player confirmed an approach by an American film company. He added, though, that he was astonished by a rumour that he would play a part without being paid. He said he had referred the company to the LTA, and if they secured the association's sanction he might agree to appear in the film.

Although the LTA declined to give their permission, at their council meeting the following January they supported a doomed motion being put by Czechoslovakia to the international federation. This called on the federation to delete the rule specifically prohibiting a player from gaining advantage by 'Posing for or permitting the taking of lawn tennis action film pictures of himself'. The British delegate, R.J. McNair, seconded the motion, in the words of the minutes, 'entirely on a matter of principle. His main point was that as amateurs were allowed to write books in which illustrations appeared, there seemed to be no logical reason for exposing them to the forfeiture of their amateur status as soon as the photographs began to move in the film.'

The fact that the federation voted 42–41 in favour of the proposal at their meeting in Paris caused some confusion. In March *Time* magazine reported that the vote meant amateurs would now be allowed to appear in films but a letter in the following issue from A.H. Chapin Jr of the Racquet Publishing Co. Inc., New York City, corrected this. He pointed out that a two-thirds majority had been necessary to pass the proposal and 'thus Perry's dream of playing in tennis movies and defending the Davis Cup for England [*sic*] went up in smoke'. Maybe, but the smoke took a while to blow away completely.

At the time Perry was still under pressure from the LTA and his father not to turn professional, both parties being horrified by the prospect of his being barred from the Davis Cup and Wimbledon. Perry's dilemma was vividly captured by a comment piece, 'Money or Fame', in the *Manchester Guardian* in October 1934. The article described as a 'complication' Perry's desire to make more than just a name for himself from the movies while continuing to play tennis as an amateur.

The Hollywood magnates, while not unsympathetic to such histrionic aspirations, have laid it down that a Fred Perry as a film actor must play tennis, at any rate if he wishes to be a highly paid actor. Of course Perry might change his name, grow a moustache, and seek to 'make good' on merits other than lawn tennis. But double life for public men is no easy task. Look at it how you will, his dilemma is complex. After all, present glory is not future glory, but £20,000 is £20,000. Happily, this is the kind of dilemma with which few of us are faced.

The stakes rose even higher in November 1934 when Mary Lawson, now engaged to Perry for eight months, told the British press that her fiancé had received the offer of 'an amazing contract' worth considerably more than £20,000 from a leading Hollywood film studio. She would not know what work it involved until he contacted her again from abroad. The *Evening Standard* thought Perry should claim the prize: 'Soon Fred Perry, Britain's number one player, will be travelling homewards from Australia, by way of Hollywood, where a £40,000 film offer is his to accept or reject. Why should he not accept and remain an amateur?' The question was rhetorical – and wishful thinking. The paper knew perfectly well why not.

The offer to which Lawson and the *Evening Standard* referred was almost certainly from RKO, the film production company renowned in the 1930s for its hit musicals. Much later, Perry wrote that RKO wanted him to sign a contract for two movies a year at $50,000 a picture – in which he would not be expected to play tennis. This was a slightly different attempt to separate his sporting life from his would-be alternative career as an actor and so avoid being seen as a shamateur, a word whose coinage in the late nineteenth century showed that Perry was treading where others had been before. Perry's putative link-up with RKO was driven by his friendship with Pandro S. Berman, the film company's supervising producer. Things went as far as a screen test in March 1935 with a view to Perry's possible appearance in *Top Hat*, a movie made famous by the dancing of Fred Astaire and Ginger Rogers. It was a month later that Perry and Lawson agreed to break off their engagement. For one thing he was determined to keep going back to America to try to break in to films while she did not want to abandon her career in Britain.

Perry also seems to have at least explored getting into films via the close friendship he was developing with Marlene Dietrich, an attachment that may have been another reason for his parting from Lawson. A more cynical interpretation would be to turn things round and surmise that the relationship with Dietrich was the consequence of his desire to be a film star. He had met Dietrich in Los Angeles, and the letter he sent to her from Australia in December 1934, in which he wrote how he longed to be back in LA, also included the leading question 'How would I look playing in a picture with the great Marlene Dietrich?' Even Perry seemed to recognise the brazenness of this suggestion and continued coyly, 'Do you think it would work or would I be an absolute flop? Maybe we could try it one of these fine days – and then maybe we could not!' In any event, nothing ever came of it.

Hollywood showed as much interest in Perry's attempts to break into acting as the British press. With his return to Los Angeles due in September 1935, Edwin Schallert, who wrote about the toings and froings of the stars for the *Los Angeles Times*, reminded his readers what had been happening.

Maybe now that Fred Perry is returning to the Coast his interrupted movie career – interrupted as a matter of fact before it was ever started – will resume again. It may be recalled that he was reported just about to sign a contract with RKO last spring, and then something happened. It was a question of whether a threat of a broken engagement with Lawson or Perry's desire to retain his amateur standing was the stronger factor in his refusal to enter into the movie agreement. Anyway, he quit town very suddenly, leaving the matter in the air.

It is understood that the RKO offer is still open. Perry's recent defeat in the singles in America [he lost to Wilmer Allison in the US Championships semi-final] might cause him to change his mind about continuing his tennis playing. Also, his marriage to Helen Vinson has altered romantic interferences, if any existed. Friends of Perry believe that he will now enter pictures. He is arriving here Tuesday.

In the end Sam Perry and the LTA, whose president Sir Samuel Hoare rang Perry from London to discuss the matter, had their way, and the RKO offer eventually lapsed. Perry agreed to suspend his film ambitions, against the advice of friends in America, because he understood those whom he supposed had his best interests at heart would work hard to find a compromise. He absolved his father of blame that this never happened on the grounds that he had done his best to prod the LTA into action. He felt less charitable about Hoare, whom he suspected had bluffed him out of making his film debut. His dislike of Hoare intensified when it was reported to him that the Harrow-educated Tory MP for Chelsea had remarked that Fred Perry 'isn't one of us'. Years later Perry accepted some responsibility for the awkward relations between him and the hierarchy at the LTA, saying that while the association never tried to understand him he did not go out of his way to understand them.

At the time, very possibly on grounds of expediency, Perry remained capable of being complimentary about the association. On his voyage back to England from the US in April 1935, when he still hoped the LTA would support his aspirations to act, Perry told a reporter who boarded the RMS *Berengaria* at Cherbourg, 'The LTA have been very good to me and the only way I can give them anything in return is by my wholehearted support in their efforts to keep Britain on the top of the world of lawn tennis.'

Perry had to wait until 1937 before fulfilling what he called his biggest unrealised ambition, when he appeared in a short film about his tennis for MGM. It was hardly the box-office blockbuster he would have hoped for and did not lead to his being offered stellar roles. He signed the contract two weeks after turning professional in November 1936. The *Los Angeles Times* described the picture as a Pete Smith one-reeler – Smith was a Hollywood producer well known for his so-called shorts – and added the likelihood was that more would follow. Despite the low-key nature of the film, its star was considered big enough for the signing ceremony to be worthy of a media presence and Perry was quoted as saying as he put his name to the contract, 'My wife Helen Vinson said that she would never marry an actor. She never counted on this.' British newspapers showed some interest in the film, one reporting that it was designed to show Perry's style of play. It added, 'Much of it will be in slow motion, so that amateurs may be able to study his strokes, but its aim will be to entertain as well as to instruct.'

Smith's speciality was 'comedy documentaries' and his desire to include some entertaining stunts led to the film taking much longer to shoot than anyone expected. He came up with a sequence in which Perry demonstrated the accuracy of his serve by directing it at an old-fashioned car horn that would honk when he hit it. Perry managed this almost straightaway but there was a blemish on the film and it took him several more hours before he could do it again.

Perry's only other skirmish with showbiz came as a result of his love of the big-band sound. In England he would spend time with the celebrated band leader Jack Hylton. He liked listening to Hylton's ensemble when depressed by an unexpected defeat, the music helping to soothe away his unhappiness. In Hollywood he was approached by a local band which had lost its leader with the idea that the group should rebrand under the name Fred Perry and his Racketeers. Perry would be paid for pretending to conduct while the set would be tennis-themed with rackets for music stands and the microphone heads cocooned in tennis balls. The idea went the way of most hare-brained schemes.

10

The great road show

None of those involved in the Ellsworth Vines–Fred Perry tour of 1937, in which Vines defended his professional title, could have hoped for a better public response to the opening match. Tickets went on sale across New York and receipts soon passed the record $30,800 taken for the first Vines–Tilden match at Madison Square Garden in 1934, and kept on rising almost to double that figure.

The press played its part in stoking up interest by publishing interviews and signed columns. Perry wrote a syndicated piece that was a curious mixture of the patronising and homespun philosophising. He compared Vines the professional to Mr Vines the amateur and concluded:

> Personally, I like him much better as plain Vines rather than 'Mr'. Since becoming a professional and earning some real money, so as to take care of himself and his family, he has become a much more interesting person. Plain Vines has shed all his shyness. He seems to have realised that possession of money makes it possible for him to hold his head up and to meet people on an equal basis . . . He feels that he means something and that the name of Ellsworth Vines is something that can stand on its own against the world . . . We shall be together a great deal in the next five months, and I am looking forward with pleasure to those months.

In an interview with the *New York Times* Vines said that although he was favourite to win the series against Perry, whom he had beaten in three of their four matches as amateurs, he had lost to Perry the last time they met, in the Davis Cup tie in Paris in 1933. 'I know what I'm up against,' Vines said. 'But I'll say now that if I lose, I'll be a pretty disappointed guy. You bet. You know, in this game it's a matter of dollars and cents. Nobody wants to pay to see a loser. And if I get a good walloping that would be the end of old boy Vinesy as a tennis attraction at the gate. So it's up to me to win and keep winning or look for another job.'

When the interviewer suggested he had a good job he would probably hate to lose, Vines agreed but said there were other things to consider. Such as? 'Well, did you ever figure that a fellow might get tired?' Vines replied. 'I've been playing tennis for about fourteen years now – ten as an amateur, four as a professional. Travel, travel, travel. I've been to Australia, China, Japan – to Europe six times. The first time it was great – and the second, too. But the sixth time wasn't so hot. I know all the big cities in this country and I've played in towns so small that it was a tight fit to get a full-size tennis court in.'

This gave a hint of how professional tours had evolved into road shows that swept across North America, through places big and small, with a canvas court rolled out wherever there was an area big enough for it and for seating the spectators. Perry recalled that the court was put down on all manner of surfaces, on one occasion directly onto ice, which meant if you stepped off the canvas you were likely to keep on going. More usually when matches were played at ice rinks, boards would be put down first, but these did not stop the cold numbing the players' lower limbs and making the tennis balls hopelessly heavy. At Asbury Park, New Jersey, where there was no way of securing the canvas court, the lines were marked straight onto a terrazzo floor that was so fast Vines' serve endangered not only Perry but people in the crowd, as a female spectator who took a smack in the eye found out.

Perry and Vines always supervised the court being marked out when it was painted straight onto a surface, which was usually when the area was too small for the canvas (so small on one occasion that Perry remembered the peculiar experience of pushing off from a wall a short distance behind him). Occasionally the baseline had to be moved forward a few inches to allow the players enough room for their backswing. Vines always insisted the service line stayed the correct distance from the net so that his big serve was not penalised. On just one occasion Perry managed to outsmart him. In El Paso on the Mexican border he returned to the venue after the court had been marked out and for a modest bribe had the service line redrawn three inches closer to the net than it should have been. Perry won easily with Vines serving a succession of faults. It was forty years before he owned up to Vines what he had done.

All this was very different from the start of the first Vines v. Perry tour in January 1937. Madison Square Garden was one of the great indoor sporting arenas of the world with plenty of room for the temporary court and the crowd of 17,630, the biggest gathering ever for a tennis match. Stars from the world of entertainment, socialites and regular tennis fans snapped up the tickets to see, as one writer put it, 'California's long, ambling Ellsworth Vines, world's ablest professional since 1933, against England's sleek, light-footed Frederick John Perry, world's ablest amateur since 1933'. Another saw the match-up as the elongated larruper of tennis balls against Fiery Fred full of the St-George-for-Merrie-England spirit and suggested that the promoters, Hunter and Voshell, should gallop up to Vines in Paul Revere costume and shout, 'Up! Up! The British are coming!' Vines said there was no need because he was wide awake. 'There are no subtleties to my game,' he added. 'I just bang away.'

The build-up continued on the night itself. So that the match started promptly at the advertised time, the curtain-raiser between the Americans George Lott and Bruce Barnes was stopped in the second set with Lott declared the winner by the unusual score of 6–2 5–5. The lights dimmed and, as a voice announced 'The challenger, Frederick J. Perry, from London, England', a spotlight picked him out entering from the north-west corner of the arena looking as spruce and meticulously primed for combat as he had for his first Wimbledon final on that July afternoon in 1934.

A far more willing accomplice to the theatrical stuff than Vines, Perry then stood to attention while a band played 'God Save the King' and the Union flag was raised to the vaulted ceiling. Perry said he sensed the emotion in the crowd and felt that Vines displayed signs of nervousness when it came to his turn to be heralded by the sounds of 'Star-Spangled Banner' while the Stars and Stripes was hoisted aloft.

Reports of what followed describe a match that did not live up to all the hoopla, possibly because both men had heavy colds but felt duty bound to play, dead or alive. One commentator quipped that the combatants played hot-and-cold tennis because Perry had a cold and Vines had a fever, his temperature topping 102 degrees. While Vines was thought to be the sicker, Perry was reckoned to have been at a disadvantage playing on a canvas court for the first time.

American newspapers reported the match under banner headlines. The widely used Associated Press account made much of Vines' many mistakes. 'Vines' best shot was into the net,' it said. Someone else wrote that Vines 'netted more than a deep-sea fisherman on the Newfoundland Banks'. Allison Danzig, New York's leading tennis writer, put it more eloquently: 'Vines could not control his wrathful speed and was lost in an unescapable morass of errors.' Perry won 7–5 3–6 6–3 6–4 but no one construed it as an early knockout by Fiery Fred, particularly given Vines' state of health.

What the match did establish beyond doubt was the tour's financial viability. With tickets priced from $1.10 to $9.90, the gross takings from the record crowd were $58,119.50. The taxman took a third of this and would remain keenly interested in the tour right the way through. He was particularly vigilant where Perry was concerned.

Not yet a naturalised American, Perry was closely monitored in case he tried to take money out of the country. So, just before the tour crossed the border into Canada, as it did from time to time, the taxman would pop up with his hand held out. In his autobiography Perry said that on these occasions the revenue authorities knew the amount of the gate receipts before the end of the match, and when he returned to the dressing room he was asked for a cheque to cover his dues.

For the January opening night in New York Perry received just over $13,000 and Vines just over $5,000, a split amicably agreed beforehand that reflected the importance of having the previous year's amateur champion as part of the venture. Hunter and Voshell trousered about $15,000.

From now until May, Perry and Vines – together with Lott and Barnes, who played preliminary singles and made up the numbers in doubles – showed remarkable stamina as travellers and tennis players. Their itinerary involved matches played on an almost nightly basis, with journeys by car or train, many of several hundred miles, in between. It is hard to reconcile this with Jack Kramer's comment that Perry 'never gave a damn about professional tennis', although it was probably aimed at Perry's attitude later on, particularly after he suffered a bad injury in 1941.

The 1937 tour was subject to a certain amount of on-the-hoof planning. Some reports before it started said there would be forty matches. In the end Perry and Vines played each other more than sixty times – and Perry also fitted in a seven-match mini-series against Tilden, returning to Madison Square Garden in late March for the opener.

Tilden, now forty-four, was reckoned to have made half a million dollars in his six years as a professional, playing an average of 200 matches a year. The New York public did not show quite the same interest as they had for the Perry–Vines match at the start of the year, but still 15,132 paid $30,433 to be there and see Perry win the first formal contest between the two of them in four sets. Hardly surprisingly, given the age difference, Perry was far too strong and athletic for Tilden.

Grantland Rice, one of the most celebrated American sports-writers of the first half of the twentieth century, had helped to make heroes of many of the great sporting figures of the 1920s, men such as the heavyweight boxer Jack Dempsey, baseball's Babe Ruth, the golfer Bobby Jones and Tilden, whom he lionised when he was indisputably the world's best tennis player. When Tilden lost to Perry in New York, Rice wrote that the defeat marked 'the end of the Golden Era of sports'. Tilden did in fact go on to win three of the seven matches but Perry was almost certainly taking on too much at this time, alternating between playing Vines on the main tour and Tilden.

Perry's account of the first Vines tour reads like the script of a classic road movie. The two men would finish matches late at night and then either jump into a car, usually Vines' enormous Buick, to drive hundreds of miles, or run for a train, still in sweaty tennis gear and without having eaten. If the journey was by train, at least there was a chance for both of them to nap before they arrived at the next venue in time to publicise their visit by talking to the local newspapers over breakfast. Then it was off to bed before doing the rounds of radio stations in the late afternoon to give their match one last plug. Often they would head off in different directions to satisfy rival stations. A Vines letter home mid-tour from Columbus, Ohio, captures a little of how hectic it was: 'Last night we got a 3.25 a.m. train and changed at Pittsburgh at 2 this afternoon. We arrived at 7 p.m., ate, shaved, and played. Tomorrow I have to make a store appearance at 12 and we then get a 1.30 train to Chicago. I believe I'll stay in town instead of Bill's place. I'd only drink plenty and stay up late.'

Small dramas occurred along the way to enliven the plot. Tilden occasionally joined the tour and, according to Perry, was a marginally scarier driver than Vines. Perry recalled the time he was driving at 80 mph and Tilden flew past him. Being a control freak, Tilden liked to reach the venue before anyone else so that he could organise the evening's schedule. On this occasion, though, his plans went awry when ten miles down the road he lost control and ended up with his car on its roof in the middle of a field. He emerged unhurt and indignant about the unmarked curve in the road. To everyone else, Perry said, the road appeared to be gun-barrel straight.

Vines also drove almost as fast as he hit a serve, and between Chicago and Milwaukee wanted to race a police car to the Illinois–Wisconsin state border after he jumped a stop sign. Perry persuaded him to pull over only for Vines to take issue with the officer's suggestion that the two tennis stars make a small donation to the police benevolent fund and the incident would be forgotten. The officer's unholstered gun and Perry's earnest counselling finally convinced Vines that the sensible thing to do would be to pay up.

Many years later Perry asserted that he and Vines never exchanged an angry word, which should probably be translated as, 'Considering we were such different characters and spent so much time together, we got on remarkably well.' Tension between the players boiled over in public on at least one occasion. During a fractious doubles match in Hartford, Connecticut the feisty extrovert George Lott shaped to take a swing at Perry but was stopped from doing so by Barnes, who grabbed his arm. The fracas took place right in front of the umpire's chair. Lott snarled at Perry, 'One of these days I'll punch you in the nose – and I guess I'll do it today.' A report of the incident by a news agency said that it was either an Anglo-American feud or a publicity stunt, but that the other players had said it was for real. 'We've been together so long we get on one another's nerves,' Lott said. During the episode Vines was heard to call Perry by his surname, which was a clear indication of his exasperation with a man whom, in public at least, he called Fred. The players had been due to travel together by car to the next venue, but Perry told the agency he was going by train. Perry seems to have patched things up better with Lott, who became a close friend, than he did with Vines.

More often, Lott contented himself with baiting Tilden, whose equilibrium was easily disturbed. Lott would sit in the crowd and shout out encouragement, but would refer to him as Tillie, which he knew riled Tilden. It all became too much for Tilden on one occasion. Before the start of a doubles match he summoned Lott to the net and told him that the crowd of several thousands expected gentlemanly behaviour from the players and he was behaving like a bum. He then threatened to break his racket over Lott's head if he did not show better manners.

A reliable match-by-match record of the Vines–Perry tour of 1937 does not exist. Perry opened a 3–0 lead when he thrashed Vines in straight sets in front of a crowd of 12,602 in Chicago, at which point Vines was admitted to hospital still suffering from the fever that had affected him on the first night of the tour and now with tonsillitis as well. The *Chicago Tribune* said that the fans who paid to watch had been swindled, which failed to get them their money back, and the nearest thing to an apology was an admission by Vines that he should not have played any of the first three matches. Very soon, though, he would rise from his sickbed restored to his old self.

Five days after leaving hospital he had levelled the series at 3–3

Perry's backhand was continually tested as opponents tried to keep the ball
from his feared forehand.

Forest Hills is packed for
the 1936 US final in which
Perry beat Don Budge.

Perry holds the US singles
trophy after winning it for keeps
with his third victory in 1936.

Perry (right) with Groucho Marx (seated), Charlie Chaplin and Ellsworth Vines before their doubles match to mark the reopening of the Beverly Hills Tennis Club, in which Perry and Vines became partners.

Stars turn out to watch Perry: Laurence Olivier, Vivien Leigh and Claire Trevor.

Perry and Bette Davis
share a table for two
at the Trocadero Club
in Los Angeles.

Perry with his first wife,
the film actress
Helen Vinson.

Perry (right) and Don Budge promote their 1939 professional tour with an unusual game of tennis at the Racquet Club in New York.

Don Budge (left), Perry, Bobby Riggs and Frank Kovacs jump the net at the Brooklyn Heights Casino in a photo shoot before their professional matches in 1941.

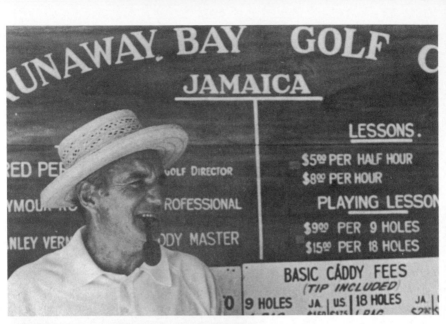

Fed up with coaching tennis, Perry had the golf concession at the Runaway Bay resort, Jamaica, in the 1960s.

Perry with Bobby, his fourth wife, to whom he was married for more than forty years.

David Wynne's statue of Perry at Wimbledon, which was unveiled by the Duke of Kent in 1984.

F. J. PERRY
WIMBLEDON CHAMPION
1934 1935 AND 1936

FRED
1909
1995

FRED PERRY

Perry had wanted the sportswear logo to be a pipe, in recognition of his smoking habit, but was persuaded the now widely recognised laurel wreath might be better.

Perry acknowledges the crowd at Wimbledon in 1993.

after winning in Pittsburgh, Detroit and Boston. The crowd at the Boston Garden was nearly 10,000 and saw one of the best matches of the tour, with Perry having a match point in the fourth set before Vines won 7–5 in the fifth. From this point on, neither player looked likely to establish a substantial advantage. Perry regained the lead 5–3 before Vines pulled ahead 7–5 and told his wife in a letter, 'It was swell hearing from you again dearest, and to show it I went out and licked Perry for the fourth consecutive time.' By the end of February Perry was in front 13–12; after forty matches they were dead level; and when they returned to play at Madison Square Garden in early May Vines led 28–27. Inevitably, this started mutterings that they were colluding to keep the public interested.

Perry was adamant that no fixing took place, and the one time they might have fiddled the outcome their competitive instincts stopped it happening. Before this particular match they decided that whoever won a properly contested first set would be allowed to win the second set and the match. 'For us it was as easy to hit the ball two inches out as two inches in,' Perry said. The reason for the intrigue was that they faced a 600-mile journey the next day, and the last thing they needed was to be battering away at each other late into the night. Perry won the first set, but at the point in the second when it was time for Vines to start missing he upped his game, apparently not finding it as easy to hit the ball wide or long as Perry made out. Vines won the second set, and although he apologised and proposed the first to drop serve in the third set should let the other go on to win, Perry was so incensed that he declined this arrangement. The marathon decider, won by Perry, ended at about midnight.

John Kieran, in the *New York Times*, gave the players the benefit of the doubt, making the point, 'they couldn't have done it much neater if they had plotted it on paper and then bisected the program with the aid of a sharp pencil and a T-square'. Kieran then applied a bit of old-school thinking in absolving Vines and Perry of fixing matches, declaring that just as the amateurs did the best they could, 'the same thing holds true in the post-graduate or professional ranks' and that Vines 'really wanted to give dashing Fred Perry a dusting on the tour'. When a reader sent a letter accusing the press of wanting to malign the players whatever happened, the *NYT* published it together with a sniffy put-down from the editor. The reader's complaint was that while the papers cried 'Fix!' because the results were so close, they would have derided the players as dumb bunnies if they had allowed the score to become one-sided. The editor retorted that the *NYT* had never suggested the results of the Vines–Perry matches were contrived 'nor is there any inclination to identify honesty as stupidity in professional games'. Even if Perry and Vines had done a little tweaking here and there, there did not seem much of an appetite on the media's part to go looking for it.

Ray Bowers, in *Forgotten Victories: A History of Pro Tennis*, applied what he called rough statistical tests to the question of whether there was any skulduggery. The results are interesting even if the science is inexact. Perry and Vines shared the first two sets thirty-seven times in their sixty-one matches in North America, well above the 50 per cent that Bowers gave as the average number of times two evenly matched players reached one set all. He also showed that when Vines was ahead by two matches or more, his win–loss record was 8–17 while at other times it was 24–12. Bowers concluded that the results of the tests were eyebrow-raising but within the limits of plausibility, particularly as it was impossible to measure mental factors such as the stimulation that being behind could give a player. 'Our suspicions therefore remain unproven,' Bowers said, 'but they remain.'

Jack Kramer, never a wholehearted admirer of Perry, came closest to stating publicly that some manipulating went on. He wrote in his book *The Game* that the promoter Jack Harris 'always told me that Elly [Vines] carried Fred to make things look close, and sell more tickets. But whenever I've asked Elly to admit that, he'd change the subject.' On the other hand, Vines, in the many letters he wrote to his wife during this tour, did not so much as hint that he waved Perry through on occasions, and he confided most things to her. Lines such as 'I thought I might get ahead of Perry last night, but I pooped out when I had the lead' and 'I beat Perry last night 6–2 8–6. Got a few let-cord shots at the right time so now I lead' suggest he was doing his best.

The match between Perry and Vines in New York on 3 May was Perry's third at Madison Square Garden since the start of the year.

The crowd this time was 6,812, much smaller than the record turnout for the tour opener in January when he had beaten Vines in four sets and well down, too, on the gathering to watch him play Tilden in March. Obviously the tour had lost some of its novelty, and the fact that Perry and Vines had just played one another in nearby Brooklyn and White Plains also contributed to the waning interest. Still, over his three matches, Perry had helped to attract close to 40,000 people to the Garden, a figure that translated into more than $100,000 in gate money.

The smallest of the three crowds saw the best match. Perry, pinning his rival back with deep groundstrokes, opened up a 4–1 lead in the first set and had a point to win it in the tenth game. He failed to do so and Vines' big serve – he was credited with twenty aces – saw him through in straight sets. The win opened his lead to 29–27 with five matches to play in the last ten days of the tour.

Vines would stay in front, winning the tour finale in Scranton on 12 May to take the series 32–29 (88–86 in sets), but in many respects Perry was the victor. He had surprised a doubting American press and public by winning far more often than they thought he would and – by prior arrangement, granted – he banked much more money from the gross receipts of $412,181 (about £80,000). John Kieran even reckoned Perry had established himself as a bigger attraction.

It has been demonstrated that Vines and Perry are about evenly matched, but Vines has been around a long while. Perry is the fresher figure, the bigger lure if other things, such as strokes and strategy, are equal, which they seem to be. For another thing . . . the dashing Britisher is really a crowd-pleaser, too. He carries a lot of colour on and off the court. But 'Old Boy Vinesy' is, as he modestly says himself, just a quiet country boy at heart and a tennis player by rare good luck.

Kieran thought, incorrectly, as it turned out, that Vines might have had enough after playing for four years as a professional. With plenty of money tucked away by now, he might decide to go off to indulge his passion for golf.

★　　★　　★

There was never any question of this happening immediately because Vines was committed to playing Perry in Britain. In early March Vines had told his wife, 'Everything is pretty definitely settled for England. Perry and I plan to sail on the *Europa* May 15 and come back on the *Queen Mary* June 16. We are guaranteed £5,000 [split between them] or about $24,000 at the present exchange rate.' Two days later he made clear his true feelings about the trip: 'Our contracts with Wembley are all settled now so I'll be going over there in May. Sure hate to, but there's too much money in it to pass up.' He wrote this soon after Sir Arthur Elvin, a friend of Perry, had sent a representative from England to the US to negotiate the participation of professional tennis's two principal players in a three-match series in London that would be grandly called the King George VI Coronation Cup. The matches would be played at the end of May at the Empire Pool and Sports Arena – later renamed Wembley Arena – a venue with which Vines was familiar. Its construction had been championed by Elvin and it was used first of all for the 1934 Empire Games swimming events. At the end of that year it also staged the first World's Invitation Men's Professional Lawn Tennis Championships, establishing it as Britain's first site for regular international tournaments for pros. Vines took part and was sufficiently impressed by winning, from an entry that also included Tilden and Dan Maskell, to tell his wife, 'Well I'm writing to you today as the new World's Indoor Champion.'

Perry and Vines, together with the rest of the troupe, sailed for England as soon as the 1937 North American tour was over. SS *Europa* was a German-built liner that could cross the Atlantic in five days. Vines, though, was more concerned with the people it was carrying. In a letter home headed 'Out to Sea Sailing to Europe' he sounded mainly downcast although there was a note of levity from the normally taciturn Californian: 'I miss you so much, and of course this boat is like all the other German boats, no young people at all. At least no good-looking ones, so guess I'll have to import a few American chorus girls or so when I next go abroad.'

A welcoming party that included tennis writers from British national newspapers was waiting when the *Europa* docked at Plymouth at 5.30 a.m. on 18 May. Players, press and family friends all then travelled together to London, where their reception indicated that for the first time in Britain professional tennis matches were stirring up interest. 'At the station we were mobbed by photographers and people wanting autographs,' Vines said. 'Some rush.' He noted, too, that the decorations put out a week earlier for the coronation of the new monarch, the event that gave its name to the trophy Vines and Perry were about to contest, 'are still up, but sort of bedraggled'.

Despite the generous reception, they would find the British divided over how to respond to tennis played by a cast of full-time professional players that for the first time included a well-known Englishman. On the one hand, the custodians of the amateur game stood fast against what they regarded as a group of outlaws, instructing clubs to have nothing to do with them. Even Perry's own club, Chiswick Park, acting under orders from the LTA, ended his member-ship, although Perry said the letter he received from the club was entirely friendly and invited him to pay visits whenever he wanted. This reflected the attitude of the public at large. They showed consid-erable interest in watching the former and reigning Wimbledon champions compete for something more than shopping vouchers worth a few quid.

Perry's first performances in his native land since joining the pros were not with a racket in his hand but as a public speaker. He was good at this, accomplished and wry, but on this occasion a display ad in the national press announced that his series of talks in the private theatre of the Harrods store in Knightsbridge promised some-thing more – they would be 'thrilling and exclusive'.

In the lecture hall and beyond, Perry gave an upbeat assessment of his first five months as a professional. He took to referring to himself as 'a partner in that very rich firm of Perry and Perry, Ltd.', but asked, as he was frequently, to confirm that he had already made £20,000, he confined himself to a smile. 'All I will say is that my tour with Vines has been very successful,' he said. 'My lawyer might be able to tell you more.' Perry was even bashful about confirming any figures to his friend the tennis writer Bruce Harris, who also asked whether it was true he would clear £4,000 from his visit to England.

Vines was far more forthcoming on financial matters, but only in the privacy of family correspondence, whose contents were not then available. As well as disclosing his guarantee for the visit to Britain, he grumbled about the UK taxman, who was as quickly onto his earnings as the American revenue had been onto Perry's. 'I have just heard from the income tax people and it looks like I'm going to have to leave about £500 to £600 here out of my £2,500, which means I'll be coming home with a lot less than expected. Probably with my earnings at Dublin I'll be back with about $11,500 only. Boy do they stick you.' In a letter written from London, he also griped about the cost of living: 'Everything is very expensive over here now. I have to pay $7.50 per day for this room and my bill for nearly eleven days is nearly $100. Boy I'm glad I'm leaving here on Thursday for other parts.'

Perry's first match as a professional in Britain took place on Tuesday 25 May 1937. Boards placed over the swimming pool transformed the vast indoor arena, a short distance from Wembley Stadium, into a tennis hall with a court that was lightning fast. Vines won the first contest in five sets, Perry giving a performance that fell short of what E.J. Sampson, of the *Manchester Guardian*, had expected:

> The incentive, at any rate, was there, but that need to show his class was absent. That he was fit to look at was certain; his clear eyes and healthy tan were eloquent. One might have expected to see him reduced to skin and bones, realising the strenuous work of the last five months, which often involved playing night after night at places hundreds of miles apart not in the open air but in covered courts. This professional game as Perry and Vines play it is certainly a young man's game. Perry during the day wears dark glasses to save his eyes for the evening's play.

Perry himself had said, 'Fred Perry, the professional, could beat F.J. Perry, Esq., the amateur, three sets to love quite comfortably', and Sampson saw evidence of this the next night, when 'the great Perry was on view, keen and keyed up, and evidently enjoying the fast and furious pace'. He won this time in four sets, and then in front of a crowd of 8,000 was successful again in straight sets, 12–10 in the third, to win the Coronation Cup 2–1.

The fact that crowds of several thousands turned up for each of the Wembley matches still failed to persuade the LTA to endorse the tour; on the contrary, they continued to do their best to stymie it. Even Edgbaston, the prestigious club in Birmingham, could not push the LTA into allowing them to stage a Perry–Vines contest, which must have severely tested Perry's resolve not to criticise openly the association. 'My contract is with Wembley Stadium and when and where provincial matches are played makes no difference,' he said. 'At the same time, if permission has been refused to Edgbaston it is a pity because I think Vines and I could have done some good to the game by playing there.'

On another occasion Perry said it would have been a popular step to let him and Vines play at LTA-affiliated clubs. 'Presumably Vines and I play tennis well,' he said, 'and there are dozens of places in England that never even see good tennis. The good amateurs never go there. If we two had played, not in only three provincial towns, but in twenty or thirty, what a flare-up of interest would have been aroused in the game.' The LTA even snubbed Perry's indirect approach to help the Davis Cup team prepare for the defence of the trophy in 1937, when Britain failed to retain the title that they had won, mainly through Perry's efforts, for the previous four years. Although Perry said that throughout European tennis 'pro was still a dirty word', across the Channel Henri Cochet, who had turned professional some time before Perry, was busily helping to prepare France's team. While the very thought of Perry so much as setting foot on Centre Court at Wimbledon would have induced a collective attack of LTA apoplexy, the French sanctioned Cochet to play an exhibition match against an amateur on the principal court at Roland-Garros.

There was a loophole in the rules of tennis's international body that the LTA might have exploited. This was an italicised footnote that said national associations could allow professional matches where they 'considered them to be necessary to the development of the game in their countries'. The LTA refusal to take advantage of this led to Perry's friend Bruce Harris ridiculing them in print. 'In other words Ruritania, where tennis is little known, may arrange such matches as a means of introducing the game there,' Harris wrote.

'Hence Cochet, I believe, was allowed to play exhibitions with amateurs in Siam. But Rochdale and Heckmondwike [in West Yorkshire], and Greenock and Elgin have not many more opportunities than Ruritania and Siam of seeing first-class lawn tennis. They [the LTA] need "waking up" in a lawn tennis sense.'

Perry and Vines managed to play just seven times in Britain, including the Wembley matches, Perry coming out on top 4–3. On two occasions they were indebted to the hospitality of football clubs, who had a relatively long history of accommodating paid sportsmen. The grass pitches were not smooth enough for tennis and so Perry's old school chum Bernard Sunley came to their aid. Perry went as far as to say the whole enterprise would have been in trouble without Sunley. The founder of the building company commissioned the making of a transportable wooden court with twenty-one-foot runbacks behind the baselines and margins of fifteen feet down each side. Sunley even provided a van and two men to pack up and drive the court to the outdoor venues.

It was driven first to Bournemouth, a town in which Perry was popular after all those victories as an amateur in the British Hard Court Championships. With the West Hants out of bounds, the wooden court was laid out at Dean Court, the ground of Bournemouth and Boscombe Athletic Football Club, and it worked surprisingly well. A crowd of 4,200 watched in bright early-summer sunshine as Vines won in four sets. Bournemouth also provided an opportunity for Vines to fit in one of his many rounds of golf during the 1937 visit to Britain. 'I have been playing golf almost every day with someone or other,' he noted after his Bournemouth round. 'We played a swell course and I shot 78. A couple of Slazenger directors accompanied us. Perry was terrible.'

They then travelled to Scotland, where they played on two successive nights at the Kelvin Hall, Glasgow, and each won a match. Vines was struck by the shipbuilding yards on the Clyde, describing as 'grand' the work being done on the *Queen Mary*'s sister ship, but enthused about little else. 'Everything closes at 10.30 so I just go to bed,' he told his wife.

On the way south they played a match at Anfield, the Liverpool FC football ground. This was just across the Mersey from Wallasey, where for two years Perry had lived during the First World War. Two decades on he fitted in a return visit at which he was feted by civic dignitaries, and the once-callow schoolboy who was now a soigné figure of international renown also visited his old junior school accompanied by Helen Vinson, who was in England filming. Bob Leach was playground prefect when the couple arrived in a Bentley. 'I had the task of keeping the lads away from Miss Vinson. She asked me what I did. I said something stupid, so she lit a cigarette and ignored me. But I didn't tell the others that. I said we'd had an interesting chat about Hollywood and they told me I was a jammy so-and-so.'

At Anfield Sunley's prefab court was set up at the Kop end, and a crowd of 10,000 turned out. A downpour delayed the start and club officials found some old football jerseys to help with the mopping-up before Perry beat Vines in four sets. They finished up with a couple of matches in Dublin, both of which Perry won, before returning to the US in mid-June. In all, in North America, Britain and Ireland, Perry and Vines played seventy singles matches and each won thirty-five.

Perry would never again play in Europe as an athlete in his prime. He was in his late thirties when he next crossed the Atlantic, a decade later – still a highly effective player but his powers diminished by a serious injury as well as age. Partly because of the effects of this injury, 1937 would be the high point of Perry's professional career, despite the difficulties encountered in the United Kingdom. The newness of it all could never be replicated, while the sheer exhaustion that he felt after travelling and playing continually for six months would stay with him as a reminder of what an exacting way of earning a living it was – and as a discouragement to doing it again too often.

Things were considerably different in 1938. Perry and Vines bought a stake in the tour, which was now managed by the impresario Jack Harris, and the itinerary was arranged partly to satisfy Vines' increasing infatuation with golf, for which he would eventually forsake tennis. He described golf as 'a very fine game for very many reasons – two of which are you don't have to run and you don't have to hit any backhands'. For a time the tour even followed the golf circuit through the southern states because Vines was set on trying to qualify for some events. He practised his golf almost as assiduously as he did his tennis. Perry remembered one occasion when Vines made him the target for his putting by getting him to stand with his heels together and toes apart on a snow-covered platform in Seattle. It was partly because of Vines' passion that Perry himself developed more than a passing interest in golf. He would eventually achieve a three handicap and turn to golf management at Runaway Bay.

The tour opened at the Pan-Pacific Auditorium in Los Angeles on 11 January 1938, when 'every motion-picture star of any prominence whatsoever' joined a crowd of more than 7,000 to watch a mediocre but exciting contest that Vines won in five sets. After six matches Vines was ahead 4–2; Perry levelled at 5–5, but after this Vines pulled away. At times Perry could not hide his frustration, which had almost certainly taken root on the 1937 tour, at what he felt was the advantage handed to Vines by the fast indoor courts on which they tended to play. The pace gave him no chance to create the angles that were a feature of his game. 'Vines is lucky,' he said on one occasion; on another he let slip that he regretted ever having turned professional.

The relationship between the two was at its most strained during this tour. They even gave up trying to conceal this and spent very little time in each other's company off court. Vines let on that what particularly irked him were Perry's very audible asides during changeovers. Triumphally, Vines wrote to his toddler daughter Carole, 'I am beating Fred Perry all of the time, so I'm still the best tennis player in the world.'

By the time they wound up the tour in Glencoe, Illinois, on 31 May, Vines was in front 49–35. The more telling figure, though, given that this was a business enterprise, was that despite a fuller programme than in 1937 gate receipts were down to around $140,000 (£28,000) – or about one third of the previous year's. If, as they must have been, Perry and Vines were sick of seeing each other across the net, the public also were tiring of watching the same two players. It was clear that Vines' fellow Californian Don Budge, now the outstanding amateur player, had to be prevailed on to turn pro.

Perry said that it was not Adolf Hitler's ambitions in Europe that persuaded him not to travel to England in 1938 to play pro matches, rather the Inland Revenue's interest in his wife's tax affairs. His marriage to Helen Vinson was now foundering and he was in no mood to go to London to settle the tax she owed for the film work she had done in England in 1936 and 1937. For one thing he professed to be at a loss as to where all the money had gone. It certainly wasn't around, he said.

Still, the cost – and stress – of the protracted process of breaking up from Vinson meant Perry had to keep busy. In the summer he took part in the first of what would later be known as the Borscht Circuits, because they were played in the mainly Jewish resorts of the so-called Borscht Belt in the Catskill Mountains. Perry remembered this particular venture as one of the occasions when Tilden's homosexuality became an issue. His roving eye for ballboys did not, understandably, go down well with their parents, and in one instance the police were called to try to stop him leaving town. Also that summer, Perry went to Montreal to prepare Canada's Davis Cup team for a match against Japan. Perry then won the US professional championship in Chicago in October, dominating the event in the absence of Vines, who had gone off to work on his golf.

Their separation meant they were back on reasonable terms when they then set off together on a tour of Latin America and the West Indies, where watching the two of them play was still a novelty. This trip was a real bonus, and yet another product of Perry's extensive network of powerful contacts. A friend who was a director of the Grace Line shipping company, which specialised in Caribbean and Latin American cruises, offered the two players a tour on one of the company's ships, the *Santa Elena*, lecturing and putting on exhibition matches at ports of call.

They played in Curaçao, Caracas, where Perry 'talked like a radio' throughout the match, and Maracaibo, then flew to Barranquilla in Colombia before rejoining the *Santa Elena* in Balboa in Panama, whose citizens must have wondered quite why they had been blessed with a Perry–Vines professional tennis match. A crowd given as 1,000 watched Vines win in four sets. The highlight of the cruise around the Caribbean was a four-day stop-off in Jamaica, an island which would feature prominently in Perry's later life. He had already been there six years before, when he won the island's singles title, but now that he was a professional the tennis authorities viewed him and Vines rather less favourably. Even in this faraway corner of the empire, tennis facilities were placed beyond their reach. With no football clubs to help them out, the cricket authorities provided the solution. An area of the outfield of Sabina Park in Kingston, where Test cricket had been played since 1930, was rolled and mown, and sizeable crowds for their two matches watched what was an unusual spectacle, the world's two most eminent professionals playing outdoors on grass.

From Jamaica, Vines and Perry went by flying boat to Cuba, taking off from Kingston harbour. They had been invited to play an exhibition match at the opening of a sports hall, and because they liked the idea of the trip had accepted without negotiating terms. Fulgencio Batista, military leader of Cuba, who had undertaken to improve the island's sports facilities, attended, and with still no mention of being paid Perry and Vines assumed their reward would be no more than the honour of playing in front of the dictator. When just before leaving they were presented with packages, Perry immediately recalled King Gustav of Sweden's signed photograph. Instead each package contained $2,000 with an invitation to return any time, which Perry said they did whenever the pro tour took them to Florida.

While Vines and Perry were away, the final details of the 1939 tour of North America were sorted out. By now Don Budge had indeed been signed up, and it was decided that he should start off by playing Vines, followed by a series against Perry. Although Perry never said so, commenting that it was simply an arrangement whereby they could play all the large cities twice and avoid the smaller arenas in the first year, the consecutive tours with his coming second amounted to a demotion. This was something an editorial in a British national spelt out in January 1939: 'It appears that Perry is not going to be given the chance of meeting Budge until Budge has had a number of matches with Vines. What it amounts to is that when the Americans are tired of watching Budge and Vines the promoters will put on

Perry and Budge. This is hardly fair on Perry. He should be given a chance to cross swords with Budge now.'

Some Americans wondered about this, too. Out of the three, Perry had the greatest appeal in terms of personality and, according to the *New York Times*, because he spoke English, he was not even classified among 'them furriners'. The paper opined that Budge did not have 'Perry's flourish and flair for gaining the favor of the populace. He lacks the vim and verve, the "savoir faire" of the dashing Britisher. Don smiles and talks readily enough when strangers corner him, but he doesn't come bounding forward under his own steam.' As for Vines, 'he goes about with a worried look on his thin face and looks for all the world like a very Gloomy Gus'.

Budge beat Vines 22–17 and Perry 28–8 in those twin 1939 tours. The eagerly awaited Budge–Vines opener at Madison Square Garden in January, when 'the Budge backhand finally met the Vines forehand', attracted 17,000 spectators and raised $47,000 for what turned out to be a disappointing contest. Budge's first stroke as a professional was also his first under lights in an indoor arena, and was a serve that landed a metre beyond the baseline. He learned quickly, though, to win 6–3 6–4 6–2 in a match that one observer reckoned would have prompted cries of 'We wuz robbed' had it been a prizefight. Maybe the memory of this was why spectators stayed away in droves when Budge returned to the Garden to play Perry on 10 March. For all Perry's supposed popularity, a crowd of fewer than 8,000 paid $18,600 for what proved an even greater anticlimax than the Vines match at the same venue. Budge immediately established his superiority over Perry by taking forty-nine minutes to win in three straight sets for the loss of four games. The massive groundstrokes flying from Budge's hefty racket thwarted Perry's desperate switching from defence to attack and back again, and set the pattern for their tour. When Budge again overwhelmed Perry the next night in front of a sparse crowd in Boston, a critic wrote, 'A snowstorm was blamed for the turnout of only 3,753, but many followers of the game were ready to believe that pro tennis had slumped worse than Perry's forehand.' Budge went on to win their first six matches in straight sets, and by the end of March was 11–2 in front. This made Perry's performance in winning six of the remaining twenty-three matches seem reasonable, but Budge spent most of them getting over a sprained ankle.

In the autumn Perry went some way to restoring his reputation. Even though he lost to Vines in the final of the US professional championship at their own Beverly Hills Tennis Club, the match was regarded as possibly the best they ever played. Vines won in four sets, securing the fourth 20–18, when a second serve by Perry bounced off the net cord and landed beyond the service line. It was a worthy contest for what turned out to be Vines' last important match. With Budge now in the ascendant Vines felt he was 'just hanging around', and with sufficient funds banked away to live off, a young family and his passion for golf overshadowing his tennis he left the game in the spring of 1940. His had been an extraordinarily successful career for someone who lacked Perry's appetite for competition and even his flair for the game; in their place Vines possessed a determination that went beyond dogged, an endlessly equable temperament that enabled him to strike the ball fluently in the tensest situation and that thing that great players of ball games have but no one quite understands – timing.

Vines' enthusiasm may also have been affected by war breaking out in Europe and tennis's profit plummetting as the news took on a very melancholy tone. The signs early on that this would be the most successful year yet for the professional circuit had been dashed.

I I

A world at war

'I abjure all allegiance and fidelity to any foreign prince, potentate,
state, or sovereignty'

The debate over whether America should join the war against
Germany and its allies dominated US public life between 1939 and
1941. Professional tennis, along with other elements of the entertainment business, managed to remain in reasonably robust health until
Japan's attack on the US fleet in the Pacific in December 1941, when
the seriousness of the situation overwhelmed even those who had
been determined to keep on enjoying themselves. And even if pro
tennis wanted to carry on regardless of what was happening in the
wider world, most of the game's young stars, including the amateurs
who were the next generation of professionals, were now in uniform
and unavailable on a regular basis.

Perry's own dilemma between 1939 and 1941 was in certain respects
a microcosm of the wider debate around him, although back in
England the establishment, that old adversary of Perry's, had little
sympathy for him or his situation. They needed no persuading of
the real reason for his deciding to stay out of the war by remaining
in the US: that he was the sort to avoid fighting for his country.
Some of the older generation, particularly, felt strongly enough to
decline ever to forgive him. This hostility largely died along with
those who harboured it but the fact that Perry was not knighted
can be construed as evidence that it never went away completely.
Over the years he moved to the forefront of high-achieving British
sportsmen as others failed to come close to emulating his success,
but still the honorary KBE, which he would have had to settle for
as he was no longer a national of a Commonwealth country, was

not forthcoming. Before the 1939–45 war only sporting administrators tended to receive knighthoods; after it, cricket's Donald Bradman and the jockey Gordon Richards were among the first to be knighted purely for sporting prowess. Based on performance, Perry stood comparison with any sporting knight.

The accusation that Perry bolted to America to be out of harm's way is at least debatable. Plenty of evidence exists that his attachment to the US began at the start of the 1930s, long before the first shots of the Second World War were fired, including him saying as early as 1934 that if he turned professional he would not return to England.

Despite this, Perry was strangely subdued in defending himself against the slur that taking out US citizenship was an act of betrayal. One close acquaintance remembered that years later Perry merely smiled cryptically when asked about it. Another explained his apparent reticence by saying that Perry was a wily operator who never felt obliged to express his true feelings about his detractors. Mostly, he was happy to keep his own counsel about those in England who defamed him but had done nothing practical to help him solve how he might stay a full-time amateur while acquiring enough money to live comfortably. When he did let rip, he did so with typical panache. He once accused the All England Club of treating him like a leper after he turned professional and moved to the US. 'I'm not sure, but I believe they dipped the door of my locker in an antiseptic,' he said.

Maybe staying put in America was the easier, safer and more agreeable option, but his decision to move there in the first place was principally so that he could be where he had started to earn his living as a professional. Come the outbreak of war in 1939 he was very firmly bound to the US by ties that included marriage, even if it was starting to fall apart. As we have seen, Perry's lawyers told him that returning to Britain might expose him to claims by the Inland Revenue relating to the earnings in the UK of his actress wife. When Perry did decide to take refuge from his domestic difficulties, he therefore headed south for Mexico rather than east across the Atlantic.

Perry did admit that September 1939, when the war started, was a difficult time for him. He had a gut feeling that he should return to Britain but felt that would have jeopardised his change of citizenship, which had not finally been sealed. This process had begun officially when he landed in Honolulu on 15 February 1935 aboard the SS *Aorangi* from Sydney. This was the date entered on the certificate of arrival made out in his name, although the document was not issued until 10 May 1938, two weeks before the *Chicago Times* published a story that he intended to seek US citizenship. Questioned about this story at the time, Perry was guarded. The newspaper reported him as saying, 'I don't know who started it. I'm not going to confirm or deny it. I'll just leave it the way it is.' Asked if he thought this might be taken as confirmation, he said, 'Not at all.'

Later Perry would give 1938 as the year he became a US citizen, although the petition for naturalisation granting him citizenship was not officially sealed by the court of the Southern District of California until two years later. Perry, who gave his address as South Lasky Drive, Beverly Hills, signed the oath of allegiance to his new homeland on 15 November 1940. It is an uncompromising document that includes the pledge 'I hereby declare, on oath, that I absolutely and entirely renounce and abjure all allegiance and fidelity to any foreign prince, potentate, state, or sovereignty, of whom (which) I have heretofore been a subject (or citizen).'

Perry's position come the end of 1939 was that he would remain where he was and join the US services if America entered the war. In the meantime, he tried to do his bit for the Allied war effort, although on one occasion his contribution and that of his fellow pros rebounded badly on them. The incident, illustrating what a sensitive issue the war had become in the US, involved a fund-raiser in aid of the Finnish Relief Fund held in a regimental armoury in Manhattan in April 1940. After it, Stanley Woodward of the *New York Herald Tribune* published what he regarded as the unacceptable expenses submitted by Perry, Bruce Barnes, Berkeley Bell, Budge, Tilden and Vines, who were 'all schooled originally in the great amateur tradition of the sport', and by three managers. Perry, who charged $312.23 for travel from Los Angeles and was paid $50 'for winning an extra match with Budge', was by no means the worst culprit, in the view of Woodward, who pointed out that Tilden asked for $400 for a journey that cost ordinary travellers $45. The charity received $4,006.60 compared to $6,774.40 paid out in expenses, figures that did not necessarily represent the bottom line. Woodward added a scathing NB: 'List of expenditures not yet complete.'

Perry's form on the professional circuit in 1940 stood up well enough. This time the competition consisted of seven round-robin events involving small groups of players. Perry entered five and won two; Budge entered six and won four. Then in 1941, with Budge's form affected by marriage and a May operation on his face, Perry had a resurgent season in which he was comfortably the best of the professional players. Accompanied by his second wife, Sandra Breaux, he emerged from south of the border to take the US professional title at the Chicago Town and Tennis Club and soon afterwards won all his matches in a four-man round-robin event on the grass courts of Forest Hills in which Budge also competed. On the low-bouncing surface Budge was outplayed by Perry, who confirmed that in matches in which cunning counted for as much as raw power he was still as good as anyone.

The Saturday of the Forest Hills event was designated 'Wimbledon Day' with proceeds being donated to the British War Relief Society of the USA. Sir Gerald Campbell, British consul-general in New York, was guest of honour and told the crowd there was a large bomb crater in the middle of the Centre Court at Wimbledon. This was only a slight exaggeration as the one bomb out of a stick of five that hit the court in October 1940 went through the roof covering the stands – two others fell elsewhere in the club grounds and the remaining two excavated bunkers in Wimbledon Park golf course – but this was clearly an occasion to lay it on a bit. Sir Gerald continued, 'It will be levelled out one day and we shall turn our heads backwards and forwards without wondering whether the Gestapo are looking and listening to what we do and say.'

At the end of 1941 Perry again agreed to leave his base in Mexico, when Budge put together a round-robin winter tour, which went ahead straight after Christmas despite the Japanese attack on Pearl Harbor on 7 December that brought America into the war.

The group for this tour included Bobby Riggs, who had won Wimbledon in 1939. Although he was not a player of the same stature as Budge or Perry – in Perry's opinion he was a bit lazy – he was still only twenty-three, which helped him to overcome the gap in class whenever they played. Riggs was also a character, whose biggest moment in tennis would come in 1973 when he brilliantly hyped up the 'Battle of the Sexes' in which he took on Billie Jean King, who at twenty-nine was twenty-six years his junior, in the Houston Astrodome. More kitsch than kosher, the match, which King won, did make tangential contact with the serious debate about sexual equality and generated an extraordinary level of interest. It made Riggs far better known than he had been for winning Wimbledon.

Perry played Riggs on the opening night of the 1941–2 tour, a gala Boxing Day occasion that attracted 11,000 to Madison Square Garden. On what would prove a fateful evening for Perry, Frank Kovacs stunned Budge by out-hitting him in the first match. The court's speed might have had something to do with the fact that it was covered in a lighter canvas than was normal, with the sheets joined by single stitching. At some point during the evening, a small section of seam came undone. No one noticed until Perry, racing for a forehand with Riggs serving for victory in a tight contest, caught his foot in the open seam. He catapulted into the air and, after landing heavily on his elbow, lay stamping his foot in agony until medical assistance arrived. He was taken to hospital, where, as Perry told it, there was some debate among the doctors about whether to open up the elbow. 'But I wouldn't let them operate,' he said. 'Once you start cutting up major joints you've got problems.'

The injury was not quite as bad as first feared and he resumed playing on 5 January 1942, but it effectively ended his competitiveness against the very best players. Being Perry, he devised his own highly original remedial routines when he returned to Mexico. They included driving industrial-sized nails into pieces of teak in order to restore strength and flexibility. Even so, he was never again able to fully straighten his arm. 'If a ball came wide across my body I couldn't push it back where it came from but only down the line. So one half of the court was closed as far as I was concerned. Opponents would exploit this, which made me look an idiot, and although I staggered through for a while I never really played seriously afterwards.'

The injury did not prevent his call-up, which took place in Santa Ana, California almost exactly a year after Pearl Harbor, although he was issued with a red armband to excuse him from saluting officers. His elbow might have excused him from joining the military at all but Perry believed that it was precisely because he was injured that he was called up. If he was unable to go around entertaining the forces by playing exhibition matches, the reasoning went, he should be put in uniform so that his propaganda potential could be exploited from within.

Also he might be useful as a physical training instructor for pilots and other sportsmen in uniform. During the war the US services had sports teams made up of big-time professional and collegiate athletes who had volunteered or been drafted. Each base would take part in various championships and a player of Perry's calibre would have been a valuable asset. For at least some of his time in the forces he was attached to the 663rd Profit Training Squadron, 'Profit' being a composite word with the last three letters being an abbreviation of 'fitness'.

He signed up with the air force, which at that time was part of the US Army. Official documents list Frederick John Perry (serial/service number(s) 19 200 432) as having joined the Army of the United States on 15 December 1942 and as having been discharged on 10 October 1945. He received two decorations, the World War II Victory Medal and World War II Service Lapel Button, both of which were awarded in recognition of service rather than anything specific that he did.

During these three years he rose no higher than staff sergeant and remained mainly in California, at Santa Ana, which was used for basic training and had no planes, hangars or runways. His stalling at such a lowly rank was partly the result of his showing the same antipathy towards the US military hierarchy as he had towards the English establishment. At one point he appeared before the interview board for the officer candidate school in Miami only for his hackles to suffer their customary Pavlovian reaction to those in charge. Feeling that he was more sophisticated than the people asking the questions – he was, after all, unusually well travelled as a result of his life as a tennis player – he did not appreciate what he perceived as their patronising attitude. His confrontational approach went down badly and he was sent away having been assessed as not US officer material.

There were occasions when he might have served his new country's war effort by travelling beyond California. At one point Major General William 'Wild Bill' Donovan, a First World War veteran who in 1941 had been put in charge of the US's intelligence operation – at this stage known as the Office of Strategic Services – threatened to put Perry on his staff. Donovan also happened to be Perry's lawyer, and the idea was that Fred would join him on a tour of the South Pacific with the prospect of receiving a battlefield commission, a system whereby an enlisted man became a commissioned officer without an increase in pay. This plan was aborted when the flow of wounded arriving at the base started to increase and Perry opted to stay put to help with rehabilitation work, which he found rewarding.

Another opportunity to leave California arose when the US government sent out a call for servicemen with knowledge of Australia to go there on a diplomatic mission. Perry, who had been to Australia four times, would have been given the posting, plus a commission, but failed his medical, the arm injury that had not prevented his conscription in 1942 now ruling him out of an overseas assignment. The anomaly was obvious and he might have been discharged at this point, but once again the military declined to let go a famous sportsman with PR potential. Perry had to wait until after the surrender of Japan in September 1945 for his release.

His discharge in October was not quite the end of his contribution to the war effort. He was just about to set off back to Mexico when Bill Tilden caught up with him at the Beverly Hills club and talked him into helping out General Holland 'Howling Mad' Smith of the US Marine Corps, a friend of Tilden, who needed entertainment for some troops stuck on a ship in San Diego, where they would remain until after Christmas. Perry protested that his damaged arm meant he could no longer strike the ball properly, but the persuasive Tilden prevailed after agreeing to Perry's request not to play flat out against him, and the enterprise was a success.

The organised tennis that did take place while Perry and others were away on military service included experiments in open events in America and Europe. The US Lawn Tennis Association introduced a wartime rule that allowed amateurs to play pros provided at least one of them was serving in the military. One such match was staged in New York in January 1944, when a crowd of 5,000 watched Lieutenant Don Budge beat Jack Kramer, who was twenty-three and establishing himself as a leading amateur. Worried that the experiment might lead to open tennis catching on, the association banned matches between amateur and pro civilians, and the opportunity to hasten the fall of the wall between the professional and amateur games vanished.

Perry would resume playing tournaments after the war, but by now it was not just his crooked arm that handicapped him. He was into his late thirties and no longer a match for the new generation led by Kramer, who would join the pros in 1947 at the height of his powers, and the effervescent Riggs. Against the older professionals, though, Perry remained competitive, and when he played in the self-styled World's Hard-Court Pro Championships at the Los Angeles Tennis Club in early December 1945 he reached the semi-finals before losing to Riggs, who then beat Budge in the final. Three weeks later he lost again to Riggs in the final of an event in Santa Barbara.

The format of two principals taking part in an extended series of matches was not revived in 1946, when the majority of professional players regrouped after their military service. Instead, Perry helped Tilden and Vinnie Richards plan a tour that reverted to the more traditional format of week-long tournaments involving groups of players. Rustling up enough competitors proved a problem, which they addressed by recruiting teaching pros regardless of competence, and the enterprise just about worked, although it did little more than cover its costs. Perry took part only when 'it was a nice warm day and the arm felt good'. Inevitably, every time he played his opponent was eager to beat the former holder of each of the four grand slam titles, and Perry suffered the frustration of opponents exploiting his restricted arm movement. 'It was a cruel way to play the game,' he said. But if his play had slipped, his feistiness remained undiminished. When a much younger opponent, Wayne Sabin, started swearing and banging balls out of the stadium at the West Side Tennis Club in New York, Perry called a halt and said, 'I won't play any more with a man who has such court manners.' He was persuaded to go on but lost.

Much more fun was a tour he undertook, also in 1946, on which warm weather was more or less guaranteed. The emphasis of the trip to the Caribbean and South America was more light entertainment than heavy-duty competition. He formed something of a double act with Frankie Kovacs, a good American player who sacrificed what he might have achieved by acting up to his reputation as the game's clown prince in much the same way that Ilie Nastase did thirty years later. A speciality was hitting one of three balls he threw into the air when serving. Perry and Kovacs played in a bullring in Bogotá as a warm-up act for the bulls and matadors waiting in the wings, but the biggest thrill for Perry on that tour came in Trinidad when a local band stopped beside a court on which he was playing and sang a calypso composed as a tribute. The lyrics included, 'We understand even the great Perry/ Had a hard time in days early/ In developing his genius to the degree/ That has him beloved universally.'

Two years after peace broke out Perry returned to Britain for the first time for more than a decade and spoke of his huge excitement when he caught a first glimpse of one of London's red double-decker buses 'because at last I knew I was back in England'. The trip would include a nostalgic visit to the Centre Court at Wimbledon, the first time he had been there since the 1936 Davis Cup challenge round. On this occasion it was to comment on the championships for the London *Evening Standard*, and from then on he went annually to the All England Club as a pundit for the BBC and newspapers.

While not everyone was speaking to him in 1947 after his absence during the war, most were, and he was still in demand as a speaker and player. He gave a series of talks on tennis at Finnigans department store in Manchester, the newspaper ads billing him as 'A Stupendous Attraction', and on the other side of the Pennines, in Scarborough, he competed in the Slazenger professional tournament, now with the initials 'USA' after his name. He had maintained his links with Slazenger which had sponsored his trip back to Britain to beef up its Scarborough event, the entries for which consisted mainly of unrecognisable names from Europe.

The competition among European pros was not nearly as stiff as in the US, and Perry, who had learned to 'fiddle his shots', as he put it, achieved some notable results, including a victory over the 1946 Wimbledon champion, Yvon Petra of France. He still struggled to hit a cross-court backhand and got by only if his opponent was not a big hitter who kept returning the ball. His biggest asset was his incomparable tennis nous, which was particularly evident when he won Scarborough for the first time in 1948. This was when he beat Petra, who at thirty-two was the younger player by seven years. Perry, noted one observer, had lost none of his zest, sting – or shrewdness. Perry assessed Petra's game while losing the first set of the final and won the next three for the loss of seven games. 'I knew a little bit more about the game than he did,' Perry said.

He won the Slazenger title again in 1950 and 1951, and it was in the same tournament in 1956, at the age of forty-seven, that he made what was probably his last singles appearance in serious competition, when Tony Mottram, the second seed, withdrew at the last minute because of injury. The news of Mottram's withdrawal 'caused some fluttering in the official dovecotes', reported the *Manchester Guardian*, 'but fortunately F.J. Perry, like a retired Wagnerian tenor hearing the call of the first notes of "Tristan", agreed to fill the breach in the draw'. Perry, who had played only three times that season and was to have appeared only in the doubles, lost in the first round in straight sets to Salem Khaled of Egypt.

Perry's association with professional tennis during the 1950s developed other strands thanks to Jack Kramer, who turned pro soon after his remarkable championship win at Wimbledon for the loss of only thirty-seven games in seven matches. For a while Kramer had a dual career as a player and promoter before an arthritic back restricted him to the latter.

Kramer's feelings about Perry did not include reservations about his shrewdness, and he engaged him as a booking agent for European tours. Perry also managed a group of players for Kramer on a visit to Europe – or rather he managed Pancho Gonzales. The other members of the group – a second American, Tony Trabert, and the Australians Frank Sedgman and Rex Hartwig – looked after themselves. Gonzales, on the other hand, while possessing certain of Perry's characteristics, such as striking good looks and a special flair for playing the game, lacked the ability to turn on the discipline when it mattered. The pair clashed repeatedly, with on one occasion Perry telling Gonzales it was perfectly all right as far as he was concerned if he went home. Gonzales reckoned he was on safe ground here. 'Who will replace me?' he asked. 'Me,' Perry said.

It is worth recording that the era of open tennis, which allowed amateurs and professionals to enter the same tournament, arrived in 1968, releasing players from having to make the sort of difficult decision that had dominated Perry's life for so long. It is also worth noting that the All England Club, that sometime villain of the Perry story, played a considerable role in ushering in this era. The club's decision at an extraordinary general meeting in 1959 to call on the LTA to stage a championship with unrestricted entry was a landmark. Nine years later, Wimbledon was the first grand slam to pay prize money. Australians Rod Laver and Tony Roche, the first men's finalists at Wimbledon in the open era, received £2,000 and £1,300, very modest rewards by today's standards but quite a hike on the gold medal and £10 prize the winner and runner-up received respectively in Perry's day.

I2

Rag trader

'Bing has been wearing his for sometime, the dirty rat'

Excited though Perry was by his return to England in 1947, he was now more visitor than native – a status imposed on him by the ninety days he was permitted, as a US citizen, to stay in the UK each year. It was a restriction he bore willingly and was simply one of several indicators – others included the permatan and mid-Atlantic accent – that he was now a fully signed up American, even if he always retained a strong sense of himself as an Englishman. The US was, and remains, not simply a favoured destination for those seeking a new life, it is also, for those with a desire to fit in, a great assimilator, and, as we have seen, it acquired in Perry a recruit who submitted readily to being absorbed into the country's culture from the early days of his first visit in 1930. Nor did the sentimental value of the trip back to England stop Perry feeling some relief when he flew out again. He could not help remarking on the contrast between the deprivations of post-war Britain, where rationing and shortages made simple things a luxury, and the high standard of living of the United States, which had been mainly isolated from the war by the thousands of miles of ocean stretching from either coast.

In time, through his association with the branded clothing company that came into being in the early 1950s, Fred Perry would again become an internationally recognised name, but his immediate aim on his return to the US in the autumn of 1947 was to establish his new career in Florida as a teaching pro.

The hotel where Perry was to teach had been done up only recently by the son of Latvian immigrants who had lived the American dream. From poor beginnings Myer Schine had built a theatre empire with his brother and was now starting up a chain of hotels. He bought his first in 1945, prompting his wife to ask, 'How can you buy a hotel when I don't even have a cook?' A year later he bought the Boca Raton Club, which had had millions of dollars lavished on it when it was built in the 1920s and was commandeered by the US government during the war. The ornate interior had been covered in protective padding and the few hundred Army Air Corps officers billeted there referred to it as 'the most elegant barracks in history'. Schine got it cheap at $3 million and turned it into an establishment that outshone even its former glory, the splendid Boca Raton Hotel and Club. The *Saturday Evening Post* said in a review at the time, 'If you were looking for the prodigal public spot on the globe, there is little argument that you need go no further than the Boca Raton Hotel and Club.' Schine and his family moved in, and the owner of the Beverly Hills Tennis Club deemed it a suitable place to teach clients how to volley and hone their groundstrokes.

Schine and Perry, both being strong characters, took a little while to smooth out their working relationship. Perry at one point walked out over the issue of guests being charged extra for use of the tennis courts. He thought this wrong when they were already paying handsomely for rooms; he also disliked having to collect money from them. Schine finally agreed, telling Perry, 'Do whatever you want.' It was the sort of instruction Perry liked, and he stayed, having what he said was a wonderfully happy time there. In due course he bought a home nearby and commuted to work along one of the waterways that are a feature of this part of Florida.

Schine assembled an impressive team of sports coaches to look after the needs of clients of the hotel and club. While Perry was there, others included the renowned Edinburgh-born golfer Tommy Armour and the Olympic diver Bill O'Brien, who coached swimming. Like Perry, Armour had become a US citizen. He was a remarkable man with an irrepressible spirit. He had regained the sight in his right eye after being blinded in a mustard gas explosion in the First World

War and won the US Open in 1927, the PGA in 1930 and the Open at Carnoustie in 1931. The author Ross Goodner wrote of him, 'At one time or another, he was known as the greatest iron player, the greatest raconteur, the greatest drinker and the greatest and most expensive teacher in golf.' It said something about the Boca Raton Hotel and Club that it was able to accommodate two personalities as big as Armour and Perry.

One thing Armour failed to do was turn Perry into a serious golfer, the former Wimbledon champion deciding that having mastered table tennis and tennis he was not prepared to make the commitment to reach the same level in another sport. Armour did manage to bring Perry's handicap down from twelve to three, the point at which Perry chose to opt for life as a social rather than a competition golfer.

Whereas tennis attracted the celebrities on the West Coast, particularly in and around Los Angeles, golf was more their thing in Florida. Although Perry's tennis courts at Boca Raton did good business, he did most of his mixing with the stars – and royalty – over in Tommy Armour's golfing empire. Danny Kaye was a frequent visitor and so was the Duke of Windsor, whose abdication had made headlines worldwide in 1936. Perry, who had once been congratulated by the future King Edward VIII on a grand slam victory when they dined coincidentally at the same London restaurant, recalled that one day when he felt particularly emboldened on the practice putting green he asked the duke whether he had regretted the events of 1936. He was told that George VI, the duke's younger brother, had done a pretty good job since replacing him.

The happy association with the Boca Raton Hotel and Club ended when it passed to new owners with whom Perry failed to form the same bond he had with Schine. The increasing amount of time he was giving to the Fred Perry clothing business was another factor in his eventually moving on, although by now he realised he had just about had it with teaching people how to play tennis.

He married a fourth time while he was at the Boca Raton hotel. Barbara Riese had been born in London and was almost exactly ten years younger than Perry also having a May birthday. She was the daughter of comfortably off parents, her father being a stock-broker and, according to Perry, a member of the Sunningdale set. Almost inevitably, given his previous form, Perry again chose a spouse with links to the world of entertainment: Riese's sister was the popular film actress Patricia Roc and her earlier marriage had been to the Hollywood director Seymour Friedman, who made films in the 1940s and '50s. Like Perry, Riese, a strikingly hand-some woman who was known as Bobby, settled first of all in California, where she went to marry Friedman when she was eighteen. Her parents were loath to let her go but consoled them-selves with the thought that America was a less dangerous place in the late 1930s than Europe.

Despite their both being Americans by now, the couple met in England at Grosvenor House, the swish hotel on Park Lane in central London. Wimbledon had started, which was why Perry was in town for broadcasting duties, while Bobby was over visiting her sick mother, the two of them staying in one of the hotel's penthouse apartments. Fred bumped into Bobby in the lobby and once again Noël Coward might have scripted the scene. 'My dear, you look dreadful,' Perry said. 'Would you like a cup of tea?'

The first of their three marriage ceremonies was in the late summer of 1953. In his autobiography Perry gave the setting as Scarborough in Yorkshire, where there was always a tournament at that time of the year, and Bobby confirmed the venue. She added that the mayor conducted the ceremony, of which no official record remains. At the same time she dismissed a news agency report that they had married in Paris in August 1953.

When they returned to the US, a problem arose over Bobby's ten-year-old son David from her first marriage. David, who was due to join the Perrys in Florida, was still with his father in California, but the authorities there did not regard the Scarborough ceremony as legal and would not allow David to leave the state. So the plan was for Fred and Bobby to put things straight by marrying in Florida before going to the West Coast. However, a complication also arose over this arrangement when they discovered it would be a year before the Florida marriage was recognised in

California, and it was out of the question as far as Bobby was concerned to wait this long before David could come to live with them. So they put the Florida wedding on hold and set off for California, stopping off to get married in Phoenix, Arizona because for some reason a marriage there was regarded as instantly legal by the California authorities. It was now all right to motor on to collect David before returning to Florida, where Bobby was finally allowed what she regarded as her proper wedding, in a civil ceremony in Delray Beach in October 1953.

Even if Perry never lost his roving eye, his marriage to Bobby was as firmly founded as the others were built on quicksand. Bunny Austin went a bit Mills and Boon after visiting them in Sussex in the 1960s, but he captured the essence of their relationship when he wrote, 'The only blots on Fred's success story were his marriage troubles. But when I met Fred in his home at Rottingdean all these were behind him. He had married an enchanting wife – gay, full of life and with an irrepressible sense of humour about herself and Fred and life generally. She was as fond of Fred as Fred was of her and of their daughter, Penny.'

Penny was born in September 1958, providing a half-sister for David, whom Fred and Bobby had adopted. In time, there would be five Perry grandchildren, David's four sons and Penny's son John Frederick, a transposition of grandfather Fred's names. Although born in Fort Lauderdale, Penny grew up mostly in England from the early 1960s, which meant that because her parents as US citizens were allowed to spend only a limited time each year in England there were long periods of separation. Penny spent at least as much time with her nanny-cum-governess, Eve Bishop, at the Perrys' house in Rottingdean as she did with her mother, so it was hardly surprising that she and Bishop became devoted to one another. She would say that as a child she had two mothers, her real one and Eve, who gave her the stability and standards that guided her through life.

Even in later life, when she settled in Florida after her 2005 marriage to Drew Evert, the brother of the outstanding women's champion Chris Evert, Penny would refer to herself, in the accent that had been modulated at private school in Brighton, as a Sussex girl who liked the outdoor life. 'I could not have faced getting married anywhere else – Rottingdean has been my life,' she said of her choice of location for marrying Drew.

Her father never tried to push her into tennis, which would have been difficult anyway because she spent all her spare time at stables indulging her passion for horses. Her mother wanted her to take piano lessons and ballet classes but Penny was always happiest with the horses or walking the dogs across the Downs. She did play some tennis from the age of twelve and remembered a couple of games of table tennis against her father, when he showed little interest in instructing her. 'Hold your bat how you want,' he told her, partly, no doubt, because that was what he had done with so much success.

As an adult, Penny became a no-nonsense sort whose strong character had helped her through her unusual upbringing unscathed. She also showed her mettle in the mid-1990s, when she was widowed by the death of her husband David and then eight months later lost her father, and again in 2002, when she had to fight a serious illness. Through all these difficulties she exhibited the stoicism that English people traditionally regard as a greater virtue than demonstrative behaviour. There were public gestures, though, of the affection she felt for her father. None was more striking than having her marriage to Drew Evert blessed under the Fred Perry statue at Wimbledon.

The Perrys moved to Fort Lauderdale shortly before Penny was born. It was here that Fred helped to establish the sports facilities at another new hotel and country club, the Diplomat at Hallandale, a resort which cost more than $20 million. Soon after this a chance meeting Perry had with his old school chum Bernard Sunley in London brought a complete change to the family's lives, particularly where they wintered.

The two old boys of Ealing County School had both been unusually successful. By now Perry's sportswear business was starting to flourish and Sunley was a builder in the major league of property development. Sunley's office in Berkeley Square, central London, was close to Perry's trading headquarters, so their meeting was not mere coincidence. Sunley took Perry to his office to show him plans of a resort he was building at Runaway Bay on the north coast of Jamaica and they cut a deal whereby Perry, having told Sunley he was not prepared to work for him but would work with him, was made the resort's director of golf.

After a false start in November 1961, when Perry arrived to find the resort a work in progress, he went regularly each winter to Runaway Bay with his family. Penny particularly remembered Christmases in Jamaica as a special time of happy reunions. As soon as school broke up, she would fly from London to Kingston. Her childhood, she said, had been influenced by the Caribbean and she never lost her love for the region.

The task of establishing golf at Runaway Bay was not always easy, the importing of essential equipment endlessly turning up unforeseen problems. And when equipment did arrive that was not always the end of difficulties. The course was to be served by the island's first motorised golf carts, which Perry himself bought to run as his own business, and the initial consignment of six duly arrived in Kingston harbour. The first one to be unloaded was winched out of the hold and, rather than being lowered gently, was dropped onto the dockside. Some weeks later Perry found a local mechanic able to fix the cart and took him onto the staff, only to have to get rid of him when it turned out he was undercutting the club's on-course bar by selling merchandise bought from a local supermarket.

In all, though, the Perrys found Jamaican winters as agreeable as those spent in Florida with the added attraction of regular visits from cricket teams, including Colin Cowdrey's MCC party in 1967–8. The peace of Runaway Bay, when Cowdrey and his team stopped there for lunch on their way from Montego Bay to Kingston, contrasted with the rather less tranquil atmosphere in which the Test match was played a few days later, a bottle-throwing riot on the fourth day bringing play to a standstill. The future of Runaway became less certain when industrial trouble led first to its being leased to a local hotelier, John Issa, and then being sold to the Jamaican government. The Perrys spent their last winter there in 1973, and then the family returned to living and wintering in the

United States. Although Perry remained a compulsive traveller right up until his death, he regarded Florida as home for most of the second half of his life. His wife Bobby and daughter Penny both still lived there in 2009, the centenary of Perry's birth.

One legacy Perry left at Runaway was the Jamaican golfer Seymour Rose, his protégé at the course, who was still running it more than a quarter of a century later. Rose became Jamaican champion, an international tour player and holder of the course record of 62.

An intriguing advertisement started to appear in newspapers and magazines in the early 1950s. Accompanied by a photograph of Fred Perry, it told 'The Story Of My Shirts'. 'It began this way . . .' the ad said. 'While watching important tennis championships, about a year ago, a former Austrian footballer asked me: "Do they have to dress this badly?"' The wording owed a certain amount to the copywriter's imagination – for a start, before the shirts Perry and Tibby Wegner had collaborated over a sweatband to be worn around the wrist – but it was accurate on two important points: Wegner's central role in the enterprise's conception and recognising that shirts were what really launched it as a major clothing company.

Wegner's first, chance encounter with Perry, which led to the foundation of Fred Perry Sportswear, could hardly have been better timed. It took place soon after the war, when Perry's playing career was coming to an end, and led to the creation of an ideal outlet for his energy and ingenuity, particularly as dress sense was something that had always interested him. Many years later, an obituary of Perry in an American magazine said that he had co-founded a profitable sportswear company that sold the kind of natty garb he favoured. The business was so successful that it defined the later years of Perry's life. In old age he happily admitted that his name was better known for shirts and sportswear than for winning Wimbledon three times. It would be untrue to add that it also gave him somewhere to channel his business acumen because, as he often said, not without justification, he had none.

In Wegner, Perry had stumbled upon a business partner who was 'a real go-getter' and as colourful and resourceful as he was; Wegner also had a quick and inventive mind. Born in Budapest in 1906, he was two when his Jewish mother took him and his brother to Vienna soon after she divorced her dentist husband. Young Theodor – or Tibby – was a keen sportsman: a good club tennis player and excellent footballer who became a part-time professional with the Jewish side Hakoah Vienna. Hakoah undertook frequent overseas tours, and Wegner went with them to the US in 1926. It was one of the most successful trips in the club's history, their match at New York City's Polo Ground attracting a crowd of 46,000. Like Perry four years later, Wegner was instantly smitten by America and in the late 1920s worked there for two years as a journalist before returning home. Back in Vienna, he did an apprenticeship in textiles and with the English he had learned in America started a business importing worsteds and tweeds from England, mainly from Yorkshire.

Just before Germany annexed Austria in 1938, after which the Nazis appropriated the Hakoah ground and the German Football Association banned the club, Wegner left for England, the move eased by links he had forged while establishing his textiles venture. He began his new life bed-and-breakfasting at the Strand Palace Hotel in London, where he shared a room with a friend to reduce costs. They fed themselves at lunch with what they managed to squirrel away during breakfast, and their evening meal depended on how well Wegner's new enterprise as a wool merchant was doing. The business must have done well because he was soon able to move out, having been joined in London by his wife – in due course there were two daughters – and by the time he met Perry he was a partner in Miller and Wegner, a wool business with its headquarters in Golden Square, close to Regent Street.

Wegner's first contact with Perry was during a visit to the Wimbledon championships. He took with him a sweatband he had invented to show to Bobby Falkenburg, the 1948 Wimbledon champion, who while playing used to dry his hands on a towel hanging from his waistband. Falkenburg was so impressed with the sweatband that he invited Wegner to the players' restaurant to meet his American colleague Jack Kramer. Wegner's prototype was a square piece of towelling attached to two thin loops of elastic, the towelling to be worn on the outside of the wrist – a device really suitable only for wiping the brow. When they entered the restaurant, they found Kramer chatting to Perry. Wegner showed Kramer the wristband and, as Wegner told a BBC Television documentary about the company, made several years later, the conversation went like this:

Kramer: 'Gee, this is great, marvellous. Can I have one, please?'
Wegner: 'Well, you can have two or three tomorrow morning. Where are you staying?'
Perry (not moving the pipe from his mouth): 'That's no damn good.'
Wegner: 'What's wrong, Mr Perry?'
Perry: 'You know, you're not a tennis player.'
Wegner: 'Yes, I am a tennis player, but not your class.'
Perry: 'You know, with a good tennis player, the sweat that runs into the playing hand, this is the dangerous sweat, not the sweat on the forehead – this is immaterial.'
Wegner: 'Mr Perry, you are talking to a textile engineer. I'm an expert in this. I'll make it for you.'
Perry: 'You just go ahead. You're one of at least fifty. I told the fifty what I want; they couldn't make it. They said it was impossible to make.'
Wegner: 'Mr Perry, where can I see you?'
Perry: 'You can meet me at Slazenger, and if you have it then we'll make a lot of money out of this.'

Perry, who had recognised the usefulness of a sweatband when at Wimbledon in 1934 he had wrapped a gauze strip around his wrist, thought no more of the meeting in the Wimbledon restaurant, not expecting to hear from Wegner again. This was to underestimate his new acquaintance's persistence.

Not long afterwards Perry was conducting a coaching course with Dan Maskell in Leicester, a textile town, where Wegner also happened to be. He was collecting the new version of the sweatband that he had had made up. It fitted perfectly with what Perry envisaged. They had some manufactured and asked the leading players to try them out. They were an instant success, and the first, faltering steps of the business were complete. Several more months elapsed, though, before Fred Perry Sportswear Limited would officially come into being on 12 August 1952.

The second paragraph of the advertisement told what happened next: 'Realising a lack of pleasing and easy sportswear, we decided to produce shirts and shorts of high class quality, superb fit for match-play, smart in design for general wear and . . . AT A POPULAR PRICE.' So, after the sweatbands came the shirts, the garment that would make the company a major international brand. Once again, though, it was not quite in the way that the copywriter described at the start of the ad. In fact, the real story was even better than Wegner simply wondering out loud to Perry whether the players had to dress so badly.

When Wegner went to Kramer's hotel to deliver his sweatbands, he asked him about the top he was wearing. Kramer told him it was his tennis shirt, which clearly offended Wegner the textiles expert. 'This is a piece of underwear,' Wegner said sniffily. 'It's made out of interlock fabric.' He pulled at it to demonstrate how it was woven to allow it to stretch. Wegner cherished Kramer's reply: 'Interlock schminterlock, I don't care what it is – the manufacturer gives me twenty-four shirts every year and when they're worn out, Tibby, they're marvellous for cleaning your boots.' Wegner protested that he should wear something better. Kramer replied, 'You mean the Lacoste shirt? He only gives me two shirts a year and I don't pay for shirts.'

Although Wegner came up with the idea to manufacture shirts that were smart but still suitable to play in, once again he was pointing in a direction that Perry had already travelled. Attention to sartorial detail had always been one of Perry's things, as he was not too bashful to remind Wegner: 'I told him I was generally regarded as the best-dressed player of my time.' Hardly surprisingly then, Perry happily went along with the plan to raise £1,000 to start up the company – after Wegner hesitated momentarily before deciding that Fred Perry would be a better brand name than Jack Kramer, given Perry's three Wimbledon wins.

Kramer's mention of Lacoste had sent Wegner racing off to

Lillywhite's, the sportswear shop on Piccadilly Circus, where he bought one of the shirts that had been pioneered before the war by Perry's near playing contemporary René Lacoste. He took the shirt to Leicester, where he asked an old contact, Frank Goodman, whether he had the machines to make a copy of it. Goodman assured him he had. 'Within a few days,' Wegner said, 'I had the first Fred Perry shirt.'

Nearly forty years later, television brought together Lacoste and Perry to chat about their shirts. Lacoste graciously tried to put Perry in his place: 'I invented the shirt; you made me a great compliment doing the same thing.' As effortlessly as he used to on court, Perry fiddled a result out of it: 'You made the back longer than the front – so between us we revolutionised it, didn't we?' In fact, Perry had a point. By pooling their talents, he and Wegner very rapidly established Fred Perry Sportswear as an equal competitor with Lacoste, and this having given the French company the best part of a twenty-year start.

The design of the shirt was not the only thing that resembled Lacoste's creation. Wegner and Perry decided there was something else they liked about the famous *chemise* – and so 'borrowed' the idea of the logo too. Just as Lacoste's sportswear became known by its crocodile emblem, the first brand identifier ever worn on the outside of a piece of clothing, Perry's would be distinguished by its laurel wreath. This symbol is now universally recognised but was thought up at no cost long before the Nike swoosh was the merest twinkle in some fantastically rewarded designer's eye.

The wreath rescued Fred Perry Sportswear from what would almost certainly have been a calamitous decision – to make the logo a pipe. Perry had had this idea because he was a pipe smoker who had once pointed out in a newspaper column that, except for Jean Borotra, Bill Tilden and Ellsworth Vines, all the top players smoked. He added that just because you wanted to become a champion did not mean 'you should give up smoking for good – you should merely act with discretion'. This might have conformed to the contemporary view of what was recognised only later as a deadly habit, but even so it did not really chime with the clean-living, outdoor life. What convinced Perry it was a bad idea was when Wegner told him he did not think the girls would like it.

Wegner first suggested the laurel wreath, which had caught his eye as part of a badge on an official touring blazer worn by Perry. It also featured on a purple silk ribbon presented to Wimbledon champions, which is why Perry sought the All England Club's permission to use it. The club owned up to having no rights to the emblem, which anyway they had dropped since the war, and with a written note from them renouncing any claim to it the logo was secured for the new line in sportswear. The original batch of shirts all had green wreaths simply because this was the colour of the mixed doubles wreath, which was the one they happened to send to the manufacturers.

Perry might not have been much of a businessman, but he was confident, gregarious and well known, and marketing was where he truly complemented Wegner's astute business sense. His own assessment of his marketing style was 'a combination of friendship and bullshit', a fairly timeless formula for moving goods, which he applied tirelessly wherever he went. This was a fair number of places. Even though he was allowed to stay in the UK for only a limited number of days each year, while he was in the country he was constantly on the move, either coaching or broadcasting, which meant there was nearly always somewhere new to peddle his clothing line.

Intentionally or otherwise, the first batch of shirts arrived during the 1952 Wimbledon championships, which was sweet timing given his association with the tournament. With access to the men's dressing rooms, Perry set about interesting the top male players in his garments. This was the time when a conveyor belt of chisel-faced champions was coming out of Australia, and players such as Lew Hoad and Ken Rosewall readily agreed to wear the styled shirts, a promotional godsend. No doubt if he had needed to, Perry would have found some way of entering the women's dressing rooms, but in the early days the range did not include shirts for females.

Although the primary target was star players, Perry did not stop there. He handed out three shirts to every male in the draw, even though the quality of the product in the early days was poor. Wegner disliked the reproduction of the logo on the original shirts, dismissing them in his distinct brand of English as 'miserable contraptions', and the quality of the fabric was not always the best, with one employee remembering that they made sure the holes in the ones they gave the players were below the waistband. But none of this really mattered, said Wegner. What mattered was that the public saw every player at Wimbledon wearing the shirt with the laurel wreath.

Wegner recalled going along to help hand them out: 'When a fellow got three shirts and went to the dressing room, the other boys said to him, "What have you got there?" He said, "Why, there's that guy outside with the funny name. He gave me three shirts, Fred Perry shirts." So they all came to me and they got their three shirts.' The media areas were also now part of Perry's domain and he worked these adroitly too. He made sure everyone got a shirt, from the commentators to the lowliest members of production, who were given theirs with an aside about how nice it would be if the cameras lingered on the laurel emblem.

'It took a year to get the shirts right,' the ad said finally. 'They were an immediate success. The world's top players wore them at Wimbledon and the crack professionals demanded them at Wembley. Now you can buy them. "Fred Perry" shirts, as worn by the stars, are in the stores and shops.' The price was 21 shillings − £1.05 − and anyone who had difficulty obtaining one was invited to write to Perry at the company's headquarters in Golden Square.

Yet again Perry's network of contacts proved invaluable when it came to expanding the market for his sportswear beyond the playing fraternity, who expected to get theirs for nothing. The business needed the public to start paying for the shirts and Perry went to see an old acquaintance, Sam Cox, chief buyer for Lillywhite's. Cox had been perplexed by customers asking for the shirts with the laurel wreath that the players had been wearing at Wimbledon. He had no idea where they came from until Perry told him they were his. Not only did he straightaway place a sizeable order but rang other retailers, including Harrods and big stores across the country. They sold well, and before long every good sports shop stocked them. In due course their popularity spread to Europe and then around the world.

A consequence of the popularity of the shirts was that the number of freebies handed out to the leading players never seemed to be enough. Regardless of being kept well supplied, the stars would turn up at major championships wearing plain old white tops, claiming their Fred Perry gear had been stolen or gone missing. Clearly they had become valuable currency for those players who were still amateur, but they were to be thwarted when the company devised a cunning countermeasure. The players now received their shirts with their two initials embroidered on them. It was bit like tagging racing pigeons. Wherever a shirt landed it was possible to identify whence it came.

The shirt with the laurel emblem became familiar to everyone, however grand. One of Perry's tales was about the opening of a clothing exhibition, when Queen Elizabeth the Queen Mother asked him why the Perry shirt was so popular and he hammed it up by telling her with a cheesy grin, 'Ma'am, it's the shirt that fits' – which had however not always been the case. The right cut for the shirt, and later the shorts, was worked out through trial, error and consultation with the players. So was the material used, as Enrique Morea, a particularly large Argentine, discovered. He was given a shirt in a material whose shrinking properties were unknown – until he ended up trapped inside it as it contracted dramatically during the course of a match.

One of the most astute marketing ploys Fred Perry Sportswear developed was dispatching shirts to celebrities – from royalty to show business personalities – around the world. Soon, not just the British royal family was familiar with the latest in sportswear. The wardrobe of the crown prince of Japan included a selection of shirts, which he wore in public, and Princess Grace of Monaco wrote thanking the company for sending her family some. The company even plied politicians with their merchandise, and John F. Kennedy became an avid wearer. Perry encountered Kennedy one day, shortly before he was sworn in as US president, on a golf course in Florida. He was sporting the laurel wreath and Perry could not resist commending the soon-to-be president on his choice of shirt, which bore the initials JK. Kennedy made a special request to have an extra letter added so that it was JFK, a three-initial honour bestowed previously only on Perry himself. Not only did Perry agree to Kennedy's request, he deferred to the president by reducing his own initials to FP. In time, the only other person to have three was Billie Jean Moffitt, later King.

The success of sending out free shirts is evident from a cuttings book stuffed with grateful letters, many of them handwritten, from the sort of names who today would expect to be handsomely rewarded for parading branded clothing in public. Oscar-winning actor Charlton Heston offered to pick his up while passing through London to save the company the problem of overseas mailing; Bing Crosby's wife thanked the company for hers and added, by way of apology, 'His, he has been wearing for sometime, the dirty rat, without even confirming receipt of them'; the actor Robert Shaw wrote to say he had thought the telephone call offering the shirts was a joke but now they had arrived 'I couldn't have had a more welcome or opportune gift.'

After men's shirts, Fred Perry Sportswear successfully added shorts and then women's shirts and shorts to its range. Next came socks, sweaters and zipper jackets. There were failures too. A cut-away football boot, universal today but not in the early 1950s, when a heavy leather boot lacing up past the ankle was standard, failed to excite its intended customers as expected, even with the name of popular England striker Tommy Lawton attached to it. And then there were the open-knit shirts for warmer weather. These sold so slowly that Wegner and Perry were delighted when staff of Ghana's airline, which occupied offices in the same building in Golden Square, agreed to buy them at cost price. The following spring, while in Paris, the two entrepreneurs gazed in astonishment at shop windows, where open-knit, the latest in chic, was on display everywhere.

Perry's own account of the clothing company concentrates on its production of sportswear. This suggests that the Perry shirt's crossover to become one of the most widely worn items of street fashion in the world – to its almost total exclusion from the sporting scene – was an unforeseen development, and yet that 1950s advertisement proclaimed it was 'smart in design for general wear'. It may be that Wegner, with his general background in textiles, always had this in mind as a possible progression.

In the BBC documentary, asked 'How did you get out of the sportswear industry into the menswear industry as well?' Wegner said it started when he introduced shirts dyed different colours to his golfing friends. They liked them and so he ordered shirts in ten different colours, forty dozen of each. What happened next is again worth telling in Wegner's own words.

I handed them over to my agents and they all brought the shirts back and said people were laughing about it. So I went down to the East End, which is the birthplace of many fashions, because there are so many races that mix there and that somehow creates fashions. I went down to one of these retailers and I said, 'Tell me, Mr Collins, why didn't you buy the coloured shirts?' He said, 'Because it's crazy, it's a man's shirt for little boys. As a boys' shirt I'll buy it, but as a grown-up shirt . . . It's a boys' shirt. You're crazy.' So I went to another Jewish retailer by the name of Gray and, I don't know, they must have spoken to each other because he said precisely the same thing. So the third one, my big customer, was a Mr Cohen and he said, 'You've been to Ronnie Gray.' I said, 'Yes.' He said, 'I fully agree with him.' I said, 'Well, in this case, phone up the other two, I want to have lunch with you.' So we went to this famous Jewish place I knew, where you have salt beef, and I said, 'I tell you what I'll do with you. On Thursday or Friday you change your windows. What does it cost to change your windows?' They said, 'Ten pounds.' I said, 'All right, there's ten pounds for you, ten pounds for you and ten pounds for you – which I want back if you are wrong.' And I said, 'This is my private telephone number just in case you need shirts on the Sunday' – because they opened on Sunday. They said, 'We'll never phone you on Sunday, and we're not going to phone you on Monday, on Tuesday, nor on any day. You'll get all the shirts back.' But still, they took them in and they made the windows. One phoned me on Sunday, 'He said, Tibby, have you got the keys for your stockroom?' I said, 'Yes, do you want coloured shirts?' He said, 'Yes.' I said, 'How many do you want?' He said, 'Well, whatever you can put in two taxis I'll accept.' So I phoned the others and this was my busiest Sunday, because all three wanted shirts.'

This was the start of the Perry shirt's metamorphosis into a fashion item. It would sell worldwide in its millions, as groups such as mods and skinheads, and the singers and bands associated with these groups, adopted it as their uniform. It also became popular with people who simply wore it because they liked it. In 2005 it did make a comeback on the tennis court when the Scottish player Andy Murray signed a contract to wear the clothing. John Flynn, managing director of Fred Perry Limited, who did the deal with Murray's agent, described the player as being a spiritual successor to Perry. 'The guy's more than just a tennis player,' said Flynn. 'He's corporate but roguish, like Fred.'

By the time the company was established as an international brand it had passed out of the hands of Wegner and Perry. The sudden growth in sales coincided with a serious illness suffered by Wegner. What precisely was wrong was never diagnosed but at one point it was thought unlikely he would survive. This led to Mackintosh, the rainwear manufacturers, buying out the company in 1964. When Wegner recovered from his illness, he was taken on by the new owners, but he said they made it very awkward for him, not purposely but because their promotional methods were very different from his, and eventually he walked away. Years later, he said he regretted having sold the company every second of his life. 'I thought I could have improved Fred Perry Sportswear enormously.'

No longer an owner, Perry retained a role in the company as the new bosses were only too aware of the eponymous founder's worth as a figurehead. He would almost certainly have negotiated a more advantageous and lasting deal had the sort of agents who operate today been around then, but in the mid-1960s the money-making possibilities that exist now for big names in sport had only just started to be exploited. The American businessman Mark McCormack was the pioneer, his International Management Group growing out of a handshake in 1960 with the golfer Arnold Palmer.

What Perry did not know he did not miss, and he happily signed up with Mackintosh to promote the clothing line during his travels, which he continued to undertake as tirelessly as ever. Perry was also retained when Figgie International Inc., a US holding company with a wide spread of interests, took over the brand in 1973. Figgie also bought Fred Perry Worldwide, an offshoot of the original company that Perry's stepson David had run. Perry described his role with Figgie 'as a sort of glad-hander, the chairman of their friendship department'. Figgie sold the company in 1995, less than a year after Perry died. The new owners were Hit Union, a Japanese company that for many years had been the exclusive distributors of Perry products in the Far East.

13

A nomad to the end

'The only change you'll notice is that I'll grunt like Jimmy
Connors when I serve'

If the world is divided into two sorts of married man, the type
whose family dominates his life and the type whose life dominates
his family, Fred Perry was indisputably a member of the second
category. The last chapter of his 1984 autobiography was entitled
'The World, My Oyster'. It was a fitting epitaph to the wanderlust
in him awakened by that first crossing to New York in 1930 and
moderated only partially by marriage and parenthood. His family
often heard him say how nice it was to keep moving on because
that way the time you spent with people was always quality time
and they never had the chance to wish you would go away.

He was well into his forties before he became a family man and
by then far too used to a roving existence to settle down completely.
His fourth marriage was a success because Bobby was more mature
than his previous three wives, as strong a character as he was, and
could handle a relationship based on mutual tolerance as well as
genuine affection. True to form, Perry spent many of the weeks of
Bobby's pregnancy with Penny on the road – he uncorked a bottle
of champagne in the press bar at Wimbledon to salute the infant's
forthcoming arrival and celebrate his siring a child who would be
born in his fiftieth year – and he kept travelling until his death far
from home in Australia.

One of Perry's more unlikely destinations, given the cold war was
at its most frigid in the late 1950s, was the Soviet Union. Before
Fred Perry Sportswear changed hands for the first time, Perry was
easy to locate at the company's headquarters in Golden Square.

It was there that a Soviet delegation sought him out in 1957. Iron Curtain countries, who had identified sporting success as a propaganda tool, needed outside help to produce players capable of challenging those from the West, and Perry seemed the obvious person to turn to where tennis was concerned. Not only was his name synonymous with tennis of the highest quality but he was from the country where the game had been invented. Also, he had a father with a political background in trade unionism and the co-operative movement.

Whether Perry was flattered by the approach from the Soviet delegation or simply had time on his hands – or both – he responded generously. He secured his new acquaintances access to Wimbledon and even arranged for them to receive a square of turf cut from Centre Court. According to Perry, this was transported back to Russia as a treasured trophy.

In due course, an invitation arrived for him to visit the Soviet Union. He was asked to take with him a group of European players to compete in the national championships, and to stay on to advise on everything from facilities to coaching methods. By now a US citizen of some twenty years, Perry took the precaution of seeking clearance from his adopted land, a wise move given the recent anti-communist hysteria led by Senator Joseph McCarthy. Once again, within Perry's wide circle of friends, whose circumference had grown with the contacts he had made while coaching at the Boca Raton Hotel, was the appropriate facilitator, and he received a letter signed by President Dwight Eisenhower. It gave him the authority to travel and told whoever it might concern that neither he nor his family should suffer any form of retribution for going behind the Curtain.

He made a second visit to the Soviet Union on a tennis mission in 1968, ten years after the first. His hosts were evidently attentive both in controlling where he went and in listening to his recommendations. These were relayed back to Moscow each evening, after which he received news of the next day's itinerary. He correctly identified the main strength and weakness of the central command system that the Soviets applied to tennis, as they did to just about everything else. Their coaching effort for juniors was impressive; their insistence on everyone playing a particular style less so. This explained why their older players enjoyed only limited success early on.

On his first trip to the Soviet Union, Perry had pressed for a grand gesture by his hosts: one of their players to be allowed out to compete at Wimbledon. Thus it was that seventeen-year-old Anna Dmitrieva became the first Russian woman to strike a ball on the courts of the All England Club – with remarkable success, too, considering how bewildering the whole experience must have been. She played in the junior tournament in 1958 and reached the final. But success at senior level would take a long time to follow. After Alex Metreveli and Olga Morozova reached Wimbledon finals in the early 1970s, progress stalled until a more tolerant attitude towards individual development, just as Perry had counselled, changed things. Most importantly, travel restrictions were also eased, allowing access to the best coaches, especially those in America such as Nick Bollettieri. As a consequence, in the 1980s and '90s players from eastern Europe started to figure prominently in the ranking lists.

Perry made his final trip to Moscow in 1994, by which time the Soviet Union was no more, to watch Russia make their first appearance in a Davis Cup final, a match they lost 4–1 to Sweden. An amusing incident took place when a tennis fan who had been a member of the KGB approached Perry with an aerial photograph of an urban setting. It had been taken by a spy satellite during the cold war and was of south London. 'There', said the Russian, pointing to a speck on the photograph, 'is the statue of you they put up at Wimbledon in 1984.'

The visits to the Soviet Union and Russia were further examples of Perry's desire – need, maybe – to travel, regardless of what he might encounter. Life in the Eastern bloc was not renowned for its conviviality, particularly on his early trips – Warsaw Pact forces dealt brutally with reformists who wanted to lighten the mood in Czechoslovakia while Perry was on his second visit to the Soviet Union – and he knew he would neither be indulged nor profit handsomely by going behind the Iron Curtain. One of the few perks he did receive came at the end of that second trip, on which he was accompanied by his wife Bobby. On leaving, at the airport he found a suitcase full of caviar nestling among their other luggage.

In the early 1950s, Egypt was another country that sought Perry's help, and on this particular mission to dispense his tennis expertise he got properly caught up in local politics. He found himself right in the middle of the revolution to overthrow King Farouk, and as a white Westerner was in some danger before an army officer was detailed to look after him. Precautions included hiding under a blanket whenever he was left alone in a car somewhere he might be spotted by unfriendly locals. He was eventually flown out of Egypt in a BOAC Hermes that happened to be on a refuelling stop at Cairo airport. It was returning home with a crew of nine but without any passengers, having flown out VIPs to Uganda, where Princess Elizabeth, soon to become Queen Elizabeth, was opening the terminal building at Entebbe airport.

Whereas the Soviets gave Perry caviar, King Farouk presented him with a fossil of a scarab, the dung beetle regarded as sacred in ancient Egypt. Perry carried the scarab loose in his pocket, occasionally taking it out to throw up and catch, until, on a visit to Sweden to assist their Davis Cup team, King Gustav asked to see it. The king pronounced it quite valuable and had it mounted in a ring for him. Perry passed it on to his wife, who wore it as a charm whenever she flew alone. Eventually, their son David took possession of it as a talisman after he survived a traffic accident in Jamaica in which he was badly injured.

Sweden was one of a number of countries to seek Perry's assistance in preparing their Davis Cup teams, but he never had more than a passing association with any of them. Other teams he dabbled in helping included those of India, Belgium, Canada and, the one that he might have been expected to be most eager to assist, Britain. A major reason why Perry did not become more deeply involved was the International Lawn Tennis Federation's tough stance on the role of professionals in the Davis Cup. Even though there had been talk for years about ending the segregation of amateurs and professionals to produce an open game, the federation's view was that until this happened there should be no compromises. Davis Cup captains had to be amateurs and were the only team officials allowed on court during a match. There were other complications.

For tax reasons, as a US citizen he could only spend a limited time in any foreign country. Also, a whole range of competing commitments, from the clothing business to broadcasting, kept him constantly on the move.

Perry's one real go at helping Britain was in 1962, when the LTA made him team manager as part of a triumvirate completed by John Barrett as captain and George Worthington, an Australian, who was coach. It proved an ill-starred appointment. The LTA dithered over accepting Perry's offer of help, a poor way to treat him at the outset. Also, the three-way arrangement was never likely to be successful, particularly as Perry was not noticeably overburdened with the sharing gene in competitive situations. Tony Mottram, a former member of Britain's Davis Cup team, pointed out at the time that as tennis was a game for individuals – and here he may well have had Perry in mind – it was not always easy for a captain acting on his own to sell ideas to his players, so 'when more than one voice of authority is to be heard the dangers are obvious'. At least one newspaper shared Mottram's scepticism: 'Whether three hands on the helm can give the clearly defined direction the team requires has yet to be seen.'

The arrangement worked well enough at first, as Britain won matches against Austria in Vienna and Brazil in Eastbourne that would have been hard to lose. Then came a severe test when the team travelled to Milan in mid-July to play Italy, one of the stronger nations. Britain lost 5–0. In January 1963 Perry received a letter from the LTA while he was wintering with his family in Jamaica in which he was told that his services would no longer be required. The experiment had not been successful, the letter said, and the association would revert to the system of an amateur captain in total control.

Perry's own comment, looking back after several years, was that it had sounded like a good idea but he never knew exactly what he was expected to do. This confusion about his role may account for why he gave 1955 as the year he served as manager, a full seven years before the actual date. Another problem, which, he said, caused a bit of a stink, had been that when he travelled to the away ties he attracted more interest than the team. The venture could not be called a success, he concluded.

A confession in his autobiography casts more light on his involvement with Davis Cup teams. He admitted he did not like coaching really good players because it was too much like hard work. They had their own way of playing and if they decided to make changes it was a protracted process that anyway might not be effective – and even if it was the coach rarely received credit. He did not say so, but an added frustration was almost certainly that he soon realised that trying to convert good players into the sort of exceptional competitor that he had been was an exercise in futility. He derived greater enjoyment from coaching club players and children.

He had a real eye for recognising potential in younger players, as he demonstrated during the Focus on Tennis campaign that he ran with Dan Maskell soon after the war. Bill Knight was one of those who, having been picked out by Perry, went on to establish himself as a Davis Cup player. 'He looked at hundreds of kids, and out of these he chose about thirty-five who provided the nucleus of the British team for the best part of a decade from 1955,' Knight said. 'He was incredibly shrewd at identifying children who could go on to achieve things, which is very difficult when you're talking about twelve- or thirteen-year-olds who had played very little tennis.'

Over time, Perry cut back his hands-on coaching and in later life, when his year took on a pattern, it featured hardly at all. From January 1978, when the international federation introduced the idea of naming its own champions – its way of competing with the rankings of the now separate men's and women's tours – Perry would go to the Masters event in New York to join Don Budge and Lew Hoad on the panel to select the ITF male world champion for the previous year. Philippe Chatrier, the federation's urbane and charming French president, thought up the world champions scheme and probably did not mind that the selection process was little more than a sinecure for old-timers he particularly admired. Next, a series of teaching clinics, broken by an extended breather in Jamaica, took Perry through to the summer and his annual trip to Europe, where he would broadcast from the French and Wimbledon championships. He would then return to America for the US Open before heading south again for some relaxation in the warmth of Florida and the Caribbean.

When he was at home he switched off completely and the family protected him from anyone wanting some of his time. He particularly enjoyed pottering around with a golf club. Although he was a low-handicap player, he was not interested in going off to compete or play a round. Penny said he just wanted to be on his own. He drove his family mad putting around the house from one wall to the other, chipping in the backyard, fiddling with his clubs and changing grips. 'It was a complete brain break, almost like a comforter,' she said.

Broadcasting was an important part of Perry's life from the late 1940s until his death. After tennis, talking was perhaps the thing he did best, and he loved the microphone. On air as a summariser and the voice of experience, he could be jocular or dismissive – or both at the same time. When a dreary match at Wimbledon was unexpectedly enlivened by an exciting rally, the commentator turned to him and said, 'What a great point.' 'Yes,' Perry said, 'it's almost woken me up.' An American critic described him as 'an outspoken, tart-tongued old-timer who speaks his piece'. His acid tongue distinguished him from other ex-players who, particularly these days, often use the commentary box to become bland spokespersons for their sport. This is a trend that has grown with the near formalisation of broadcasting as a career extension for athletes. Perry was, as ever, a trailblazer and remained a pungent commentator to the end, never opting for mealy-mouthed platitudes even if his remarks caused offence.

No one could question his credentials to talk about tennis. He could do it in his sleep, which was just as well. The quip about nearly waking him up might not have been far from the truth. He was quite capable of dozing off in the commentary box, but could retrieve the situation with aplomb. He learned to respond to a dig in the ribs with a generalisation that fitted any situation. This bought him a few moments to remember where he was and deliver some pertinent and insightful comment. Most of the time, though, he was alert and never mundane. His commentaries helped to popularise tennis just as his shattering of the class barrier to become a champion had done.

He started doing radio commentaries with Max Robertson in 1948, and this was the broadcast medium that he preferred. Above all, it gave him endless opportunities to dip into his deep well of anecdotes. A reviewer who praised the BBC's coverage of Wimbledon said, 'We get a far better range of gossip on radio, with all those small personal stories of players' histories and foibles, especially from the eternal Fred Perry, who must spend weeks at a time chatting on Florida patios.'

When in the 1960s Perry did a stint with ITV, which for a few years shared televising Wimbledon with the BBC, he remarked that the trouble with television was that there was very little need to utter a word – no good for a chatterbox such as himself.

Frank Keating, who went on to become a highly regarded print journalist, was responsible for luring Perry to television. 'In the mid-1960s I was a pink-shirted tyro ITV editor of outside broadcasts in London,' Keating recalled. 'They ordered me to take on the BBC at Wimbledon. I panicked. Somebody said, "Just hire Fred." I did.'

Keating said Perry introduced him to every face at Wimbledon and almost every blade of grass on Centre Court, and 'although our little ITV production tent up on the hill looked like that of the English army at Agincourt compared with the BBC's whole caravan of fortnight's camping, because of Fred in our team the world came to visit us'. Unlike the English army at Agincourt, though, ITV with Perry as their Henry V found the odds against them insurmountable, with only one channel and very little archive material. Perry never did manage to replace his old friend Dan Maskell, BBC's lead commentator, as the television voice of Wimbledon.

Without archive footage to fill in when it rained, ITV did at times give Perry the opportunity to talk rather more than he gave the medium credit for, to the point where even he nearly dried up on one occasion. Towards the end of a particularly long rain interruption, he surprised his fellow commentator, Emlyn Jones, by asking him how many people he thought there were in the studio. Jones did a quick count and came up with a number. 'In which case,' said Perry, 'why can't we get a cup of tea around here?' Cups were duly brought and the discussion about afternoon tea went on longer than the subject deserved. The end of the transmission came just in time to save him from further irrelevant extemporising.

'He was tremendous, original and full of quick-fire one-liners in his mid–Atlantic accent,' Keating said. 'Any ratings ITV got were solely due to him.' Only Perry, for example, could have enhanced the commercial broadcaster's output by facilitating an unscheduled appearance by Bing Crosby. He had spotted Crosby outside Wimbledon trying to buy tickets off a tout. He intervened and arranged for him to be admitted, and when Crosby wondered how he could thank Perry the answer was obvious, allowing ITV a rare scoop over the BBC. In later years, when he was one of the senior citizens of the media community, Perry became an avuncular figure. His advice and encouragement were appreciated by young broadcasters intimidated by having to work alongside such an eminent colleague.

Not just broadcasters enjoyed the convivial side of his nature during Perry's stints at Wimbledon. He loved to entertain or join in enthusiastically when being serenaded at functions marking his various anniversaries. In 1984 he hosted a gathering of 350 people in the members' enclosure at the All England Club to mark both his seventy-fifth birthday and the fiftieth anniversary of his first Wimbledon singles title, and five years later the International Tennis Federation put on an eightieth-birthday party for him at the club. There was the informal partying, too. For years he organised an unscheduled add-on to the Wimbledon Ball when it was held at the Grosvenor House Hotel on the second Saturday of the tournament. Perry would take those still standing to a West End nightclub, outings that would last until daybreak, when breakfast was served before the revellers headed home.

The geniality did have its limits, though, on occasion being replaced by the edge that had made him such a great competitor. He was once asked by a young acolyte at BBC Television Centre to stay on at Wimbledon after hours to appear as a guest on Terry Wogan's chat show. Half an hour before the show he was told he was no longer required. He immediately contacted the BBC's director general and told him that he was no longer available to take part in any other BBC programmes, a stance he steadfastly observed.

If the BBC harboured any resentment it did not last. It had certainly disappeared by the time of Perry's death in 1995, after which Sir Roger Cary, who worked for corporate affairs at the BBC's radio headquarters in central London, suggested in an internal memo that the corporation become involved in helping to organise the thanksgiving service at St Paul's Cathedral. In his note, Cary, who said that he and his mother had been 'ardent listeners' to radio commentaries when Perry was in his playing prime, challenged a view of him expressed in a number of obituaries. 'These have tended to suggest that Fred's great triumph for England was something of an irritant to an older generation of Lawn Tennis Association members. If so, this is very much at variance with my own personal memories,' Cary, a well-connected Old Etonian, wrote. 'I accept that Robert Riseley's father, then Deputy Chairman of Wimbledon, may have an attitude that was partly shaped by the views of the debenture holders. But by the mid-1930s most people were overjoyed that on the tennis court England [sic] was at last toppling the French dominance of Cochet and his team.' Cary also wrote, 'The Englishman who gave my mother anxiety was Bunny Austin, because he could be prickly and challenge line calls (!). My memory is that Perry was a great British hero, although I totally accept that as war approached he temporarily fell from grace through (a) trouble in his marriage and (b) turning professional, which was certainly regarded as something that only Americans did: a far cry from the world of the Duke of York and Louis Greig.'

Cary's suggestion that the BBC be involved in the thanksgiving service was not only accepted but Cary himself was given a role. 'It was a great honour to find myself lent to Wimbledon to help them mount the service,' he wrote in reply to Lord Annan, who had thanked Cary for the offer of a ticket to the service.

Throughout his life Fred Perry was insatiably sociable, indisputably a lady's man but just as much a man's man as well. The man who shaped him was his father, and Sam Perry was clearly a strong-minded, opinionated individual. Some children respond to a robust parent or parents by becoming timid, others by developing the same strong character. In Fred's case strength meant very early on renouncing the political ambition and politics that had driven his father.

After his father, the main men in Perry's life in his early years were inevitably those he played tennis against, and for them there were two Fred Perrys – the ultra-competitive version and the cordial, companionable model. The line between the two might not always have been clear but there does seem to have been a distinct difference. What was remarkable was that he was able to switch between these opposing personas so effortlessly – one minute the ruthless tournament player, the next affability itself. Both moods, though, contained that constant in Perry's character, a knowingness that meant those tricks he did miss were not really tricks.

He certainly knew how to work a crowd. John Kieran, in a column in the *New York Times* in 1939, wrote, 'He's a ready talker and a good mixer. He can be the life of any party. He can walk up to a microphone without showing signs of aphasia or palsy, and he doesn't run away and hide from photographers. Those are among the things that make a public figure popular and certainly a great tennis player must be considered a public figure in these times.' This surefootedness did desert Perry at times, notably in his early relationships with women – before he brought his emotions under the control of his head – and in business matters. This may seem contrary to the success of the Fred Perry clothing line, which continues to flourish to this day, but as we have seen a major part of the business's early success can be attributed to the venture's co-founder Tibby Wegner, and when Perry sold his stake in 1964 he almost certainly did miss what was undeniably a trick by failing to negotiate a permanent stake in the brand. The fact is, the astute side of Perry's character was reserved mostly for matters social and sporting and, as he himself remarked, he was not much of a businessman.

His relationships with fellow players invariably followed a sequence: a wariness bordering on dislike to start with followed by a friendship that became a lifelong bond. This was particularly true of two of his great American rivals, the charming and debonair Sidney Wood and Frank Shields, who was film-star handsome and, if possible, a more irresistible magnet for women than Perry. Perry even sorted things out with George Lott, the American whose irritation with the English intruder turned almost to blows during a doubles match in 1937.

Wood, who never uttered a word without a mischievous twinkle in his eye, even in late old age, said that early on he found Perry hard to take. He confirmed Perry's sarcastic banter during matches, including the 'Very clevah' quip that so infuriated opponents. 'He'd really give it you,' Wood said. 'Frank Shields and I both felt the same way about Fred early on, and we all ended up bosom friends, which is the way it should be, of course.' Wood told how Perry later went out of his way to encourage and help him as a broadcaster and try to find him more TV work. 'He was very loyal,' Wood said.

Don Budge also came round to liking Perry after finding him hard to take in his playing prime. Perry was 'the one player who was able to get my goat on a more regular, if less emotional, basis' than Pancho Gonzales, who 'could force me to the peak of my rage'. Things became particularly bad, Budge said, when he and Perry toured together as professionals. 'He took to calling me J. Donald God, and the thing that especially annoyed me was that he would never use that name unless there were others around to hear it.' Later on, Budge made regular visits to the Montego Bay Racquet Club in Jamaica, 'a couple of coves away' from Perry at Runaway Bay, and the old animosity soon evaporated. Now, said Budge, he could 'be the most engaging player of all on court'.

Perry's relationship with the less outgoing Ellsworth Vines veered from close to cordial to cool, as is clear from the many mentions of Perry in Vines' letters to his wife. To an extent this is unsurprising: Perry was never going to bond with a man whose bearing, according to one American scribe, was not the type that caused onlookers to sing 'For He's a Jolly Good Fellow'. On the other hand, John Kieran reckoned that Vines' Gloomy Gus look made him appear more unapproachable than he was, and anyone who broke through it would find him modest and very natural and obliging.

Jack Kramer, from the generation that followed Perry, was the one player who never really tempered his criticism, although his beef was mainly with the way Perry conducted himself as a player once he had passed his glory days as an amateur. In his book *The Game* Kramer wrote that Perry's attitude when it came to playing for money was opportunistic, and that he was selfish and egotistical.

Kramer remembered his first encounter with Perry when they appeared on the same day on the closing weekend of the 1936 Pacific Southwest tournament in Los Angeles. He played a junior match in the morning and was given a front-row seat to watch Perry and Budge contest the final of the main men's event in the afternoon. Although the match went to four sets, Kramer said, 'Perry quit in the third set. I was only fifteen, but I was old enough to tell when somebody gave up. And Perry tanked [tennis jargon for threw the match], I could see that . . . As a kid, that really hurt me – that a star player could do that sort of thing. But the trouble with Fred was that it never seemed to hurt him to lose, especially when he didn't think that a match was important.' Soon after this Perry quit the amateur game and, according to Kramer, never gave a damn about professional tennis. 'He was through as a player the instant he turned pro.' Kramer maintained this line into old age. 'Pro tennis meant more to Vines and to Budge than Fred, and I don't understand the reason why,' he said. 'Fred never really played as well as a professional as he did when he was an amateur.'

Kramer's antipathy towards Perry might have softened had it not been for the 1973 Wimbledon boycott by seventy-nine members of the newly formed Association of Tennis Professionals, the first players' union. As the ATP's executive director, Kramer effectively led this boycott over Wimbledon's decision to bar Nikki Pilic because he had declined to play a Davis Cup tie for Yugoslavia. Kramer was incensed by Perry's decision to denounce the players' action in newspaper articles. He accused Perry of protecting his British image rather than backing the association's principled stand.

Beyond tennis, Perry had an enormous number of friends and acquaintances. One of these was the Hollywood actor Robert Montgomery, who became a star when Norma Shearer chose him to star opposite her in *Private Lives* in 1931. On a visit to London three years later, Montgomery received a guided tour of the capital from Perry. The mode of transport was Perry's Austin Seven, whose sliding roof had to be kept open because Montgomery was so tall. What must have made the sight even more comical was that Montgomery, in trying to dress the British way, wore a bowler hat.

Perry quickly understood that developing strong friendships offered the possibility of a little leverage here or there. He also soon realised that some of those who wanted to be his friends were interested only because of the kudos of being associated with one of the greatest sportsmen of a generation – and he would go along with this for something in return. There were limits, though. On one occasion in 1935 he went out to dinner in London with his Hollywood friends Ben Lyon and Bebe Daniels and, among others, a new acquaintance, Horace Dodge, the son of the co-founder of the eponymous automobile business. The conversation turned to Perry's prolonged dilemma over whether to turn professional, during which the question cropped up of how much money would be involved. Someone mentioned £100,000, a sum that Dodge instantly dismissed as trifling. Perry took this as a condescending slight on his worth and left, instantly cutting himself off from a well-stashed contact and a possible useful friend.

In time, too, disenchantment set in with Hollywood. There were two views of the capital of the film world. The sanguine one was nicely summed up by Sidney Wood. 'It was a small community. You knew everybody,' Wood said, in his winningly light way. 'They weren't celebrities, they were just people who were either nice or not nice. A lot of them were really wonderful, close friends. Gary Cooper was my closest friend; an absolute sweetheart.' The other view Perry himself glimpsed in 1935 on his first visit to Hollywood outside late summer, when tennis had slipped down the agenda. He quickly discovered, he said, what a strange place it could be. He found himself wondering about a town where for a few weeks of the year a tennis star having dinner with a film star was big news and for the rest of the year it meant nothing at all. The failure of his marriage to Helen Vinson added to his disillusion with the West Coast and his eventual decision to go east.

When he returned to England after the war, Perry took quiet satisfaction from the fact that through his sporting success he was now accepted in the sort of English society that otherwise would have spurned him. Even so, he never joined their club. He was happy to live apart from them in America, and when in England was perfectly content with his unobtrusive home in Rottingdean.

At the top end of this society was royalty, who, through their patronage of Wimbledon, became part of Perry's life from quite early in his tennis career. Perry admitted to being overawed to the detriment of the way he played, when George V turned up unexpectedly at Wimbledon in 1930 to watch that first match he played on Centre Court against the Yorkshire doctor Colin Gregory. However, by the time of his next encounter with the king, who this time was accompanied by Queen Mary, Perry was a confident man of the world at ease in anyone's presence, however majestic. This was the occasion after his first Wimbledon success in 1934, when the king, having missed the men's final on the Friday, asked Perry to join him and his wife in the royal box for the women's final the next day. Perry recalled that the king noticed he was suffering from the previous evening's celebrations and his dash up to Wimbledon from Eastbourne, and invited him to sit down almost straightaway rather than prolong the standing part of their public appearance. Thus His Majesty got me off the hook, recalled Perry, who was conscious that for once he was having difficulty maintaining the pose of the soldier-straight athlete.

Forty-three years later Perry had another royal audience at Wimbledon, this time with George V's granddaughter Queen Elizabeth, whose visit marked her silver jubilee and the tournament's hundredth anniversary. The queen was no tennis fan – horse racing was her thing – and she would not be seen again at Wimbledon during the twentieth century. Nor would what she witnessed that day in 1977: a British player – Virginia Wade, on this occasion – winning a singles title.

Perry, who sat next to the queen at tea, was just the man to carry on a conversation with the monarch about something that did not interest her. He could dress up any story to engage a listener, even one determined to be bored by it, and when the queen wondered indifferently about the presentation ceremonies in the 1930s, his response ensured that 'she appeared to be most intrigued'. For a start, he told her, in complete contrast to the stage-managed presentations that now take place on Centre Court, followed by the champion's victory parade in front of the stands, there was no ceremony in his day whatsoever. All he received, he said, was a voucher for ten pounds to be spent at a jeweller's (a better story than the gold medal that in fact he received). He did not even see his two trophies, the Challenge Cup and the Renshaw Cup, until he was escorted into the vaults of the Bank of England to be photographed with them in 1947.

One last engagement with the British royal family at Wimbledon took place in 1984, the fiftieth anniversary of Perry's first Wimbledon win, when David Wynne's statue of him and the Fred Perry Gates were unveiled by the Duke of Kent. Wynne discarded nearly 700 photographic images of Perry before deciding on one that he considered suitable, and Perry said the unveiling ceremony meant more to him than all the prize money in the world.

One measure of the affection Britain has for its sports stars, apart from a summons to appear on a BBC talk show such as *Wogan* – albeit rescinded – is the interest shown if his or her trophies and other career spoils are ever sent for sale. Perry's cups, salvers, prizes and gifts kept cropping up at auction, mostly at Christie's in South Kensington, central London. In addition there were two main sales, both of which stirred up considerable interest.

The first was when the Perrys had a big clear-out of lesser treasures early in 1976. They gave away some of them, including items to the Wimbledon museum, and the rest were sold at auction, the £1,270 raised being donated to charities. Bobby Perry told the press that looking after them all at their home in Rottingdean was no longer something they could manage. 'Cleaning them was absolutely ghastly,' she said, 'and we had to have special cupboards for keeping them.' There was also the constant anxiety that they might be burgled.

The second and much bigger sale was that of 'The Fred Perry Collection' at Christie's in June 1997, two years after Perry died. It caused some comment in the press, who especially enjoyed the undercurrent of controversy. This, suitably enough, involved Wimbledon. Even though he had passed on, Perry was still able to embarrass the club. The discomfort was summed up by the first paragraph of the *Guardian*'s report on the sale: 'Some of triple Wimbledon champion Fred Perry's most precious trophies have been sold to an American museum at an auction where the All England Club bought just a dented cigarette box.' In fairness to the club, its interest lay only in Wimbledon-related items, which fetched much higher figures than expected – tennis memorabilia prices were at a peak at this time – but this did not stop the *Guardian* commenting, 'The [Wimbledon] museum's parsimony will be seen as the final snub to the champion from the club in a lifetime of such episodes.'

In time, Wimbledon regained some of the items it had held until purchased by outside collectors at the second auction. They bought back two of the three Renshaw Cups that Perry had received for his Wimbledon triumphs, which had attracted the liveliest bidding, going for £36,800 and £25,300, and also reclaimed miniature replicas of the Challenge Cup and the President's Cup that Wimbledon presented to Perry in the 1970s. The racket Perry used to win his first Wimbledon title in 1934, which fetched £23,000, might also have found its way back to the All England Club had they thought to ask.

There were audible gasps from the audience as the bidding for the racket rattled past the estimate of £1,000–1,500 and set a record for such an item sold at auction. Frank Lowe, who was knighted in 2002 for his services to advertising and charity, made the winning bid by phone from behind the Members' Stand at Lord's cricket ground, where he was watching England play Australia. He said several years later that someone from the All England Club should have asked him for the Perry racket, but no one ever did, and eventually he gave it as part of a collection of rackets to the Queen's Club, where in 1979 he had inaugurated the Stella Artois Championships. For Queen's to have ended up with the racket in a showcase must be especially galling for Wimbledon, given Perry's warm-up routine for the All England Club Championships ignored Queen's in favour of representing Chiswick Park at the Middlesex championships.

The Americans who attended the 1997 auction targeted things that had nothing directly to do with Wimbledon, including the US LTA Challenge Cup, which Perry won outright after securing his third US title in 1936. This was bought for £36,700 by the Tennis Hall of Fame, based in Newport, Rhode Island, whose representative made her objective clear by keeping an arm raised throughout the bidding.

Perry's health in old age was generally good until he had a major scare in 1983, when what he described as a dry cough and sore throat turned out to be pleurisy. This was discovered only when his condition suddenly worsened while he was on commentary duty on the first Monday of Wimbledon and he was taken to the Nuffield Hospital in Brighton. Up until then he had not missed a day at the championships since 1947.

Afterwards, Perry liked to joke about what happened. 'When the X-rays came up I asked the doctor how my lungs were looking. "Like London airport on a foggy day," he said.' When he was about to leave hospital – saying his goodbyes to the nursing staff, in fact – he collapsed and had to be readmitted with what turned out to be a blood clot that went to the lung. He might well have died had he not been where he was with doctors and nurses on hand to treat him. Perry said they took Bobby aside at the hospital and told her, 'We think we can save Fred.' He knew how close it was. 'If I wasn't at death's door, I wasn't far away.' By the end of Wimbledon he had recovered sufficiently to send a telegram to the champions' dinner: 'Thanks for all your kind messages. Was match points down but happy to say am now a break up in the final set.'

He had a related alarm the following year in Florida, when it was discovered he had a residue in the lung, but once given the all-clear he resumed his wandering life. This included yet more tournaments, broadcasting, advising on tennis matters and promoting the Perry clothing label. Old age frustrated him but failed to dampen his spirit. He liked to tell the story of the comedian in Jerusalem who introduced him as 'Fred Perry, who won Wimbledon so long ago the Dead Sea wasn't even sick'. It also amused him that a doctor had advised him: 'Look, Fred, just concentrate on breathing in and breathing out – and don't let anything else bother you.' Perry certainly gave credence to the idea that chirpiness in the face of deteriorating health keeps you going longer. His daughter said he never really thought about his age. 'In fact, I think he thought he was immortal. It never occurred to him that he might not be around for the next trip or whatever.'

Aged eighty, he was interviewed for a newspaper column entitled 'Me and My Health'. 'People ask me if I feel my age and the answer is no. But then don't forget I have a vivacious wife and with five grandchildren and two homes (Sussex seafront and Florida) there's always something going on. Bobby says she's falling apart but I'm kept going by my ego. Could be. Fred Perry Sportswear is flourishing. I fly all over the world and still drive (medium blue Cadillac).' He said also that he had not hit a ball over a net for years. If he did pick up a racket it was while lecturing to children, and he would knock balls through hoops into buckets of water to hold their attention. He liked to walk a couple of miles when he could and enjoyed plenty of sleep, plus a siesta. 'I just lie on top of my bed and I'm off.' He answered his own question about whether it was time to give up working. 'No, I've got to have somewhere to hang my hat and work keeps me young. Luckily my memory is good – though I often forget where I put my glasses – and so is my hearing. Actually I often hear things I'm not supposed to hear.' On another occasion he gave this explanation for keeping up what would have been a punishing schedule even for a much younger man: 'If I had to say, "What am I going to do today? Maybe I'll wander over and see Charlie and then watch some TV and then take a nap," I wouldn't have stayed alive for two weeks.'

Perry was back working for BBC Radio at Wimbledon in 1984 and did not miss another day at the tournament before his death. Right up until the end he remained defiant about his mounting health problems. He had a heart condition that required a triple-bypass operation in Fort Lauderdale in December 1992. The surgeons also fitted him with a new valve and pacemaker, which he took as another excuse for waggishness. 'They used some part of a pig's anatomy,' he said, 'so the only change you'll notice in me is that I'll now grunt like Jimmy Connors when I serve.' Such humour was almost certainly part defence mechanism against the signs of his mortality that were all around now and even he must have recognised. His great friend Dan Maskell died while Perry was recovering from the heart surgery. His family did not tell him straightaway because of the effect it might have had on his recuperation. Towards the end he also developed late-onset diabetes and had an ulcerated toe removed. 'They wanted to save the bloody toe,' he told a reporter, 'but that would have meant spending four weeks in bed, taking antibiotics. So I told them, "To hell with that – take it off. I'm not going to be bouncing around Centre Court any time soon."'

Perry died in Melbourne shortly after the 1995 Australian Open, which he attended. There was a certain poetic aptness that the old warrior was at one of the grand slam championships, the one he had won sixty-one years before, at which he had established his reputation around the world.

Towards the end of the tournament he had slipped and hurt himself in the bathroom of his hotel. In pain, he dressed for dinner. He insisted on attending a reception that night in honour of Ken Rosewall and the late Lew Hoad, two of the greatest of Australia's many outstanding players. Journalists recalled him passing their table and saying, 'Christ it hurts.' The next day he was X-rayed and later admitted to Epworth Hospital with four cracked ribs. Even then no one suspected his death was imminent. Several friends went to see him in hospital, including John Parsons of the *Daily Telegraph*. Parsons said there was little indication of how rapidly or gravely his condition would decline. He hardly had time to sit down before Perry launched into tennis talk, wanting to analyse the Australian women's final, in which Mary Pierce of France had beaten Spain's Arantxa Sanchez-Vicario. He had watched the match on his bedside TV, at changeovers switching to check on the progress of Mike Atherton's England cricket team playing in Adelaide.

'Now then,' he asked Parsons, 'can you tell me why the Sanchez girl didn't try a few loopers to try to win the initiative back from Pierce?' His mind was sharp and he was eager to keep the conversation going. He regretted that modern players received so much help with all aspects of their lives off the court that they were unable to think enough for themselves on it; he felt also that players had lost sight of the need to express themselves and entertain.

There was a huge difference between opinions such as these coming from him rather than anyone else. Through his play Perry had expressed himself memorably and entertained hundreds of thousands of people around the world. And won.

Bobby Perry was by her husband's bedside when he died of acute renal failure on 2 February 1995. Doctors told her to keep talking to him so that he would drift and relax in his final moments.

He had already died by the time Penny passed through Bangkok on her way to be with her father, but the news was kept from her. Her mother met her at Melbourne airport and, assuming she had been told, suggested they went to the hotel. Penny said that she wanted to go straight to the hospital to see her father. 'She looked horrified and then told me he had gone,' Penny recalled. 'If I went to the hospital there were press there and things needed to be done.' Penny still insisted they went to the hospital.

'I walked into the hospital, spoke to the nurses and told them that I needed ten minutes with my father.' After this, she rang her son's school in England to make sure that when he woke up he heard the news first from the headmaster. She was then ready for the press conference.

Epilogue

'He did not forget his roots'

Fred Perry would almost certainly have enjoyed the outrageous pun 'Perry goes out to a big service', which was the headline to one national newspaper's account of 'A Service of Thanksgiving for the life of Fred Perry' at St Paul's Cathedral in London.

Only in the preparation for and the execution of his many tennis battles had he been an earnest man. One of his greatest sadnesses was the premature death of his mother, Hannah, which he blamed partly on her stressful existence as a politician's wife. This loss removed any ambition he might have had to pursue the sort of career that so absorbed his father. Instead he had exploited his rare capacity for playing competitive tennis and devoted the time left over to exploring the lighter side of life. Of his handsome facial features, his eyes said the most about him, gleaming with intensity during a match or twinkling with barely suppressed merriment in most other circumstances.

Perry would also have approved of the remark made by the actress Patricia Roc, his sister-in-law – still a beauty at eighty – while helping to arrange his funeral service, which took place at St Margaret's Church, Rottingdean on Monday 27 February. The priest, Father Martin Morgan, apologised to her for all the practical details that had to be dealt with, to which she replied, 'Well, darling, I perfectly understand, because if we fuck this up we can never put it right.'

The choice of venue for the funeral was significant. After all Perry had died a US citizen. Penny said at the ceremony that his attachment to Britain and his adopted Rottingdean had never faltered. 'He did not forget his roots,' she said. 'He felt he belonged here, even though he was not here for much of his life.'

The church was packed; outside it rained heavily. One of his old wooden rackets lay alongside his coffin. 'I guess there will be laughter in heaven. Can there be a more Wimbledon day than this?' Father Martin said. He recalled Perry's charm, skill, honesty and integrity, and described him as a one-off. Perry was also characterised as a gentleman, a posthumous accolade that would have caused him more amusement, given how the gentry had viewed this upstart son of a cotton mill worker.

A cremation followed the service, and Perry's ashes were taken to Wimbledon to be placed beneath the plaque in front of his statue.

The service of thanksgiving took place on the Thursday before the 1995 Wimbledon championships, 22 June, and Sir Christopher Wren's great cathedral at the top of Ludgate Hill was filled, as *The Times* noted, not with his peers because 'nobody in British tennis and few in world tennis have come close to rivalling Fred Perry's triumphs'.

A colour photograph of Perry in the order of service gave a reminder of how in old age, with the once-taut planes of his face now filled out and his hair grey and thinned, he looked just as striking as he had sixty years earlier. A poem, 'To Fred Perry' by the BBC commentator Max Robertson, contained the rather good line 'to fight with gut and not conform'.

Four Wimbledon champions – Virginia Wade, Martina Navratilova, John Newcombe and Pete Sampras – read verses from Rudyard Kipling's 'If', the poem whose lines 'If you can meet with Triumph and Disaster/ And treat those two impostors just the same' are inscribed above the doorway that leads onto Centre Court at Wimbledon. Two of his friends and broadcasting colleagues, John Barrett and Emlyn Jones, read passages from reports recalling highlights of his playing career.

Tony Trabert, the American who won the Wimbledon men's title in 1955, gave the address. Perry 'was simply fun to be around' – warm, friendly and a bit of a rascal who was not above sarcasm. He told the story of the day Perry walked into a locker room and said, 'Thank God I'm not playing me today.'

Bibliography

Bowers, Chris, *The Book of Tennis* (London 2002)

Bowers, Ray, *History of the Pro Tennis Wars* (website)

Budge, Don, *Don Budge: A Tennis Memoir* (New York 1969)

Carbery, Thomas F., *Consumers in Politics: A History and General Review of the Co-Operative Party* (Manchester 1969)

Collins, Bud and Hollander, Zander, *Bud Collins' Encyclopedia of Tennis* (New York 1980)

Earl of Suffolk and Berkshire, Peek, Hedley and Aflalo, F. G. (eds), *Encyclopaedia of Sport* (London 1897)

Fein, Paul, *Tennis Confidential II* (2008)

Harvey, Charles (ed.), *Almanack of Sport* (London 1966)

Huggins, Mike and Williams, Jack, *Sport and the English* (London 2006)

Johnson, Joseph, *Grand Slam Australia* (Melbourne 1985)

Kendall, Allan, *Australia's Wimbledon Champions* (Sydney 1995)

Kramer, Jack, *The Game: My 40 Years in Tennis* (New York 1979)

Little, Alan, *Suzanne Lenglen: Tennis Idol of the Twenties* (London 1988/2007)

Little, Alan, *Wimbledon Compendium* (London annually)

McCauley, Joe, *The History of Professional Tennis* (London 2003)

Maskell, Dan, *Oh, I Say!* (London 1988)

McLean, Ron, *Country Cracks: The Story of N.S.W. Country Tennis* (Newcastle, NSW 1984)

Metzler, Paul, *Tennis Style and Stylists* (Sydney 1969)

Millman, A.E. (Ted), *A History of Professional Tennis 1919–1984* (Cheltenham 1984)

Mills, Alan, *Lifting the Covers* (London 2005)

Montagu, Ivor, *Perry Wins a World Championship* (London 1933)

Naudet, Jean-Jacques and Riva, Maria, *Marlene Dietrich: Photographs and Memories* (New York 2001)

Olliff, John, *Olliff on Tennis* (London 1948)

Olliff, John, *The Romance of Wimbledon* (London 1949)

Perry, Fred, *Fred Perry: An Autobiography* (London 1984)

Perry, Fred, *My Story* (London 1934)

Perry, Fred, *Perry Wins!* (London 1935)

Phillips, Caryl (ed.), *The Faber Book of Tennis: The Right Set* (London 1999)

Reid, Aileen, *Brentham: A History of the Pioneer Garden Suburb* (London 2000)

Robertson, Max (ed.), *The Encyclopedia of Tennis* (London 1974)

Seddon, Peter, *Tennis's Strangest Matches* (London 2001)

Shine, Ossian, *The Language of Tennis* (Manchester 2003)

Tinling, Ted, *Sixty Years in Tennis* (London 1983)

Vines III, Ellsworth, *The Greatest Athlete of All Time* (Los Angeles 2004)

Wallis Myers, Prue A., *Wallis Myers: A Testament to Tennis* (Melbourne 2004)

Index